READING MODERNISM'S READERS

Edinburgh Critical Studies in Modernist Culture

Series Editors: Tim Armstrong and Rebecca Beasley

Available

Modernism and Magic: Experiments with Spiritualism, Theosophy and the Occult
Leigh Wilson

Sonic Modernity: Representing Sound in Literature, Culture and the Arts
Sam Halliday

Modernism and the Frankfurt School
Tyrus Miller

Lesbian Modernism: Censorship, Sexuality and Genre Fiction
Elizabeth English

Modern Print Artefacts: Textual Materiality and Literary Value in British Print Culture, 1890–1930s
Patrick Collier

Cheap Modernism: Expanding Markets, Publishers' Series and the Avant-Garde
Lise Jaillant

Portable Modernisms: The Art of Travelling Light
Emily Ridge

Hieroglyphic Modernisms: Writing and New Media in the Twentieth Century
Jesse Schotter

Modernism, Fiction and Mathematics
Nina Engelhardt

Modernist Life Histories: Biological Theory and the Experimental Bildungsroman
Daniel Aureliano Newman

Modernism, Space and the City: Outsiders and Affect in Paris, Vienna, Berlin and London
Andrew Thacker

Modernism Edited: Marianne Moore and the Dial Magazine
Victoria Bazin

Modernism and Time Machines
Charles Tung

Primordial Modernism: Animals, Ideas, Transition (1927–1938)
Cathryn Setz

Modernism and Still Life: Artists, Writers, Dancers
Claudia Tobin

The Modernist Exoskeleton: Insects, War, Literary Form
Rachel Murray

Novel Sensations: Modernist Fiction and the Problem of Qualia
Jon Day

Hotel Modernity: Corporate Space in Literature and Film
Robbie Moore

The Modernist Anthropocene: Nonhuman Life and Planetary Change in James Joyce, Virginia Woolf and Djuna Barnes
Peter Adkins

Asbestos – The Last Modernist Object
Arthur Rose

Visionary Company: Hart Crane and Modernist Periodicals
Francesca Bratton

Modernist War Poetry: Combat Gnosticism and the Sympathetic Imagination, 1914–19
Jamie Wood

Abstraction in Modernism and Modernity: Human and Inhuman
Jeff Wallace

odernism and Religion: Between Mysticism and Orthodoxy
Jamie Callison

Modernism, Material Culture and the First World War
Cedric Van Dijck

Reading Modernism's Readers: Virginia Woolf, Psychoanalysis and the Bestseller
Helen Tyson

Forthcoming

Modernism and the Idea of Everyday Life
Leena Kore-Schröder

Sexological Modernism: Queer Feminism and Sexual Science
Jana Funke

Micromodernism: Rethinking Literary History in the Long 1930s
Tim Armstrong

www.edinburghuniversitypress.com/series/ecsmc

READING MODERNISM'S READERS

Virginia Woolf, Psychoanalysis and the Bestseller

Helen Tyson

EDINBURGH
University Press

Edinburgh University Press is one of the leading university presses in the UK. We publish academic books and journals in our selected subject areas across the humanities and social sciences, combining cutting-edge scholarship with high editorial and production values to produce academic works of lasting importance. For more information visit our website: edinburghuniversitypress.com

Edinburgh University Press Ltd
The Tun – Holyrood Road
12(2f) Jackson's Entry
Edinburgh EH8 8PJ

Typeset in 10/12.5 Adobe Sabon by
IDSUK (DataConnection) Ltd, and
printed and bound by CPI Group (UK) Ltd,
Croydon, CR0 4YY

A CIP record for this book is available from the British Library

ISBN 978 1 3995 2209 0 (hardback)
ISBN 978 1 3995 2211 3 (webready PDF)
ISBN 978 1 3995 2212 0 (epub)

CONTENTS

FIGURES

ACKNOWLEDGEMENTS

This book began as a PhD funded by the Arts and Humanities Research Council in the English Department at Queen Mary University of London, where I had the privilege and great pleasure of being supervised by Jacqueline Rose and Peter Howarth. I am so grateful to Jacqueline and Peter – their insight, careful readings and re-readings, their faith in the project, and their unfailing generosity continue to inspire me in my teaching and research. To Jacqueline and Peter: thank you – I would not be where I am today without your care and support. My PhD examiners, Isobel Armstrong and Lyndsey Stonebridge, helped me to see what I was trying to do in new ways, and their own work continues to make me think this is all worth doing. To Isobel and Lyndsey: thank you. I'm also grateful to the many people that made the English Department at Queen Mary such a vibrant and creative place to do a PhD, and to those who taught me and read my work along the way – especial thanks to Paul Hamilton and Suzanne Hobson for reading and responding to my work at crucial moments.

Since joining the University of Sussex in 2016, I've learnt from many brilliant colleagues and friends who changed the way that I thought about and wrote this book. Thanks to Peter Boxall, Natalia Cecire, Sara Crangle, Vicky Lebeau, Nicholas Royle, Sam Solomon, Bethan Stevens, Pam Thurschwell, Hope Wolf and many more. Thank you in particular to Peter Boxall for reading this book in its entirety and giving me a much-needed boost of confidence. And thank you especially to Hope Wolf for your friendship and for our many conversations about modernism and much more.

I thank David Bradshaw for introducing me to and teaching me how to read Virginia Woolf.

Thank you to Shaul Bar-Haim and Elizabeth Coles for helping me to think and write about psychoanalysis. Thank you to Akshi Singh for friendship in the Marion Milner archive. And thank you to Roberta Klimt for many years of reading and friendship.

Thank you to Karen Watson and colleagues at the University of Sussex Special Collections and the Keep; to the archivists at the Henry W. and Albert A. Berg Collection of English and American Literature at the New York Public Library; to Ewan O'Neill at the British Psychoanalytical Society; and to Darren Clarke at the Charleston Trust.

Thanks to the Society of Authors as the Literary Representative of the Estate of Virginia Woolf for permission to quote from Virginia Woolf's reading notebooks, and to the Estate of Vanessa Bell and DACS for permission to reproduce the images on the front cover and in Chapter 1. Chapter 1 is an extended and revised version of an article I first published as 'Reading Childishly? Learning to Read Modernism: Reading the Child Reader in Modernism and Psychoanalysis', *Textual Practice*, 31.7 (2017), 1435–57, https://doi.org/10.1080/09 50236X.2016.1237997. Chapter 4 is an extended and revised version of an article I first published as '"Forebodings about fascism": Marion Milner and Virginia Woolf', *Feminist Modernist Studies*, 4.1 (2021), 1–21, https://www.tandfonline.com/doi/abs/10.1080/24692921.2020.1848334. I am grateful to the publishers for permission to print the extended versions of these articles here. I'm very grateful to Giles Milner for his generosity in granting permission to cite from Marion Milner's notebooks and to reproduce her drawings, which appear here by permission of the Marsh Agency Ltd, on behalf of the Estate of Marion Milner.

I'm grateful to Jackie Jones at Edinburgh University Press for receiving my initial proposal so enthusiastically, and to Tim Armstrong and Rebecca Beasley for offering such insightful editorial suggestions, and for steering the book through to publication. Thanks also to Elizabeth Fraser for all of her help in getting the book to press.

Trying to finish this book while having a baby during a pandemic was not easy, but the love and friendship of my friends and family made this possible, while Grace's wild passion for life kept me going. To Joseph, Grace and now Iris – thank you.

SERIES EDITORS' PREFACE

This series of monographs on selected topics in modernism is designed to reflect and extend the range of new work in modernist studies. The studies in the series aim for a breadth of scope and for an expanded sense of the canon of modernism, rather than focusing on individual authors. Literary texts will be considered in terms of contexts including recent cultural histories (modernism and magic; sonic modernity; media studies) and topics of theoretical interest (the everyday; postmodernism; the Frankfurt School); but the series will also reconsider more familiar routes into modernism (modernism and gender; sexuality; politics). The works published will be attentive to the various cultural, intellectual and historical contexts of British, American and European modernisms, and to interdisciplinary possibilities within modernism, including performance and the visual and plastic arts.

INTRODUCTION: READING
MODERNISM'S READERS

In Virginia Woolf's 1931 novel *The Waves*, Neville goes to a bookcase and takes down a book. 'Certainly,' Neville comments, 'one cannot read this poem without effort':

> To read this poem one must have myriad eyes, like one of those lamps that turn on slabs of racing water at midnight in the Atlantic, when perhaps only a spray of seaweed pricks the surface, or suddenly the waves gape and up shoulders a monster. One must put aside antipathies and jealousies and not interrupt. One must have patience and infinite care and let the light sound, whether of spiders' delicate feet on a leaf or the chuckle of water in some irrelevant drainpipe, unfold too. Nothing is to be rejected in fear or horror. The poet who has written this page [. . .] has withdrawn. There are no commas or semicolons. The lines do not run in convenient lengths. Much is sheer nonsense. One must be sceptical, but throw caution to the winds and when the door opens accept absolutely. Also sometimes weep; also cut away ruthlessly with a slice of the blade soot, bark, hard accretions of all sorts. And so (while they talk) let down one's net deeper and deeper and gently draw in and bring to the surface what he said and she said and make poetry.[1]

---

[1] Virginia Woolf, *The Waves*, ed. by Michael Herbert and Susan Sellers (Cambridge: Cambridge University Press, 2011), pp. 158–9. All further quotations from the novel are from this edition.

He may read 'half a page of anything', but Neville's description of the 'effort' involved in reading 'this poem' echoes a distinctly modernist experience of reading. A modernist aesthetics of impersonality leaves the reader at sea: 'The poet' – like the narrator of this, Virginia Woolf's most elusive and 'impersonal' novel – 'has withdrawn'.[2] There are, in this poem, as in many a modernist poem, 'no commas or semicolons', and 'The lines do not run in convenient lengths'. 'Much is sheer nonsense.'[3] For Neville, who is also a classicist and a literary scholar, this scene of reading is at once arduous, immersive and disorientating. The experience of reading is compared, in a metaphor that itself demands the kind of reading it describes, to a lamp turning on 'slabs of racing water', suggesting that the images, affects and meanings of the poem are, for the most part, submerged in the racing current, popping up perhaps only fleetingly like the 'spray of seaweed' that 'pricks the surface', but at other times surging forth violently, as when 'suddenly the waves gape and up shoulders a monster'. Neville is a cautious reader, his 'sceptical' attitude echoing the emotional reserve upheld by the formalist literary critics and scholars of whom Woolf was herself so suspicious, but he also finds himself letting down his 'net deeper and deeper', sinking the mind like a fishing net into the poem, in order to 'bring' latent images and feelings 'to the surface', to connect different voices ('what he said and she said'), and 'make poetry'.[4] There's an echo between the poem that Neville reads – where 'the poet has withdrawn' – and the text that we are reading, where Woolf has banished the narrative voice to a mere 'he said', 'she said'. But both the poem and Woolf's novel also present their readers with deeply involving and immersive experiences of reading. In this scene of reading, Neville finds himself immersed within the depths of the poem, reflecting back at Woolf's own reader something like their own experience of reading *The Waves*. By framing the scene of reading in this way, Woolf both offers a description of what it is like to encounter a difficult modernist text like *The*

---

[2] On modernism and impersonality see Maud Ellmann, *The Poetics of Impersonality: T. S. Eliot and Ezra Pound* (Brighton: Harvester, 1987). In 'Poetry, Fiction and the Future', Woolf wrote: 'we long sometimes to escape from the incessant, the remorseless analysis of falling into love and falling out of love, of what Tom feels for Judith and Judith does or does not altogether feel for Tom. We long for some more impersonal relationship.' Virginia Woolf, 'Poetry, Fiction and the Future' (1927), in *The Essays of Virginia Woolf*, ed. by Andrew McNeillie and Stuart N. Clarke, 6 vols (London: Hogarth Press, 1986–2011), IV, pp. 428–41 (pp. 435–6).

[3] On modernism, difficulty and 'nonsense', see Leonard Diepeveen, *The Difficulties of Modernism* (London: Routledge, 2003), p. 14, p. 47.

[4] On Woolf's critical response to the professionalisation of literary criticism and literary studies, see Melba Cuddy-Keane, *Virginia Woolf, the Intellectual, and the Public Sphere* (Cambridge: Cambridge University Press, 2003).

Waves, while also enacting and soliciting her own reader to participate in this process of literary immersion.

* * *

This book focuses on the portraits of reading staged within modernist, psychoanalytic and popular writing from the early twentieth century. In chapters focusing on modernist novels by Virginia Woolf and Marcel Proust, on popular novels by Ethel M. Dell, and on psychoanalytic writing by Sigmund Freud, James Strachey, Melanie Klein and Marion Milner, I argue that a staged, fictionalised encounter with literary texts lies at the heart of early-twentieth-century culture. In close readings of these portraits of reading, *Reading Modernism's Readers* argues that the scene of reading reveals some of our culture's most powerful and enduring fantasies about the role of literature in psychic, social and political life. In the scenes examined within this book, fictional and imagined readers entertain overdetermined, overlapping and frequently conflicting fantasies in which literature appears not only as a source of pleasure and enchantment, but also (and often at the same time) as a buttress of scholarly patriarchal authority, a source of consolation, a vehicle of fantasy and escape, a refuge from modernity, and a repository of communal belonging. In modernist novels, in bestsellers, and in psychoanalytic writing from the early twentieth century, the scene of reading appears as a stage on which writers depict, scrutinise and enact the dominant fantasies of reading in early-twentieth-century culture. These portraits of reading also function in a similar way to what Charles Altieri has described as the 'projected readers' of modernism – the 'ideal' readers imagined in and projected by modernist texts, as a way of modelling and shaping how we, as readers, respond imaginatively and psychologically to this difficult form of writing.[5] In this book, I show how writers – Woolf especially – challenged dominant ideas about the function of literature in our psychic, social and political lives, while at the same time imagining, soliciting and enacting powerful alternative scenes, in which the act of reading appears as a potential source of communal feeling and democratic belonging.

Existing critical accounts of modernism and reading have been divided. One highly polemical, and still popular, account views modernism as a reactionary, antagonistic, anti-democratic assault on the newly literate mass readers of the early twentieth century. For John Carey, one of the most vocal of modernism's critics, difficult modernist writing took the form of a 'hostile reaction to the

---

[5] Charles Altieri, 'Modernist Innovations: A Legacy of the Constructed Reader', in *Modernism*, ed. by Astradur Eysteinsson and Vivian Liska, 2 vols (Amsterdam and Philadelphia: John Benjamins, 2007), I, pp. 67–86 (pp. 67–9).

unprecedentedly large reading public created by late nineteenth-century edu-cational reforms': 'The purpose of modernist writing', Carey argues, 'was to exclude these newly educated (or "semi-educated") readers, and so to preserve the intellectual's seclusion from the "mass."'[6] In another account, Leo Bersani criticises modernism as a politically naïve, historically blind and ethically devoid attempt to seduce the reader into an evasive claim to cultural redemp-tion.[7] And yet another account – in contrast – defends modernist writing as a radical form of estrangement, in which the difficulty presented to the reader is understood as the only viable form of political resistance against the pernicious incursions of capitalist and fascist mass-cultural deception. For critics work-ing in the tradition following Theodor Adorno, Viktor Shklovsky and Bertolt Brecht, difficulty, defamiliarisation and disenchantment represent powerful forms of political resistance in a world that continues to be threatened by the forces of capitalist consumption and fascism. In one striking instance of this critical tradition, Vicki Mahaffey invokes Hannah Arendt to argue that 'the Holocaust was facilitated by a widespread abdication of interpretative power', and claims that the difficulty of modernist writing represents a challenge to the reader to exercise such 'interpretative power': 'modernist writers', Mahaffey claims, 'saw reading as a microcosmically political enterprise, an exercise in resisting totalitarian dictation by an author.'[8]

[6] John Carey, *The Intellectuals and the Masses: Pride and Prejudice among the Literary Intelligentsia, 1880–1939* (London: Faber and Faber, 1992), p. vii. One of the earliest articulations of this argument appears in Max Eastman, 'The Cult of Unintelligibility', *Harper's Monthly Magazine*, 518 (April 1929), 632–86.

[7] Leo Bersani, *The Culture of Redemption* (Cambridge, MA: Harvard University Press, 1990).

[8] Vicki Mahaffey, *Modernist Literature: Challenging Fictions* (Oxford: Blackwell, 2007), p. 23, p. 196. For other examples of this tradition, see Theodor Adorno, 'Why Is the New Art So Hard to Understand?' (1931), in *Essays on Music*, trans. by Susan H. Gillespie, ed. by Richard Leppert (Berkeley: University of California Press, 2002), pp. 127–34 (pp. 131–2); Theodor Adorno, 'Trying to Understand Endgame' (1958), in *Notes to Literature: Volume One*, trans. by Shierry Weber Nicholsen, ed. by Rolf Tiedemann (New York: Columbia University Press, 1991), pp. 241–75; Theodor Adorno, *Aesthetic Theory*, trans. by Robert Hullot-Kentor, ed. by Gretel Adorno and Rolf Tiedemann (London: Continuum, 2009), pp. 1–8, pp. 232–60 (p. 237); Viktor Shklovsky, 'Art as Technique', in *Russian Formalist Criticism: Four Essays*, ed. by Lee T. Lemon and Marion J. Reiss (Lincoln: University of Nebraska Press, 1965), pp. 3–24 (p. 12, p. 13, p. 18); Leo Bersani and Ulysse Dutoit, *Arts of Impoverishment: Beckett, Rothko, Resnais* (Cambridge, MA: Harvard University Press, 1993), pp. 8–9. On the differences between Brecht's *Verfremdung*, Russian Formalism's *ostranenie*, and the shock effects of the avant-garde, see Ben Brewster, 'From Shklovsky to Brecht: A Reply', *Screen*, 15.2 (1974), 82–102 (p. 96, p. 97), and Stanley Mitchell, 'From Shklovsky to Brecht: Some Preliminary Remarks towards a History of the Politicisation of Russian Formalism', *Screen*, 15.2 (1974), 74–81.

And yet, as I argue in this book, these tenacious critical accounts fail to attend to the ways in which the scene of reading, as it is portrayed in modernist literature, in bestselling novels, and in psychoanalytic writing, already unsettles the crude oppositions of later criticism. In this book, I show how modernist writers both imagined and shaped their own readers through scenes of reading that challenge the enduring arguments that modernism is simply elitist, redemptive, or, on the contrary, produces unequivocally radical forms of estrangement. Reading the reader in modernism and in the bestselling romance novel via the insights of psychoanalysis is, I claim, the sharpest riposte to the entrenched dichotomies of existing debates about modernism. Focusing on portraits of reading in modernist novels, psychoanalytic writing and popular novels, I argue that these scenes of reading function in a similar way to Altieri's 'projected' or 'ideal' readers of modernism – the readers who are not only depicted in, but also shaped through the formal qualities of literary texts.[9] Writing about the role of solace in contemporary literature, David James cites Steven Mullaney's distinction 'between narrative *representations* of emotional states [. . .] and the narrative process and phenomenology' of the reader's involvement in 'affecting plots'. In narrative representations of emotional states, the reader is 'presented with an example, a model, or an illustration of an affective state', whereas the 'narrative process and phenomenology' of the reader's investment in 'affecting plots' is a process through which the reader is 'modelled or shaped or reconfigured as much by his or her own reading [. . .] as by a represented state of being, capable of imitation'.[10] For James, whose subject is the afterlife of modernist consolation in contemporary literature, this distinction facilitates his own disaggregation between three analytic 'tiers': 'the stylistic and diegetic lives solace leads *in* representation, the role it plays compositionally for some writers [. . .] and the myriad responses that consolation (including its unacceptability) may arouse in readers.'[11] In this book, my analysis focuses both on the readers that are represented in modernist and popular novels, and on the ways that those novels seek, through formal experimentation, to shape, model and even reconfigure their own readers. In what follows I argue that the readers represented in literary texts and the readers projected and shaped by those texts are intimately linked. Focusing on portraits of readers that explore what James describes elsewhere as the 'myriad forms of readerly attention' – from scholarly close reading to reading

---

[9] Altieri, 'Modernist Innovations', pp. 67–9.

[10] Steven Mullaney, *The Reformation of Emotions in the Age of Shakespeare* (Chicago: University of Chicago Press, 2015), pp. 24–5, cited by David James, *Discrepant Solace: Contemporary Literature and the Work of Consolation* (Oxford: Oxford University Press, 2019), p. 10.

[11] James, *Discrepant Solace*, p. 10.

for pleasure, for escape, or for solace – this book focuses on how modernist and popular novels didn't just represent but also performed their own scenes of reading.[12]

Despite a longheld assumption that the practices of close reading and practical criticism associated with the rise of literary studies in Britain and America privileged the idea of the poem as autonomous, Peter Howarth has recently argued that the account of close reading developed by some of its earliest practitioners in fact celebrated a form of modernist reading in which the experimental form of the poem can be 'read as a dramatic *anticipation* of its historical readership'.[13] 'To write like a modernist', Howarth argues, 'is to be preternaturally aware of the efforts of your future readers.'[14] Modernist poetry demands the enactment of a certain kind of close reading, because 'the reader is the theatre or venue in which the poem unfolds its present-tense performance'.[15] In modernist novels, too, I argue, the portrait of reading foregrounds the ways in which modernist novelists imagined the scene of reading as a kind of performance. In reading these scenes, we, as readers, are solicited to reflect on our own processes of reading, and on the individual, social and cultural fantasies that shape our reading. Like Altieri, and like John Lurz, I am interested in what Lurz describes as the 'determining role played by reading' in modernist texts.[16] Although I share both Altieri's and Lurz's interest in the ways that modernist writing imagines its own scenes of reading, *Reading Modernism's Readers* aims, unlike these publications (which in Altieri's case perpetuates the 'great divide' model of modernism, and in Lurz's case focuses on the scene of reading as a 'meditation on transience and temporal progress'), to bring psychoanalytic insight to the troubled politics of readerly identification in the historical landscape stretching from the First World War to the rise of totalitarianism and fascism in the 1930s.[17]

Although Virginia Woolf's writing takes centre stage in this book, her novels are read alongside and in conversation with writing by (amongst others) Marcel Proust, Sigmund Freud, James Strachey, Melanie Klein and

---

[12] David James, 'Introduction', in *Modernism and Close Reading*, ed. by David James (Oxford: Oxford University Press, 2020), pp. 1–16 (p. 7).

[13] Peter Howarth, 'Close Reading as Performance', in *Modernism and Close Reading*, ed. James, pp. 45–68 (p. 65).

[14] Howarth, 'Close Reading', p. 65.

[15] Howarth, 'Close Reading', p. 49.

[16] John Lurz, *The Death of the Book: Modernist Novels and the Time of Reading* (New York: Fordham University Press, 2016), p. 1.

[17] Lurz, *The Death of the Book*, p. 1. On the 'great divide' model of modernism, see Andreas Huyssen, *After the Great Divide: Modernism, Mass Culture, Postmodernism* (Bloomington: Indiana University Press, 1986).

Marion Milner (a psychoanalyst, artist and writer who was, I argue, as much a 'modernist' as Woolf or Proust), and in relationship to the popular novels of Ethel M. Dell. Throughout the twentieth century and beyond, one of the most powerful and enduring narratives about modernism has been the idea that modernism is defined in opposition to the feminine and infantile satisfactions of popular culture. In writing from the 1920s and 1930s, this argument appears repeatedly in relationship to the popular novelist Ethel M. Dell, whose readers were imagined by her many critics (including Woolf) as hopelessly addicted and voracious gluttons. In Chapter 2, I offer a close analysis of the scenes of consumption in Dell's novels, revealing how these scenes trouble the dominant critical narrative about Dell and her readers as the monstrous and gluttonous other to literary modernism. Reading Dell's scenes of consumption alongside the formalist criticism of the Bloomsbury art critics Clive Bell and Roger Fry, I challenge the polarised division between popular and modernist readers, turning to James Strachey's account of the unconscious drives underpinning all modern scenes of reading.

For Virginia Woolf, although modernist writing may have been difficult, this difficulty was bound up in the quest for a new, more equal relationship between writer and reader. Announcing, famously, that 'on or about December 1910 human character changed', Woolf's 1924 essay 'Character in Fiction' traced the shifting relationships not only between 'masters and servants, husbands and wives, parents and children', but also between writers and readers.[18] Commenting on the difficulties that she encountered in reading T. S. Eliot and James Joyce, Woolf described Eliot's 'obscurity' and 'confess[ed]' that

> As I sun myself upon the intense and ravishing beauty of one of his lines, and reflect that I must make a dizzy and dangerous leap to the next, and so on from line to line, like an acrobat flying precariously from bar to bar, I cry out, I confess, for the old decorums, and envy the indolence of my ancestors who, instead of spinning madly through mid-air, dreamt quietly in the shade with a book.[19]

This 'obscurity', Woolf insisted, was a necessary symptom of the 'smashing' and 'crashing' of defunct literary traditions that propped up a false hierarchy between writers and readers.[20] Modernist writing may have been 'dizzy[ing]', but, Woolf argued, the immersive and absorbing qualities of modernist writing appeared as a solicitation to the reader to become an active participant, to

[18] Virginia Woolf, 'Character in Fiction' (1924), in *Essays*, III, pp. 420–38 (p. 421, p. 422).
[19] Woolf, *Essays*, III, pp. 434–5.
[20] Woolf, *Essays*, III, p. 433.

forge a 'close and equal alliance' with the writer.[21] Reminding her readers of their 'duties and responsibilities', Woolf wrote:

> In your modesty you seem to consider that writers are of different blood and bone from yourselves [. . .] Never was there a more fatal mistake. It is this division between reader and writer, this humility on your part, these professional airs and graces on ours, that corrupt and emasculate the books which should be the healthy offspring of a close and equal alliance between us.[22]

For Woolf, as critics including Melba Cuddy-Keane, Anna Snaith, Kate Flint and Beth Rigel Daugherty have all argued, the scene of reading was a site of democratic possibility and dialogic exchange in which writers and readers might participate collectively in what Woolf described, in her 1940 lecture to the Brighton branch of the Workers' Educational Association, as the 'common ground' of literature.[23] In the essay based on this talk, Woolf looked to a time when there would be 'no more towers and no more classes'.[24] Arguing that public libraries might serve to fertilise such a terrain, Woolf exhorted her listeners to 'trespass', for 'Literature is no one's private ground; literature is common ground'.[25]

Virginia Woolf was committed to the scene of reading as a site of democratic community. Like Isobel Armstrong, whose arguments in *The Radical Aesthetic* I explore in detail in Chapter 3, Woolf was critical of the drive to mastery she saw in institutionalised forms of reading practised by the 'critic and the scholar'.[26] And yet, in her writings from the 1930s, the vision of literature as a 'common ground' is increasingly threatened by its proximity to fascist fantasies of aesthetic unity and oceanic oneness. In this book, I explore the

---

[21] Woolf, *Essays*, III, p. 436.

[22] Woolf, *Essays*, III, pp. 435–6.

[23] Virginia Woolf, 'The Leaning Tower' (1940), in *Essays*, VI, pp. 259–83 (p. 274, p. 278). On Woolf's relationship with her readers, see Cuddy-Keane, *Virginia Woolf*; Beth Rigel Daugherty, '"You see you kind of belong to us, and what you do matters enormously": Letters from Readers to Virginia Woolf', *Woolf Studies Annual*, 12 (2006), 1–12; Beth Rigel Daugherty, ed., 'Letters from Readers to Virginia Woolf', *Woolf Studies Annual*, 12 (2006), 13–212; Anna Snaith, 'Wide Circles: The *Three Guineas* Letters', *Woolf Studies Annual*, 6 (2000), 1–10; Anna Snaith, ed., 'The *Three Guineas* Letters', *Woolf Studies Annual*, 6 (2000), 11–168. And on Woolf's reading practices see Kate Flint, 'Reading Uncommonly: Virginia Woolf and the Practice of Reading', *The Yearbook of English Studies*, 26 (1996), 187–98; Hermione Lee, *Virginia Woolf* (London: Vintage, 1997), pp. 402–15.

[24] Woolf, *Essays*, VI, p. 274.

[25] Woolf, *Essays*, VI, p. 278.

[26] Woolf, 'The Common Reader' (1925), in *Essays*, IV, p. 19; Isobel Armstrong, *The Radical Aesthetic* (Oxford: Blackwell, 2000).

tensions between a modernist belief in cultural experience as an enactment of democratic community, and a deep-rooted set of anxieties about the political risks for readers who became immersed in politically dubious fantasies of oceanic oneness. Writing about modernist poetry's roots in Friedrich Schiller's idea of aesthetic education as a means of reharmonising an alienated society, Peter Howarth argues that 'By disorienting and bewildering, [modernism] attempts to immerse its reader in a kind of unity unavailable to detached thought, and recreate lost forms of collective being'.[27] In this way, modernism 'becomes a training in democratic feeling'.[28] In this book, I am interested in what happens when, as Howarth puts it, 'this very expansiveness' becomes both modernism's 'attraction and its chief political problem'.[29]

At the heart of modernist culture, I argue, lies an ambivalent fascination with, and an anxiety about, the pleasures, the possibilities and the potential perils of the act of reading in an age dominated by the psycho-politics of mass culture and what Hannah Arendt would describe as the 'fungus'-like growth of fascism.[30] In the scenes of reading and other forms of cultural encounter examined in this book, reading often appears as a process in which the boundaries between self and object, reader and book, dissolve, producing what Marion Milner describes as a 'dread of annihilation merging into a deep delight'.[31] The scenes of reading that I explore in this book are sensuous, immersive, affect-laden. But this is no simple celebration of textual emancipation – this is not another turn in the revolution of poetic language.[32] The scene of reading is, increasingly in the 1930s, shadowed by these writers' anxieties about the psycho-politics of an age of mass identification and looming totalitarianism. To dive deep into the modernist text is, I argue, to encounter the fragile border between rapturous forms of identification and the troubling psycho-politics of fascism.

---

[27] Peter Howarth, *The Cambridge Introduction to Modernist Poetry* (Cambridge: Cambridge University Press, 2012), p. 31.

[28] Howarth, *The Cambridge Introduction*, p. 16.

[29] Howarth, *The Cambridge Introduction*, p. 31.

[30] Defending her argument about the 'banality of evil', Hannah Arendt wrote that 'It can overgrow and lay waste the whole world precisely because it spreads like fungus on the surface'. Hannah Arendt, 'Letter to Gershom Scholem', in *The Jewish Writings*, ed. by Jerome Kohn and Ron H. Feldman (New York: Schocken, 2007), p. 471, cited in Lyndsey Stonebridge, *The Judicial Imagination: Writing After Nuremberg* (Edinburgh: Edinburgh University Press, 2011), p. 30.

[31] Marion Milner, *A Life of One's Own* (Hove: Routledge, 2011), p. 151.

[32] Julia Kristeva, *Revolution in Poetic Language*, trans. by Margaret Waller (New York: Columbia University Press, 1984). On the ways that Kristeva's idea of the semiotic has been used to think about 'rhythm' in Woolf's writing, see Lyndsey Stonebridge, *The Destructive Element: British Psychoanalysis and Modernism* (Basingstoke: Macmillan, 1998), pp. 80–1.

PSYCHOANALYSIS AND THE MODERNIST SCENE OF READING

The links between psychoanalysis and modernism, especially 'Bloomsbury' modernism, are both direct and oblique.[33] In the early decades of the twentieth century, the artists and writers of Bloomsbury shared its famous squares with Freud's first English translators, patients and fellow psychoanalysts. As the site of one of Britain's earliest psychotherapeutic clinics (which was partly funded by the writer May Sinclair), and as the setting for Melanie Klein's first London lectures in 1925, Bloomsbury was home to numerous psychoanalysts, including Virginia Woolf's brother and sister-in-law, Adrian and Karin Stephen.[34] In 1924, Virginia and Leonard Woolf became the publishers of the largest library of psychoanalytic writing in English, taking over the entire International Psycho-Analytical Library, and publishing the works of Freud and other psychoanalysts in translations by (amongst others) their friends James and Alix Strachey.[35] '[A]ll the psycho-analyst books have been dumped in a fortress the size of Windsor castle in ruins upon the floor,' Woolf wrote:

[33] See Helen Tyson, '"Freudian Fiction" or "Wild Psycho-Analysis"? Modernism, Psychoanalysis, and Popular Fiction, 1900–1920', in *British Literature in Transition, 1900–1920: A New Age?*, ed. by James Purdon (Cambridge: Cambridge University Press, 2021), pp. 365–80; Sanja Bahun, 'Woolf and Psychoanalytic Theory', in *Virginia Woolf in Context*, ed. by Jane Goldman and Bryony Randall (Cambridge: Cambridge University Press, 2012), pp. 92–109; Matt ffytche, 'The Modernist Road to the Unconscious', in *The Oxford Handbook of Modernisms*, ed. by Peter Brooker et al. (Oxford: Oxford University Press, 2010), pp. 410–28; Lyndsey Stonebridge, 'Psychoanalysis and Literature', in *The Cambridge History of Twentieth-Century Literature*, ed. by Laura Marcus and Peter Nicholls (Cambridge: Cambridge University Press, 2004), pp. 269–85; Stephen Frosh, 'Psychoanalysis in Britain: "The Rituals of Destruction"', in *A Concise Companion to Modernism*, ed. by David Bradshaw (Malden: Blackwell Publishing, 2003), pp. 116–37; Sally Alexander, 'Psychoanalysis in Britain in the Early Twentieth Century: An Introductory Note', *History Workshop Journal*, 45 (1998), 135–44; R. D. Hinshelwood, 'Psychoanalysis in Britain: Points of Cultural Access, 1893–1918', *International Journal of Psycho-Analysis*, 76 (1995), 135–51.

[34] On the Brunswick Square Medico-Psychological Clinic, see Theophilus Boll, 'May Sinclair and the Medico-Psychological Clinic of London', *Proceedings of the American Philosophical Society*, 106 (1962), 310–26; Suzanne Raitt, 'Early British Psychoanalysis and the Medico-Psychological Clinic', *History Workshop Journal*, 58.1 (2004), 63–85; Philippa Martindale, '"Against all hushing up and stamping down": The Medico-Psychological Clinic of London and the Novelist May Sinclair', *Psychoanalysis and History*, 6.2 (2004), 177–200. On the reception of Freud's ideas in the British press, see Dean Rapp, 'The Reception of Freud by the British Press: General Interest and Literary Magazines, 1920–1925', *Journal of the History of the Behavioural Sciences*, 24 (1988), 191–201; Dean Rapp, 'The Early Discovery of Freud by the British General Educated Public, 1912–1919', *Social History of Medicine*, 3.2 (1990), 217–43.

[35] J. H. Willis, Jr, *Leonard and Virginia Woolf as Publishers: The Hogarth Press, 1917–41* (Charlottesville: University Press of Virginia, 1992), pp. 297–328.

We are publishing all Dr Freud, and I glance at the proof and read how Mr A. B. threw a bottle of red ink on to the sheets of his marriage bed to excuse his impotence to the housemaid, but threw it in the wrong place, which unhinged his wife's mind,—and to this day she pours claret on the dinner table. We could all go on like that for hours: and yet these Germans think it proves something—besides their own gull-like imbecility.[36]

Fifteen years later, on 29 January 1939, Woolf recorded in her diary: 'Barcelona has fallen: Hitler speaks tomorrow; the next dress rehearsal begins; I have seen Marie Stopes, Princesse de Polignac [. . .] & Dr Freud in the last 3 days.'[37] As Europe sat waiting for Hitler's next speech – the speech in which he would announce his 'prophecy' of the 'annihilation of the Jewish race' – Virginia and Leonard Woolf visited Sigmund Freud.[38] The ageing father of psychoanalysis, seeking refuge in London from Nazi-occupied Vienna, gave Virginia a narcissus. The conversation, Woolf wrote, was 'difficult'.[39] They felt 'like patients on chairs', sitting opposite 'A screwed up shrunk very old man', 'an old fire now flickering'.[40] They discussed Hitler, Freud's books, fame, guilt and the war. By this point, the Woolfs had been Freud's publishers for fifteen years, and yet it was only after Freud's death in 1939 that Woolf would finally, against 'the monotonous boom of the war', begin seriously to read Freud.[41] On 2 December, Woolf wrote in her diary: 'Began reading Freud last night; to enlarge the circumference. to give my brain a wider scope: to make it objective; to get outside. Thus defeat the shrinkage of age. Always take on new things. Break the rhythm &c.'[42] By the end of that week she was 'gulping up Freud'.[43] 'Freud is upsetting,' she wrote:

> reducing one to whirlpool; & I daresay truly. If we're all instinct, the unconscious, whats all this about civilisation, the whole man, freedom &c? His savagery against God good. The falseness of loving one's neighbours. The conscience as censor. Hate . . . But I'm too mixed.[44]

---

[36] Virginia Woolf, *The Letters of Virginia Woolf*, ed. by Nigel Nicolson and Joanne Trautmann, 6 vols (London: Hogarth Press, 1975–1980), VI, p. 202.

[37] Virginia Woolf, *The Diary of Virginia Woolf*, ed. by Anne Olivier Bell and Andrew McNeillie, 5 vols (London: Hogarth Press, 1977–1984), V, p. 202.

[38] Adolf Hitler, Speech to the Reichstag, 30 January 1939, cited by Nikolaus Wachsmann, 'The Policy of Exclusion: Repression in the Nazi State, 1933–1939', in *Nazi Germany*, ed. by Jane Kaplan (Oxford: Oxford University Press, 2008), pp. 122–49 (p. 144).

[39] Woolf, *Diary*, V, p. 202.

[40] Woolf, *Diary*, V, p. 202.

[41] Woolf, *Diary*, V, p. 238.

[42] Woolf, *Diary*, V, p. 248.

[43] Woolf, *Diary*, V, p. 249.

[44] Woolf, *Diary*, V, p. 250.

For Elizabeth Abel, Virginia Woolf's antipathy towards psychoanalysis is connected to a distinctively English and 'singularly literary version of psychoanalytic discourse' that was, in large part, constructed by 'Bloomsbury' writers and
translators, and 'which intensified both its appeal and its potential threat to
writers of imaginative texts'.[45] The affinities between psychoanalysis and literature were, of course, already present, albeit in a sometimes anxious form,
in Freud's own writing. Having recounted the final case in *Studies on Hysteria*
(1893), Freud found it 'strange' that 'the case studies I write should read like
short stories and that, as one might say, they lack the serious stamp of science'.[46]
Despite this hesitation, Freud returned frequently to literary examples: he
'turn[ed] to the poets' when he reached an impasse or difficulty in his own thinking, and, of course, one of the central concepts of psychoanalysis, the Oedipus
complex, is itself rooted in Freud's argument that the force of the Greek tragedy,
and later *Hamlet*, depends upon the reader or spectator being 'compell[ed]' to
'recognize our own inner life, where those impulses, though suppressed, are still
present'.[47] Following the 1925 publication of Freud's *Collected Papers*, there
was a lengthy and heated debate in the reviews and letters pages of the *Nation
and Athenaeum*, in which, as Abel notes, both detractors and defenders of psychoanalysis relied on the 'recurrent term', 'Imagination'.[48] Later that year, the
Nation published a two-part essay by the psychoanalyst James Glover on 'Freud

---

[45] Elizabeth Abel, *Virginia Woolf and the Fictions of Psychoanalysis* (Chicago: University
of Chicago Press, 1989), p. 15. On Woolf and psychoanalysis, see also Jan Ellen Gold-
stein, 'The Woolfs' Response to Freud: Water Spiders, Singing Canaries, and the Second
Apple', in *Literature and Psychoanalysis*, ed. by Edith Kurzweil and William Phillips (New
York: Columbia University Press, 1983), pp. 232–55; Bahun, 'Woolf and Psychoanalytic
Theory', pp. 92–109; Perry Meisel, 'Woolf and Freud: The Kleinian Turn', in *Virginia
Woolf in Context*, ed. by Jane Goldman and Bryony Randall (Cambridge: Cambridge
University Press, 2012), pp. 332–41; Maud Ellmann, 'A Passage to the Lighthouse', in
A Companion to Virginia Woolf, ed. by Jessica Berman (Oxford: John Wiley & Sons,
2016), pp. 95–108; Maud Ellmann, 'On Not Being Able to Paint: *To the Lighthouse*
via Psychoanalysis', in *Virginia Woolf*, ed. by James Acheson (London: Palgrave, 2017),
pp. 106–24.

[46] Sigmund Freud and Josef Breuer, *Studies on Hysteria* (1893–95), in *The Standard
Edition of the Complete Psychological Works of Sigmund Freud*, trans. and ed. by James
Strachey et al., 24 vols (London: Hogarth Press and the Institute of Psycho-Analysis, 1953–
74), II, pp. 135–81 (p. 160).

[47] Sigmund Freud, *New Introductory Lectures on Psycho-Analysis* (1933 [1932]), *Standard
Edition*, XXII, pp. 1–182 (p. 135); Sigmund Freud, *The Interpretation of Dreams* (1900–
1901), *Standard Edition*, IV–V, p. 263. See Rachel Bowlby, *Freudian Mythologies: Greek
Tragedy and Modern Identities* (Oxford: Oxford University Press, 2009).

[48] Abel, *Virginia Woolf*, p. 15. See also John Forrester and Laura Cameron, 'A Psychoanalytic
Debate in 1925', in *Freud in Cambridge* (Cambridge: Cambridge University Press, 2017),
pp. 363–431.

and His Critics'. Reiterating a claim often attributed to Freud himself, Glover insisted that the idea of the unconscious 'must be credited to literary genius long before Freud'.[49] Writing admiringly of Freud's 'great subtlety of mind', Leonard Woolf described a 'broad and sweeping imagination more characteristic of the poet than the scientist or the medical practitioner'.[50]

For a number of modernist writers, one of the primary issues at stake in their often hostile encounters with psychoanalysis was the question of reading and interpretation. In a 1920 review of what – despite not, at that stage, having read any Freud – she called 'Freudian Fiction' (she was reviewing J. D. Beresford's novel *An Imperfect Mother*), Virginia Woolf complained 'that the new key is a patent key that opens every door. It simplifies rather than complicates, detracts rather than enriches'.[51] The characters in such fiction, Woolf claimed, are 'some of the very numerous progeny of Dr Freud' – 'all the characters have become cases' and 'We', the readers, are obliged to adopt 'the professional manner of a doctor intent upon his diagnosis'.[52] Writing in 1922, T. S. Eliot complained similarly of the reductive vision of a new 'psychoanalytic type' of novel that claimed to lay bare 'the soul of man under psychoanalysis'.[53] D. H. Lawrence was outraged by the 'vicious half-statements of the Freudians'.[54] Katherine Mansfield complained of 'the sudden "mushroom growth" of cheap psycho analysis', and, in *Finnegans Wake*, James Joyce mocked the 'yung and easily freudened', issuing a 'word of warning' to his readers to be wary of making 'freudful mistake[s]'.[55] These writers were anxious about what

---

[49] Leonard Woolf wrote to T. S. Eliot to recommend Glover as the 'best English psycho-analyst'. James Glover, 'Freud and His Critics: I', *Nation and Athenaeum*, 38.5 (31 October 1925), 180–2 (p. 181); *The Letters of T. S. Eliot*, ed. by Valerie Eliot, Hugh Haughton and John Haffenden, 5 vols (London: Faber and Faber, 1988–2009), II, p. 651, pp. 702–5; Victoria Glendinning, *Leonard Woolf: A Biography* (New York: Free Press, 2006), p. 236. See also Lionel Trilling, *Freud and the Crisis of Our Culture* (Boston: Beacon Press, 1955), pp. 15–16; Adam Phillips, 'Poetry and Psychoanalysis', in *Promises, Promises: Essays on Literature and Psychoanalysis* (London: Faber and Faber, 2000), pp. 1–34.

[50] Leonard Woolf, 'Review of Freud's *Psychopathology of Everyday Life*', *New Weekly*, 1.13 (June 1914), 12; reprinted in *A Bloomsbury Group Reader*, ed. by S. P. Rosenbaum (Oxford: Blackwell, 1993), pp. 189–91 (pp. 189–90).

[51] Virginia Woolf, 'Freudian Fiction' (1920), in *Essays*, III, pp. 195–8 (p. 197).

[52] Woolf, *Essays*, III, p. 196.

[53] T. S. Eliot, 'London Letter: August 1922', *Dial*, 73 (September 1922), 329–31 (p. 330).

[54] D. H. Lawrence, *The Letters of D. H. Lawrence, Volume II: 1913–1916*, ed. by George J. Zytaruk and James T. Boulton, 2nd edn (Cambridge: Cambridge University Press, 2002), p. 655.

[55] Katherine Mansfield, *The Collected Letters of Katherine Mansfield*, ed. by Vincent O'Sullivan and Margaret Scott, 5 vols (Oxford: Oxford University Press, 1984–2008), IV, p. 69; James Joyce, *The Restored Finnegans Wake* (1923–39), ed. by Danis Rose and John O'Hanlon (London: Penguin, 2010), pp. 91–2, p. 320.

Paul Ricœur, writing some forty years later, would refer to as a 'hermeneutics of suspicion'.[56] Modernist writers were troubled by what they perceived as a symptomatic theory of reading at the heart of psychoanalysis – a theory in which literature, treated like a patient, is subordinated to the interpretative mastery of the psychoanalytic reader, who sets about exposing the unconscious life of fictional characters, or, worse, diagnosing their author.[57] This modernist refutation of psychoanalysis is, however, more often than not a critique of what Freud himself described as '"wild" psycho-analysis' – it is a critique of the most reductive and simplified version of psychoanalysis.[58] For both Woolf and Mansfield, their critique of psychoanalysis was derived not so much from a sustained engagement with psychoanalytic writing or practice, but from a critical reading of popular 'Freudian Fiction' (in Woolf's words) and 'cheap' novels (in Mansfield's). These 'wild' or, to borrow Shoshana Felman's term, 'vulgar' forms of psychoanalysis were not only offensive to the sensibilities of modernist writers, but also a travesty of Freud's own portrait of the human mind.[59]

Freud's relationship to interpretation was fraught. Despite his admittedly troubled allegiance to Enlightenment scientific ideals, and despite his own sometimes 'vulgar' or 'wild' readings of literary texts, Freud was, nonetheless, alert to the contradictions and tensions inherent in his commitment to unravelling unconscious aspects of the human psyche that, by definition, retreat from the analyst's grasp. Mansfield's complaint about the '"mushroom growth" of cheap psycho analysis' is uncannily reminiscent of one of the most famous moments in which Freud can be seen to hesitate before the limits of interpretation. In *The Interpretation of Dreams*, Freud observed:

> There is often a passage in even the most thoroughly interpreted dream which has to be left obscure; this is because we become aware during

---

[56] Paul Ricœur, *Freud and Philosophy: An Essay on Interpretation*, trans. by Denis Savage (New Haven: Yale University Press, 1970), pp. 33–4.

[57] See also Allon White, *The Uses of Obscurity: The Fiction of Early Modernism* (London: Routledge & Kegan Paul, 1981), p. 45, p. 167, n. 52.

[58] Sigmund Freud, '"Wild" Psycho-Analysis' (1910), *Standard Edition*, XI, pp. 219–28.

[59] See Shoshana Felman, 'Turning the Screw of Interpretation', *Yale French Studies*, 55/56 (1977), 94–207 (pp. 106–8); Shoshana Felman, 'To Open the Question', *Yale French Studies*, 55/56 (1977), 5–10. On literature and psychoanalysis, see also Maud Ellmann, ed., *Psychoanalytic Literary Criticism* (London: Longman, 1994); Helen Small and Trudi Tate, eds, *Literature, Science, Psychoanalysis, 1830–1970: Essays in Honour of Gillian Beer* (Oxford: Oxford University Press, 2003); Laura Marcus and Ankhi Mukherjee, eds, *A Concise Companion to Psychoanalysis, Literature, and Culture* (Oxford: Wiley, 2014). On '"Wild" Psycho-Analysis', see also Tyson, '"Freudian Fiction"'; Shaul Bar-Haim, Elizabeth Coles and Helen Tyson, 'Introduction: Wild Analysis', in *Wild Analysis: From the Couch to Cultural and Political Life*, ed. by Shaul Bar-Haim, Elizabeth Coles and Helen Tyson (London: Routledge, 2021), pp. xxi–xlvi.

the work of interpretation that at that point there is a tangle of dream-thoughts which cannot be unravelled [. . .] This is the dream's navel, the spot where it reaches down into the unknown. The dream-thoughts to which we are led by interpretation cannot [. . .] have any definite endings; they are bound to branch out in every direction into the intricate network of our world of thought. It is at some point where this meshwork is particularly close that the dream-wish grows up, like a mushroom out of its mycelium.[60]

Mansfield's strange echo (whether intentional or not) of Freud's description of the 'obscure' 'navel' of the dream acts as a reminder that Freud's writings are as much a testament to what Woolf described as the 'dark region of psychology' as to the sovereign powers of the analyst.[61]

Despite these historical tensions between modernism and psychoanalysis, in this book I argue that psychoanalysis offers a unique set of insights into the modernist and early-twentieth-century scene of reading. For Mary Jacobus – from whom I borrow the evocative phrase 'the scene of reading' – the psychoanalytic concepts of introjection and projection, the inner world, transference, and the transitional object all offer a vivid language for describing 'the plunge into observation, self-observation, and memory involved in reading'.[62] In Jacobus's work, the term 'the scene of reading' (which itself evokes Jacques Derrida's essay on 'Freud and the Scene of Writing') describes 'a scene in which imagining an open book in an empty room gives rise to a series of equivalences, such as "inside the book" and "inside me"'.[63] For Jacobus, psychoanalysis – especially the tradition of object relations psychoanalysis – offers a peculiarly resonant account of what Alix Strachey called 'the idea of insideness', facilitating Jacobus's exploration of the question of how, when we read, 'things get, so to speak, from the outside to the inside—simultaneously establishing the boundary between them and seeming to abolish it'.[64] Taking this account of psychoanalysis and the 'scene of reading' into an analysis of the specifically modernist and early-twentieth-century scene of reading, I argue that modernist writing and psychoanalysis shared a historically specific fascination with the intimate psychic processes of reading.

In modernist and psychoanalytic writing from the first part of the twentieth century, we find attempts to reckon with and to reimagine the role of literature in a darkening world. As we shall see in what follows, the psychoanalytic

[60] Freud, *The Interpretation of Dreams*, p. 525.

[61] See Tyson, '"Freudian Fiction"'.

[62] Mary Jacobus, *Psychoanalysis and the Scene of Reading* (Oxford: Oxford University Press, 1999), pp. 11–12.

[63] Jacobus, *Psychoanalysis*, p. 18.

[64] Alix Strachey, 'A Note on the Use of the Word "Internal"', *International Journal of Psycho-Analysis*, 22 (1941), 37–43, cited by Jacobus, *Psychoanalysis*, p. 19.

concepts of fantasy, identification and reparation were all forged within, and in part as a response to, the violent historical landscape of the 1910s, 1920s and 1930s. As critics and historians including Lyndsey Stonebridge, Jacqueline Rose, Adam Phillips, Stephen Frosh, Sally Alexander and Michal Shapira have all noted, the psychoanalytic theory of aggression can be historically situated: it is no coincidence that psychoanalysts writing in the wake of the First World War, during the Second World War, and in its aftermath were drawn to theorise a violently destructive aspect of psychic life, and nor is it a coincidence that, in these years, psychoanalysts also sought to theorise forms of psychic and aesthetic reparation and repair.[65] Describing the 'traffic' of Kleinian ideas with inter-war rhetoric about reparation following the Treaty of Versailles, Stonebridge writes:

> This traffic can no more simply be described as proof that psychoanalysis may be understood as the sum of historical contingencies that produced it (which is true), than it can be put forward as testament to the efficacy of psychoanalysis as a form of historical interpretation (which is also true): the relation between psychoanalysis and history is, notoriously and rightly, more complex.[66]

Psychoanalytic ideas forged in the early twentieth century were both shaped by and can help to offer powerful analyses of that historical moment.[67] In this book, I argue that these psychoanalytic ideas also offer a distinctive way of understanding the fantasies that underpinned the scene of reading in this era.

THE SCENE OF READING AND THE CULTURE OF REDEMPTION

In a 1905 essay, 'On Reading', Marcel Proust wrote that

> There are [. . .] certain circumstances, pathological circumstances one might say, of spiritual depression, in which reading can become a sort of curative discipline entrusted with the task of continually leading a lazy

---

[65] See Stonebridge, *The Destructive Element*, p. 5, pp. 31–2; Jacqueline Rose, *Why War? Psychoanalysis, Politics and the Return to Melanie Klein* (Oxford: Blackwell, 1993), pp. 135–230; Adam Phillips, 'Bombs Away', *History Workshop Journal*, 39.45 (1998), 183–98; Stephen Frosh, 'Psychoanalysis in Britain', pp. 116–37; Sally Alexander, 'D. W. Winnicott and the Social Democratic Vision', in *Psychoanalysis in the Age of Totalitarianism*, ed. by Matt ffytche and Daniel Pick (London: Routledge, 2016), pp. 114–30; Michal Shapira, *The War Inside: Psychoanalysis, Total War, and the Making of the Democratic Self in Postwar Britain* (Cambridge: Cambridge University Press, 2013); Sally Alexander and Barbara Taylor, 'Introduction', in *Psyche and History: Culture, Psychoanalysis, and the Past*, ed. by Sally Alexander and Barbara Taylor (London: Palgrave, 2012), pp. 1–10.

[66] Stonebridge, *The Destructive Element*, pp. 31–2.

[67] See also Bar-Haim, Coles and Tyson, 'Introduction: Wild Analysis', pp. xxv–xxix.

spirit, by means of repeated excitations, back to an inner life. Books then play for the person in these circumstances a role analogous to that played by psychotherapists for certain neurasthenics.[68]

For Leo Bersani, the idea of literature as a 'sort of curative discipline' is typical of a modernist and psychoanalytic faith in art as a form of reparation or, to cite Bersani's term, 'redemption'. In *The Culture of Redemption*, and elsewhere, Bersani criticises modernist and psychoanalytic writers for conspiring to produce a redemptive account of cultural experience, in which 'great masterworks' are supposed to 'save us—save us from our lives, which in some way are failed lives in need of repair or redemption'.[69] For Bersani, this modernist 'culture of redemption' presents art as a form of compensation for the devastations and desolations of personal and historical reality, soliciting readers and spectators to turn a dangerously blind eye to the 'catastrophes of history'.[70]

In the critical literature on modernism, the idea that art or literature might offer forms of reparation, consolation or solace vies with claims about the power of art to bring about political as well as personal transformation in the reader.[71] A modernist and critical faith in reading as a source of radical transformation, as well as the need to defend the role of literary studies in universities, has resulted in a deep suspicion of forms of reading that, it is claimed, soothe or comfort with illusions, rather than expose injustice, shatter complacency and demystify illusion. For Bersani, although modernist writers like Proust and Joyce were complicit with the 'culture of redemption', writers like Samuel Beckett produce a kind of writing in which the reader experiences a form of self-shattering. In his critique of the culture of redemption, Bersani celebrates instead a form of art that shatters the insistence on 'identity as authority'.[72] In the 'first pages of Freud's essay on narcissism', and in certain modernist artists and writers, Bersani finds a 'self-*jouissance* that dissolves the person and thereby [. . .] erases the sacrosanct value of selfhood, a value that may account for human beings' extraordinary willingness to kill in order to protect the seriousness of their statements'.[73] Writing with Ulysse Dutoit, Bersani argues that 'the only way to escape the irresistible thrill of exercising a hyperbolic (personal and cultural) ego is to exaggerate, with a Beckettian obstinacy, our forlornness, our divested, even derelict condition'. Seeking 'to imagine a form of political and cultural resistance and renewal consistent with

---

[68] Marcel Proust, 'On Reading' (1905), in *On Reading*, trans. and ed. by Damion Searls (London: Hesperus, 2011), pp. 24–5.

[69] Bersani and Dutoit, *Arts of Impoverishment*, pp. 3–4.

[70] Bersani, *The Culture of Redemption*, p. 22.

[71] For a summary of these debates see James, *Discrepant Solace*, pp. 14–16, pp. 44–5.

[72] Bersani, *The Culture of Redemption*, p. 3.

[73] Bersani, *The Culture of Redemption*, pp. 3–4.

self-divestiture and the renunciation of authority', Bersani and Dutoit locate this form of 'cultural resistance' in the fragmented and inhospitable world of the Beckettian text.[74] And yet, there is no guarantee that shattered readers go on to bring about positive change in the world.[75]

Both modernist writers and psychoanalysts were attracted to the idea of art as a form of reparation in the war-torn and increasingly fractious Europe of the 1920s and 1930s. And yet, these writers also encountered forms of violence and destruction that rendered these fantasies of literary reparation fragile and precarious. For Woolf and Melanie Klein, in their writing from the 1930s, the scene of reading was also increasingly threatened by the destructive fantasies that animated European fascism. In Klein's writing, although she sketches the framework for a reparative theory of reading, the scene of reparation nonetheless remains haunted by the forms of psychic and historical violence that it is trying to contain. In Woolf's *The Waves*, similarly, the characters repeatedly turn to poetry and to art in an attempt to find consolation in the wake of their friend Percival's death. And yet, in *The Waves*, as I argue in Chapter 3, the scene of reading is overdetermined, the desire for consolation bound up with troubling fantasies of masculine authority, imperial power and proto-fascist unity. By framing the act of reading in this way, Woolf challenges her readers to reflect critically on the fantasies that shape our own investments in literature, not only revealing a conflicting desire for a fragile form of reparation, but also warning against the potential dangers of a redemptive view of art.

'FOREBODINGS ABOUT FASCISM'[76]

In *Civilization and Its Discontents* (1930), Freud responded to Romain Rolland's description of what he called the 'oceanic feeling' with scepticism.[77] 'Normally', Freud observed, 'there is nothing of which we are more certain than the feeling of our self, of our own ego.'[78] 'This ego', Freud claimed, 'appears to us as something autonomous and unitary, marked off distinctly from everything else.'[79] This 'appearance' of a unitary self is, Freud argued,

---

[74] Bersani and Dutoit, *Arts of Impoverishment*, pp. 8–9.

[75] For critical responses to Bersani, see Maud Ellmann, 'Failing to Fail', *Essays in Criticism*, 65.1 (1995), 84–92 (p. 91), and Eve Kosofsky Sedgwick, 'Paranoid Reading and Reparative Reading', in *Touching Feeling: Affect, Pedagogy, Performativity* (Durham, NC: Duke University Press, 2003), pp. 123–51. On the political dangers of 'radical desubjectivization', see Mikkel Borch-Jacobsen, *The Freudian Subject*, trans. by Catherine Porter (London: Macmillan, 1989), pp. 26–7.

[76] Marion Milner, *An Experiment in Leisure* (Hove: Routledge, 2011), p. 82.

[77] Sigmund Freud, *Civilization and Its Discontents* (1930), *Standard Edition*, XXI, pp. 57–146 (p. 64).

[78] Freud, *Civilization*, p. 65.

[79] Freud, *Civilization*, p. 66.

'deceptive', serving only as a 'kind of façade' for the deep recesses of uncon-scious life.[80] And yet, when we think about the ego in relation to the outside world, it 'seems to maintain clear and sharp lines of demarcation'.[81] There is, Freud argued, 'only one' (although he quickly added another) exception to our certainty of existing as an autonomous, unitary self, and that is the state of being in love:

> At the height of being in love the boundary between ego and object threatens to melt away. Against all the evidence of his senses, a man who is in love declares that 'I' and 'you' are one, and is prepared to behave as if it were a fact.[82]

'Pathology', Freud added, has also 'made us acquainted with a great number of states in which the boundary lines between the ego and the external world become uncertain or in which they are actually drawn incorrectly':

> There are cases in which parts of a person's own body, even portions of his own mental life—his perceptions, thoughts and feelings—, appear alien to him and as not belonging to his ego; there are other cases in which he ascribes to the external world things that clearly originate in his own ego and that ought to be acknowledged by it.

'Thus', Freud acknowledges reluctantly, 'even the feeling of our own ego is subject to disturbances and the boundaries of the ego are not constant.'[83]

For Marcel Proust, Virginia Woolf, Marion Milner, and even for Freud him-self, the scene of reading offered a seductive experience of the oceanic feeling. In his essay on reading, Proust described reading as a 'friendship without ego', while, for Freud, the 'innermost secret', the 'essential *ars poetica*' of the creative writer, lay 'in the technique of overcoming the feeling of repulsion in us which is undoubtedly connected with the barriers that rise between each single ego and the others'.[84] Woolf wrote similarly, in terms that are at once erotic and ambivalent, that 'the state of reading consists in a complete elimination of the ego, and it's the ego that erects itself like another part of the body I don't dare to name'.[85] For Woolf this annihilation of the masculine ego is pleasurable, but

---

[80] Freud, *Civilization*, p. 66.

[81] Freud, *Civilization*, p. 66.

[82] Freud, *Civilization*, p. 66.

[83] Freud, *Civilization*, p. 66. See also Jacobus, *Psychoanalysis*, p. 20.

[84] Proust, 'On Reading', p. 35; Sigmund Freud, 'Creative Writers and Day-Dreaming' (1908 [1907]), *Standard Edition*, IX, pp. 141–53 (p. 152).

[85] Woolf, *Letters*, V, p. 319.

also besets her with a violence, transforming into something more like depression and hinting at the sinister aspect of such dissolution: 'It's a disembodied trance-like rapture that used to seize me as a girl, and comes back now and again [. . .] with a violence that lays me low.'[86] In the scenes of reading, and in the various forms of cultural encounter that populate Woolf's, Proust's and Milner's writing, all three writers explore states in which the boundaries between the individual ego and the cultural object seem to dissolve, creating sensuous experiences of pleasure and communal feeling. And yet, just as Freud's own reluctance to identify with the 'oceanic feeling' may itself have been informed by the forms of mass psychology that lurk in the historical background to *Civilization and Its Discontents*, for Woolf and for Milner the fantasy of literature as a source of oceanic feeling was as terrifying as it was alluring.[87] Although in both her novels and her essays Woolf celebrates literature as the 'common ground' of democratic life, the scenes of reading that populate her writing in the 1930s are also fearful of the perilous forms of self-abandon and communal submission that would be encouraged under fascism.[88]

In 1939, as Hitler spread his tentacles across Europe, Woolf finally began 'gulping up Freud', noting, as she did, the affinities with her own analysis of a 'subconscious Hitlerism' lurking in Britain.[89] In *Three Guineas*, published in 1938, Woolf had traced a line between the patriarchal group fantasies that animated English imperialism and the forms of misogyny that underpinned European fascism, insisting that the latent 'germ' of fascism could be found embedded within the day-to-day structures of British life as much as in the speeches of Hitler and Mussolini.[90] In this epistolary essay, Woolf traced the male desire to dominate to a 'powerful and widespread subconscious motive', to 'very ancient and obscure emotions [. . .] which the Professors have only lately brought to the surface and named "infantile fixation", "Oedipus complex", and the rest'.[91] Bizarrely, but in a manner that is characteristic of her

---

[86] Woolf, *Letters*, V, p. 319. On Woolf's presentation of reading as 'linked to the pleasures of sexuality, but without the threats and dangers attendant on assertive masculine participation', see Flint, 'Reading Uncommonly', p. 187.

[87] On the relationship between the oceanic feeling and fascism, see Alice Kaplan, *Reproductions of Banality* (Minneapolis: University of Minnesota Press, 1986), p. 13, and Jessica Berman, *Modernist Fiction, Cosmopolitanism, and the Politics of Community* (Cambridge: Cambridge University Press, 2011), p. 139. See also Daniel Pick, 'Freud's *Group Psychology* and the History of the Crowd', *History Workshop Journal*, 40.1 (1995), 39–62; and Jacqueline Rose, 'Introduction', in Sigmund Freud, *Mass Psychology and Other Writings*, trans. by J. A. Underwood (London: Penguin, 2004), pp. vii–xlii.

[88] Woolf, *Essays*, VI, p. 274.

[89] Woolf, *Diary*, V, p. 249.

[90] Virginia Woolf, *Three Guineas* (1938), in *A Room of One's Own and Three Guineas*, ed. by Anna Snaith (Oxford: Oxford University Press, 2015), pp. 135–6, p. 201.

[91] Woolf, *Three Guineas*, p. 200, p. 204.

ambivalence towards psychoanalysis, Woolf's footnotes make no direct reference to Freud, plucking the phrases '"infantile fixation" [. . .] and the rest' from an Oxford theologian rather than any of the psychoanalysts that Woolf was publishing at the Hogarth Press.[92] Woolf's reading notes for 'Freud. Groups Psy. & The Ego', however, suggest that when she did read Freud directly in 1939, she found much to confirm and to stimulate her own analysis of the intimate relationship between patriarchal group psychology, the masculine 'instinct' to fight, and the fantasies underpinning fascism.[93] Copying out a quotation from Freud's chapter on 'The Herd Instinct', in which Freud notes how the 'individual' is 'ruled' by 'attitudes in the group mind' that 'exhibit themselves' in forms such as 'class prejudices' and 'public opinion', Woolf commented: 'Suppose we add sex prejudice?'[94] Following another quotation, in which Freud describes how 'the woman' (the 'prize of battle & the allurement to murder') was 'turned in to the seducer & instigator to the crime', Woolf posed a series of questions: 'The origin of sex hatred? What wd. happen if the male accepted the woman as his equal? & then had no scapegoat?'[95] Pursuing this line of thought, Woolf wrote:

> The present war is very different.
>
> For now the male has also considered his attributes in Hitler, & is fighting against them. Is this the first time in history that a sex has turned against its own specific qualities? Compare with the womans movement.
>
> [. . .] That was said to be a defiance of womanhood. She replied How do you know?
>
> At any rate she has changed . . .
>
> [. . .] In the present war we are fighting for liberty. But we can only get it if we destroy the male attributes. Thus the womans part is to achieve the emancipation of man. In that lies the only hope of permanent peace.[96]

[92] Woolf, *Three Guineas*, pp. 199–201. Woolf cites Canon Laurence William Grensted, 'Appendix I: Certain Psychological and Physiological Considerations', in *The Ministry of Women, Report of the Archbishops' Commission on The Ministry of Women* (London: Church Literature Association, 1936), pp. 79–87.

[93] Transcribed from Virginia Woolf, Holograph Reading Notebooks, RN1.21, p. 3, Virginia Woolf Collection of Papers, Henry W. and Albert A. Berg Collection of English and American Literature, New York Public Library, Astor, Lenox and Tilden Foundations; Woolf, *Three Guineas*, pp. 184–5. With thanks to the Society of Authors as the Literary Representative of the Estate of Virginia Woolf for permission to cite from the reading notebooks.

[94] Woolf, Holograph Reading Notebooks, p. 3; the quotation corresponds to Sigmund Freud, *Group Psychology and the Analysis of the Ego*, trans. by James Strachey (London: International Psycho-Analytical Press, 1922), p. 82.

[95] Woolf, Holograph Reading Notebooks, p. 4; Freud, *Group Psychology*, pp. 113–14.

[96] Woolf, Holograph Reading Notebooks, pp. 4–5.

If reading Freud confirmed Woolf's view that a line can be drawn between the fantasies of masculinity underpinning patriarchal society and those underlying the dictatorships of fascist Europe, it also, as these notes suggest, reinforced her view that it was through their position as 'outsiders' that women might stand against tyranny and 'achieve the emancipation of man'.[97] In her 1940 essay 'Thoughts on Peace in an Air Raid', Woolf wrote of the 'subconscious Hitlerism' that threatened to dominate women's as well as men's minds.[98] 'Hitler', Woolf wrote, is 'Aggressiveness, tyranny, the insane love of power made manifest': 'Destroy that', Woolf argued, repeating the observations from her reading notes, 'and you will be free'.[99] 'Hitlers', she asserted, 'are bred by slaves', suggesting that it was only through thinking 'against the current' that women might 'free ourselves from tyranny' and thereby 'free men from tyranny'.[100]

In *Three Guineas*, Woolf both modelled and made an argument for a form of feminist critique, celebrating the critical and imaginative possibilities of the position of the outsider. In her reading of *Antigone*, Woolf suggests that, like Antigone, women might transform their own position as outsiders into a critique and a potential reimagining of the reigning structures of patriarchal, imperialist and fascist oppression. And yet, as I show in Chapter 4, although, in *Three Guineas*, Woolf imagines the scene of reading as an enactment of feminist solidarity with the 'Outsiders' Society', in *The Years*, the scenes of reading explore literary encounters in which the reader struggles to extricate herself from the fantasies that permeated British fascism in the 1930s. In the scenes of reading depicted in *The Years*, Woolf challenges those critical accounts that celebrate modernism as a form of writing that pushes the reader into the position of a critical outsider. Despite Woolf's own call for women and – implicitly – for other marginalised people to think 'against the current', in *The Years*, the scenes of reading explore risky forms of identification that don't necessarily yield the reader a safe position outside of the fantasies and structures that dominated Europe in the 1930s.[101] For Woolf, the scene of reading appeared as a risky site of encounter with the forms of mass psychology that dominated individual, social and political life in the 1930s.

* * *

[97] Woolf, *Three Guineas*, pp. 183–91, p. 252, n. 48; Woolf, Holograph Reading Notebooks, p. 5.

[98] Virginia Woolf, 'Thoughts on Peace in an Air Raid' (1940), in *Essays*, VI, pp. 242–8 (p. 243, pp. 245–7, n. 1). See also Abel, *Virginia Woolf*, p. 165, n. 44; John Mepham, *Virginia Woolf: A Literary Life* (London: Macmillan, 1991), pp. 195–8; Lee, *Virginia Woolf*, pp. 722–6.

[99] Woolf, *Essays*, VI, p. 243.

[100] Woolf, *Essays*, VI, p. 243.

[101] Woolf, *Essays*, VI, p. 243.

In the chapters that follow, I begin with the seemingly blissful immersion of childhood reading, and go on to explore the compulsive reading of popular romance, serious scholarly reading inside universities, as well as various forms of reading for comfort, for solace, or for escape. The first chapter, 'Modernism and the Childhood Scene of Reading', focuses on portraits of childhood reading in the writing of Virginia Woolf, Marcel Proust and Sigmund Freud. For many literary critics in the 1920s and 1930s, the difficulties of modernism appeared as a solicitation to the reader to, in Q. D. Leavis's words, 'respond as an adult'.[102] And yet, by tracking the figure of the child reader within modernism, psychoanalysis and literary critical debates about 'mature' and 'infantile' readers, this chapter argues that the dominant narrative about modernism as a route to maturity overlooks the modernist fascination with the figure of the child reader. The figure of the child reader, I suggest, functions as one of what Charles Altieri has described as the 'projected readers' of modernism – those 'ideal' readers imagined in and constructed by modernist texts, as a way of modelling how we might respond imaginatively and psychologically to this difficult form of writing.[103] But there is, of course, a fundamental disavowal at work in such representations of the child reader in works that are so evidently not written for children to read. We, as adult readers, are solicited to identify as a child. What happens, I ask, when we do so? What is it that we are being encouraged to identify with? For a number of critics, the child reader is a suspicious figure, a figure of fantasy and wish-fulfilment, ripe for ideological and political indoctrination. And yet, although Freud, Woolf and Proust do all draw on the idea of childhood reading as a site of indulgent pleasure, fantasy and wish-fulfilment, all three also complicate this image, depicting the strange temporal shifts and the enigmatic identifications at work in both the childhood and the modernist scene of reading. Freud, Woolf and Proust were all alert to, and draw our attention to, the cultural fantasy of childhood as a site of innocence, pleasure and wish-fulfilment. In Proust's and Woolf's writing, the scene of reading exposes the ways that this fantasy of childhood malleability intersected with the politics of imperialism and fascism. And yet, both Proust and Woolf offer their own alternatives to the dominant image of childhood reading as a site of political indoctrination.

In the second chapter, 'Strange Taboos and Detrimental Diets: Reading Ethel M. Dell', I turn to the figure of the romance reader in early-twentieth-century culture. The figure of the romance reader as a voracious and unthinking glutton is, I argue, a fantasy figure that found one of its most striking articulations in critical imaginings of the bestselling novelist Ethel M. Dell and

---

[102] Q. D. Leavis, *Fiction and the Reading Public* (London: Chatto & Windus, 1932), p. 230.
[103] Altieri, 'Modernist Innovations', pp. 67–9.

her readers. Dell's bestselling novels were condemned by critics including Q. D. Leavis and George Orwell as 'detrimental diet', 'suet pudding', to be 'suck[ed] down' by addicted female readers.[104] And yet, in Dell's first novel, *The Way of an Eagle* (1912), the opening meeting between the hero and heroine takes the form of a violent encounter, in which the heroine – who we know is already dependent on opium – is forcibly drugged by the man who, we also know, she will come to love and marry by the close of the novel. I explore the historical reverberations between Dell's scene of forcible drugging and the contemporary accounts of suffragette forcible feeding, arguing that Dell's writing stages a set of questions about women's agency, hunger and desires that trouble the critics' insistence that such novels straightforwardly engendered a passive form of degenerate, engorged femininity in their readers. Examining the fantasies of the gluttonous reader surrounding, and staged by, Dell, I ask, what is repressed in the construction of this voracious glutton as modernism's monstrous 'other' reader? Turning to James Strachey's 1930 essay on 'Some Unconscious Factors in Reading', I show how a psychoanalytic account of the fantasies that drive the act of reading unravels the attempts of highbrow modernists to disavow the desires of 'hungry girl clerks and housemaids'.[105]

Chapter 3, 'Reading *The Waves*, Reading You: Virginia Woolf and the Culture of Redemption', focuses on Virginia Woolf's 1931 novel *The Waves*. *The Waves* is the most intensely poetic, and challenging, of Woolf's novels. And yet, although even Woolf herself worried about the difficulties that this novel presented to its readers, in this chapter I argue that the figure of the reader is at the heart of *The Waves*. In a plan dated 13 June 1930, Woolf sketched out the episodes of the book from 'The garden', through 'school', 'College', 'London', 'Maturity', 'Death' and 'Love', to a final section devoted to 'Books. & sensation'.[106] Although there is no final episode dedicated to 'Books. & sensation', scenes of reading appear throughout both the drafts and the final text of *The Waves*: 'Books. & sensation' is up there, in the final text as much as in the plan, with 'Death' and 'Love'.

In *The Waves*, the characters indulge in overdetermined, and often conflicting, fantasies in which literature appears as a buttress of scholarly patriarchal authority, a source of consolation, a vehicle of grief, a refuge from the horrors

---

[104] Leavis, *Fiction*, pp. 53–4; George Orwell, 'Bookshop Memories' (1936), in *The Collected Essays, Journalism and Letters of George Orwell*, ed. by Sonia Orwell and Ian Angus, 4 vols (Harmondsworth: Penguin, 1970), I, pp. 273–7 (p. 275); James Strachey, 'Some Unconscious Factors in Reading', *International Journal of Psycho-Analysis*, 11 (1930), 322–31 (p. 326).

[105] Roger Fry, *The Artist and Psycho-Analysis* (London: Hogarth Press, 1924), p. 11.

[106] Virginia Woolf, *The Waves: The Two Holograph Drafts*, transcr. and ed. by J. W. Graham (London: Hogarth Press, 1976), p. 400.

of mass modernity, and as a reservoir of communal belonging. Throughout the novel, the characters articulate their desires for various forms of cultural redemption. In *The Waves*, the longing for redemption appears, not only in the characters' turns to poetry and paintings in the wake of Percival's death, but also in Neville's fantasy of poetry as a scholarly refuge from the horrors of mass modernity, and in Louis's vision of poetry as a source of proto-fascist community. In these scenes, however, far from participating in the 'culture of redemption', Woolf challenges the dominant fantasies in early-twentieth-century culture about the role of literature in psychic, social and political life. Turning to Melanie Klein's work, I show how although the scene of reading might appear as a powerful site of reparation, for both Woolf and Klein, the reparative powers of reading were rendered increasingly fragile in a period dominated by psychic and historical violence. In *The Waves*, Woolf stages a series of scenes of reading that disrupt the characters' longings for different forms of cultural redemption, while also modelling and enacting the alternative (and still potentially reparative) processes of reading that Woolf's modernist writing demands from her own readers. And yet, although these projected scenes of reading do seek to imagine alternatives to the dominant models of reading in early-twentieth-century culture, *The Waves* also enacts an ambivalent struggle with the different forms of reading that it both diagnoses and seeks to reimagine, charting the perils of literary identification in an age of incipient fascism.

In the final chapter of this book, '"Monsters Within and Without", or, "Forebodings about Fascism": Marion Milner Reads Virginia Woolf', I focus on portraits of reading from Woolf's 1937 novel, *The Years*, alongside the portraits of reading, and other forms of cultural encounter, in Milner's 1937 book, *An Experiment in Leisure*. In her first book, *A Life of One's Own* (1934), Milner had asked the apparently simple question: 'What do I like?'[107] This experiment in finding out 'What does a woman want?' was cast not as a record of solipsistic introspection, nor even, as in Freud's *The Interpretation of Dreams*, as a path on the 'royal road' to the interpretation of the unconscious, but instead as a new 'method' – a method that Milner offered up to her reader as a way of freeing himself or herself from the shackles of the 'borrowed mass-produced ideal[s]' foisted upon us in capitalist modernity.[108] By 1937, however, when Milner published *An Experiment in Leisure*, the question 'What do I like?', and the urgency of answering it, had shifted. Writing against

---

[107] Milner, *Life*, p. xxxiv.

[108] Freud to Marie Bonaparte, quoted in Ernest Jones, *Sigmund Freud: Life and Work*, II (London: Hogarth Press, 1955), p. 468, cited by Maud Ellmann, 'New Introduction: The Thing that Lives Us', in Milner, *Experiment*, pp. xiii–xlii (p. xiii); Freud, *The Interpretation of Dreams*, p. 608; Milner, *Life*, p. xxxiv.

the backdrop of a rising current of nationalism and fascism across Europe (written in Spain on the eve of the Spanish Civil War, the book also records Milner's responses to Mussolini's aggressions in Abyssinia and the 1930s hunger marches in Britain), there was a new urgency for Milner in 1937, in understanding the apparent ease with which not only Hollywood movie makers, but now also European dictators, might manipulate individual desires.

For Milner, the question of 'what I like' became fraught with anxiety in an era when individual desires were understood to be prey to the manipulations of capitalist mass-production and fascism. In Milner's writing, what might at first appear as a whimsical project in self-analysis becomes a political project in extricating the self from the polluted desires of early-twentieth-century political life. In the portraits of reading written into *The Years*, Woolf too explores the fear that entering into the pleasures of the text might leave the reader prey to the emotional manipulations of fascism. Beginning with a discussion of Milner's early writing, this chapter then moves on to an analysis of the troubled scenes of reading in *The Years*. The chapter concludes by considering how we might view these writers as resistant to the 'monsters' (as Milner describes them) that they traced both inside and outside the mind in 1930s Europe.[109]

In the scenes of reading examined in this book, Woolf, Proust and Milner scrutinise – and frequently both implicitly and explicitly criticise – the ideas of scholarly mastery underpinning early-twentieth-century practices of close reading. Like other books about modernist literature, *Reading Modernism's Readers* is itself a work of close reading that is intimately bound up with and shaped by the critical practices that it takes as its subject-matter. And yet it is also, I suggest, a book that aims to learn from the scenes of reading enacted within modernist literature. By presenting us with these self-reflexive scenes of reading, modernist writers solicit their own readers to confront the more troubling fantasies at work within early-twentieth-century culture, and beyond, about the role of literature in our psychic, social and political lives. Not only do these scenes challenge many of our existing critical accounts about modernism (that it is elitist, redemptive, or, in contrast, that it produces unequivocally radical forms of disenchantment and defamiliarisation), but they also provide a counter-argument to that age-old, and recently much-trumpeted, claim that empathetic identification in the act of reading is, in itself, a moral or political good.[110] In the conclusion, this book takes

---

[109] Marion Milner, *On Not Being Able to Paint* (Hove: Routledge, 2010), p. 41.

[110] For a philosophical argument about the relationship between reading, empathy and the moral imagination, see Martha Nussbaum, *Love's Knowledge: Essays on Philosophy and Literature* (Oxford: Oxford University Press, 1990). Popular iterations of this argument are abundant; see, for example, Claudia Hammond, 'Does reading fiction make us better people?', BBC, 3 June 2019, https://www.bbc.com/future/article/20190523-does-reading-fiction-make-us-better-people (accessed 27 October 2023).

up modernism's legacies in contemporary literature, addressing increasingly urgent questions about how – and why – we read today, in a period dominated once again by the rise of far-right politics, and by so-called 'fake news' and 'alternative facts'.[111]

---

[111] The phrase 'alternative facts' was used by Donald Trump's advisor Kellyanne Conway on 22 January 2017 to defend the false claims made by the president's press secretary about the crowds at the presidential inauguration. See Rachael Revesz, 'Donald Trump's presidential counsellor Kellyanne Conway says Sean Spicer gave "alternative facts" at first press briefing', *The Independent*, 22 January 2017, https://www.independent.co.uk/news/world/americas/kellyanne-conway-sean-spicer-alternative-facts-lies-press-briefing-donald-trump-administration-a7540441.html (accessed 27 October 2023).

I

MODERNISM AND THE CHILDHOOD SCENE OF READING

MODERNISM AND THE CHILD READER

When literary criticism seized on modernist literature it prided itself on the reading of difficult modernist texts as a route to maturity.[1] Lamenting the 'loss in maturity' between popular writers of the eighteenth century and those of later eras, Q. D. Leavis, writing in *Fiction and the Reading Public* (1932), bemoaned a pervasive appeal to what she described as an 'adolescent and child-hood sensibility' that had

> accustomed the reading public to habits of diminished vigilance, provoked an uncritical response and discovered the appeals which have made the fortunes of Sir James Barrie and Mr. A. A. Milne, the reputation of the Poet Laureate [the children's author John Masefield], and the success of most later nineteenth-century and twentieth-century bestsellers.[2]

Discussing the challenges posed to readers by Virginia Woolf's novel *To the Lighthouse*, Leavis wrote of the necessity of enquiring 'why the conditions of

---

[1] This is a revised and extended version of an article published as Helen Tyson, 'Reading Childishly? Learning to Read Modernism: Reading the Child Reader in Modernism and Psychoanalysis', *Textual Practice*, 31.7 (2017), 1435–57, https://doi.org/10.1080/09502 36X.2016.1237997.

[2] Leavis, *Fiction*, p. 230.

the age have made it inaccessible to a public whose ancestors have been competent readers of Sterne and Nashe'.[3] For Leavis, a stultifying mass culture was to blame:

> The training of the reader who spends his leisure in cinemas, looking through magazines and newspapers, listening to jazz music, does not merely fail to help him, it prevents him from normal development, partly by providing him with a set of habits inimical to mental effort.[4]

The modern reader, stymied by cinemas, magazines, newspapers and jazz, is, in Leavis's view, obstructed from 'normal development', unable to attain the mental maturity required by this difficult adult novel. In contrast to this infantilised and infantilising mass culture, F. R. and Q. D. Leavis advocated a form of literature that would require readers to 'respond as an adult'.[5]

Modernist literature, especially, was valorised for the demand it made upon its readers – a demand that they grow up, and join that 'very small minority' that F. R. Leavis described as the 'critically *adult* public', leaving behind their fellow citizens to wallow, childlike, in the infantile satisfactions of popular culture.[6] As Ben Knights has argued, throughout the 1920s and 1930s in Britain the 'Scrutineers' championed a rhetoric of mature masculinity, working hard to establish the study of literature as a form of 'heroic reading', warding off 'Peter Pan-like' regressive wishes in the reader.[7] Following I. A. Richards's lectures on 'Practical Criticism' in the 1920s, 'Cambridge English', as developed by Leavis and his colleagues, set itself at odds with the traditional model of philological research, revolutionising the study of English in British universities, which would increasingly embrace practical criticism, close reading and literary critical models of study as opposed to the older philological, linguistic research-based traditions.[8] This new form of literary criticism and institutionalised

---

[3] Leavis, *Fiction*, p. 223. See also F. R. Leavis on 'maturity' in *The Great Tradition* (Harmondsworth: Penguin, 1972), p. 48, pp. 55–6.

[4] Leavis, *Fiction*, p. 224.

[5] Leavis, *Fiction*, p. 230.

[6] F. R. Leavis, 'Mass Civilization and Minority Culture' (1930), in *Education and the University: A Sketch for an 'English School'*, 2nd edn (Cambridge: Cambridge University Press, 2011), pp. 141–71 (p. 159, my emphasis).

[7] See Ben Knights, 'Outlaws and Misfits: The Identities of Modernist Criticism', *Modernist Cultures*, 14.3 (2019), 337–56; Ben Knights, *Pedagogic Criticism: Reconfiguring University English Studies* (Basingstoke: Palgrave, 2017), pp. 19–52; Ben Knights, 'Reading as a Man: Women and the Rise of English Studies in England', in *Gendered Academia: Wissenschaft und Geschlechterdifferenz 1890–1945*, ed. by Miriam Kauko, Sylvia Mieszkowski and Alexandra Tischel (Gottingen: Wallstein Verlag, 2005), pp. 65–81 (pp. 78–9).

literary study, Knights argues, 'like the modernism on which to a considerable extent it drew [. . .] was designed to estrange the text, to awaken readers from their conformist trance', and to help them on 'the difficult but necessary journey towards emotional and intellectual maturity'.[9]

And yet, despite the literary critics' emphasis on modernism as a route to maturity, modernist writers were repeatedly drawn to the figure of the child. From the vivid depiction of childhood in the novels of Henry James to the opening pages of James Joyce's *A Portrait of the Artist as a Young Man* (1916), May Sinclair's *Mary Olivier: A Life* (1919) and Virginia Woolf's *The Waves* (1931), to Roger Fry's 1917 exhibition of children's drawings, Walter Benjamin's radio broadcasts for children, Gertrude Stein's books for children, and Virginia Woolf's, Amy Lowell's and Harriet Monroe's championing of child poets, the child appears as a key figure in modernist culture.[10] Although a

---

[8] Ben Knights, 'English on Its Borders', in *English Studies: The State of the Discipline, Past, Present, and Future*, ed. by Niall Gildea, Helena Goodwyn, Megan Kitching and Helen Tyson (Basingstoke: Palgrave Macmillan, 2015), pp. 15–24. On Leavis, 'Scrutiny' and the history of English studies, see Chris Baldick, *The Social Mission of English Criticism 1848–1932* (Oxford: Clarendon Press, 1983), p. 162; Christopher Hilliard, *English as a Vocation: The 'Scrutiny' Movement* (Oxford: Oxford University Press, 2012), pp. 9–13; Francis Mulhern, *The Moment of 'Scrutiny'* (London: Verso, 1981), pp. 329–31. On the role of extramural study in the foundation of English literature degrees, see Alexandra Lawrie, *The Beginnings of University English: Extramural Study, 1885–1910* (Basingstoke: Palgrave, 2014).

[9] Knights, 'English on Its Borders', p. 18.

[10] James Joyce, *A Portrait of the Artist as a Young Man*, ed. by Seamus Deane (London: Penguin, 2000), pp. 3–4; May Sinclair, *Mary Olivier: A Life* (London: Virago, 1980), pp. 3–4; Woolf, *The Waves*, pp. 5–20; Roger Fry, 'Children's Drawings' (1917), in *A Roger Fry Reader*, ed. by Christopher Reed (Chicago: University of Chicago Press, 1996), pp. 266–70; Henry James, *The Turn of the Screw* (1898), in *The Turn of the Screw and Other Stories*, ed by T. J. Lustig (Oxford: Oxford University Press, 2008), p. 140. On Walter Benjamin and childhood, see Walter Benjamin, 'A Glimpse into the World of Children's Books' (1926), trans. by Rodney Livingstone, in *Selected Writings: Volume 1, 1913–1926*, ed. by Marcus Bullock and Michael W. Jennings (Cambridge, MA: Belknap Press of Harvard University Press, 2004), pp. 435–43; Walter Benjamin, 'Toys and Play' (1928), trans. by Rodney Livingstone, in *Selected Writings: Volume 2, Part 1, 1927–1930*, ed. by Michael W. Jennings, Howard Eiland and Gary Smith (Cambridge, MA: Belknap Press of Harvard University Press, 2005), pp. 117–21; Jeffrey Mehlman, *Walter Benjamin for Children: An Essay on His Radio Years* (Chicago: University of Chicago Press, 1993); Daniela Caselli, 'Attack of the Easter Bunnies: Walter Benjamin's Youth Hour', *Parallax*, 22.4 (2016), 459–79. On Gertrude Stein's writing for children, see Gertrude Stein, *The World Is Round*, illus. by Clement Hurd (New York: Harper, 2013); Dana Cairns Watson, 'Building a Better Reader: *The Gertrude Stein First Reader and Three Plays*', *The Lion and the Unicorn*, 35 (2011), 245–66. On Woolf's patronage of the child poet Joan Adeney Easdale, see Emily James, 'Virginia Woolf and the Child Poet', *Modernist Cultures*, 7.2 (2012), 279–305. On Monroe's and Lowell's championing of the child poet,

number of critics denigrated what Wyndham Lewis condemned as the 'child cult' of the early twentieth century, both modernist and psychoanalytic writers were fascinated by the figure of the child, and in particular by the figure of the child reader.[11] At the centre of Virginia Woolf's 1927 novel *To the Lighthouse*, and at the centre of Lily Briscoe's painting, Mrs Ramsay sits reading Grimm's fairy tales to her youngest son, James. In this poignant, lyrical and Oedipally charged invocation of the pleasures and consolations of the maternal scene of reading, Mrs Ramsay's words are, for James, as well as for many of Woolf's own readers, rhythmical and consoling. Like the 'soothing tattoo' of the waves on the beach, which provide for Mrs Ramsay her own 'old cradle song', Mrs Ramsay's words beat out their own rhythm, 'like the bass gently accompanying a tune, which now and then ran unexpectedly into the melody'.[12] While *To the Lighthouse* describes Lily Briscoe's attempt to paint this Madonna-like scene of Mrs Ramsay reading Grimm's fairy tales to James, Marcel Proust's narrator in *À la recherche du temps perdu* (1913–27) similarly evokes luxurious and seductive memories of his mother's bedtime stories. In the opening pages of *À la recherche*, Proust's narrator recalls both his childhood attachment to his mother's bedtime reading, and the absorbing experience of solitary childhood reading. In their fiction and their non-fiction, both Virginia Woolf and Marcel Proust, authors of some of modernism's most notoriously challenging prose, return repeatedly to the figure of the child reader. Focusing on the scene of childhood reading in the writings of Sigmund Freud, Virginia Woolf and Marcel Proust, this chapter argues that the image of the child reader is of crucial significance within both literary modernism and psychoanalysis.

In the scenes of childhood reading that I examine in this book, Freud, Woolf and Proust all demonstrate a preoccupation with the image of the child reader and with the child's dream or fantasy life. Why is it, I want to ask, that these writers turn to these images of the child reader? And what relationship are they positing between childhood, fantasy and reading? Do Woolf and Proust present the child reader as in some way an ideal reader of modernism? Is there something about the child – perhaps something about the child's capacity for daydream, fantasy and the imagination – that makes him or her in some way a better reader than the jaded adult? In modernist literature, the figure of the

see Harriet Monroe, 'Two Child Poets', *Poetry: A Magazine of Verse*, 16.4 (1922), 222–7 (p. 224, p. 225); Amy Lowell, 'Preface', in Hilda Conkling, *Poems by a Little Girl* (New York: Frederick A. Stokes Co., 1922).

[11] Wyndham Lewis, 'The Revolutionary Simpleton', *Enemy*, 1 (January 1927), cited in Sianne Ngai, *Our Aesthetic Categories: Zany, Cute, Interesting* (Cambridge, MA: Harvard University Press, 2012), pp. 68–9.

[12] Virginia Woolf, *To the Lighthouse*, ed. by David Bradshaw (Oxford: Oxford University Press, 2008), p. 16, p. 48.

child reader appears as an ideal or projected reader – one of what Charles Altieri has referred to as the 'projected readers' of modernism, the 'ideal readers' who are both imagined in and 'constructed by' modernist texts as a way of modelling how we, as readers, might respond both imaginatively and psychologically to this difficult form of writing.[13] Of course – as I noted in the introduction – there is a fundamental disavowal at work in representations of child readers in novels that are so evidently not written with child readers in mind. There is a little-known history of modernist writing *for* children and of modernist writing *by* children, but young children certainly don't read *The Waves* or *À la recherche du temps perdu*.[14]

MODERNISM, PSYCHOANALYSIS AND 'THE CHILD'

In *The Interpretation of Dreams* (1900) and the related essay 'On Dreams' (1901), Freud described his son, aged eight, 'deep in a book of legends about the Greek heroes'.[15] That night he dreamt 'he was driving in a chariot with Achilles and that Diomede was the charioteer'; 'it was easy to see', concludes Freud, 'that he had taken the heroes as his models and was sorry not to be living in their days.'[16] Typically, of course, the image of the child reader invokes precisely this kind of pure, uninhibited identification in the realm of fantasy, utter suspension of disbelief – which is one reason why the image at first seems so out of place within difficult modernist texts. Writing on the figure of the child in modernism, Daniela Caselli has drawn attention to the ways in which '*the*' child is frequently summoned as an idealised figure of pure identification, unperturbed by what she describes as the 'estranging project of literary modernism'.[17] In a close reading of a scene from *Mrs Dalloway*, Caselli describes 'the child' as a figure in whom we, as readers, imagine a fleeting 'respite' from the difficulties of modernism.[18] In 'the child', Caselli argues, we find a momentary 'shift from modernism' – 'understood here as a theory and practice of the split self', as a literary form which, through formal difficulty, estranges and startles its readers – to an idealised realism in which language is imagined as

[13] Altieri, 'Modernist Innovations', pp. 67–9.

[14] On modernist writing *for* children, see Gertrude Stein, *The Gertrude Stein First Reader and Three Plays* (Dublin: Maurice Fridberg, 1946); Stein, *The World Is Round*; Watson, 'Building a Better Reader'. On Woolf and the child poet Joan Adeney Easdale, see James, 'Virginia Woolf and the Child Poet'. On Monroe's and Lowell's championing of the child poet, see Monroe, 'Two Child Poets'; Lowell, 'Preface', in Conkling, *Poems by a Little Girl*.

[15] Freud, *The Interpretation of Dreams*, p. 129; Sigmund Freud, 'On Dreams' (1901), *Standard Edition*, V, pp. 629–86 (p. 645).

[16] Freud, 'On Dreams', p. 645.

[17] Daniela Caselli, 'Kindergarten Theory: Childhood, Affect, Critical Thought', *Feminist Theory*, 11 (2010), 241–54 (pp. 242–3).

[18] Caselli, 'Kindergarten Theory', p. 243.

a transparent window on to the objects of the real world.[19] 'The child', writes Caselli, '*is* identification.'[20]

For Caselli, as for many modernist writers, the figure of the child as pure identification is politically suspect, suggesting not just the vulnerability of the child to ideological and emotional manipulation but also contributing to a tradition in which the figure of childhood innocence is itself employed as a kind of political exhortation.[21] Pointing to the ways in which the figure of the innocent child operates in political life, Caselli cites a passage from Walter Benjamin, in which he describes Bertolt Brecht's appeal to an ahistorical concept of childhood as a healing power in the face of Nazi barbarism. Arguing in favour of including *Children's Songs* in *Poems from Exile*, Brecht exhorts Benjamin:

> We must neglect nothing in our struggle against that lot. What they're planning is nothing small, make no mistake about it. They're planning for thirty thousand years ahead. Colossal things. Colossal crimes. They stop at nothing. [. . .] They cripple the baby in the mother's womb. We must on no account leave out the children.[22]

'While he was speaking like this', Benjamin writes, 'I felt a power being exercised over me which was equal in strength to the power of fascism.'[23] For Benjamin, Caselli notes, 'falling back on the power of childhood marks the dropping of dialectical thought: the rhetoric of fascism and that of its resistance coincide in the child'.[24] For Caselli, similarly, the idea of the child as having unique access to unmediated forms of pure identification and wish-fulfilment risks a kind of nostalgic yearning for childhood enchantment that is at odds with the estranging work of modernism.

This idealised image of the child as a figure of identification and immediate wish-fulfilment is, of course, itself an adult fantasy, a fantasy that masks a series of evasions concerning our vexed adult relationships to sexuality, language, and material and historical reality. As Jacqueline Rose has pointed out,

---

[19] Caselli, 'Kindergarten Theory', p. 242.

[20] Caselli, 'Kindergarten Theory', p. 242.

[21] Caselli, 'Kindergarten Theory', p. 245.

[22] Walter Benjamin, 'Conversations with Brecht', in *Understanding Brecht*, trans. by A. Bostock (London: Verso, 1998), pp. 105–21 (p. 120), cited by Caselli, 'Kindergarten Theory', pp. 245–6.

[23] Benjamin, 'Conversations with Brecht', p. 120, cited by Caselli, 'Kindergarten Theory', p. 246.

[24] Caselli, 'Kindergarten Theory', p. 250. See also Lee Edelman, *No Future: Queer Theory and the Death Drive* (Durham, NC: Duke University Press, 2004), and Kathryn Bond Stockton, *The Queer Child: Or, Growing Sideways in the Twentieth Century* (Durham, NC: Duke University Press, 2009).

we use this fantasy of the child 'to hold off a panic' – a 'threat' posed by Freud's writing about childhood and the unconscious 'to our assumption that language is something which can simply be organised and cohered, and that sexuality, while it cannot be removed, will eventually take on the forms in which we prefer to recognise and acknowledge each other'.[25] For Rose, the idealised image of the innocent child and the fantasy of childhood access to unmediated and pure forms of identification is a kind of sham, a screen behind which adults hide their own fears about the unruliness of sexuality, language and history.

The figure of the child reader is an overdetermined figure in early-twentieth-century literary culture – an idealised figure of innocence, identification and pleasure, but also a spurned figure for the infantilisation of mass culture, or, worse, a figure of vulnerability to imperialist and fascist ideologies.[26] In the scenes of childhood reading that appear in the writings of Freud, Woolf and Proust, all three writers appeal to the child reader's indulgence in a rich dream life. And yet, this is no simple fantasy of naïve wish-fulfilment or retreat from the difficulties of modernism. As we shall see in what follows, in their representations of childhood and of childhood reading, Freud, Woolf and Proust all draw their reader's attention to the fantasies that underpin our cultural fascination with the figure of the child, exposing the myths that accrue to this heavily freighted image, while also offering nuanced accounts of the child's encounter with books. In Freud's writing, he reveals the powerful role of fantasy in shaping our adult fascination with the child, while also drawing attention to the non-linear, fragmented and shifting temporality of the childhood scene of reading. In their portraits of childhood reading, both Woolf and Proust are alert to the perils of idealising childlike identification and challenge our cultural fantasy of the child's blissful immersion in books. Like Freud, both Woolf and Proust produce rich, complex and strange accounts of the child's encounter with books, drawing attention to the temporal shifts and the enigmatic psychic leaps at work in childhood and the modernist scene of reading.

FREUD, THE 'WOLF MAN' AND THE CHILDHOOD SCENE OF READING

In Freud's portrait of his eight-year-old son reading and dreaming about the Greek heroes, he offers a typical image of the child reader as a figure of immediate identification and wish-fulfilment. But in 1924 the literary critic I. A. Richards invoked a very different portrait of the Freudian child. In his canonical book

---

[25] Jacqueline Rose, *The Case of Peter Pan, or The Impossibility of Children's Fiction* (Basingstoke: Macmillan, 1984), p. 10.

[26] On the figure of the 'vulnerable child', see Douglas Mao, *Fateful Beauty: Aesthetic Environments, Juvenile Development, and Literature 1860–1960* (Princeton: Princeton University Press, 2008), p. 8. See also Denise Riley, *War in the Nursery: Theories of the Child and Mother* (London: Virago, 1983).

Principles of Literary Criticism, a foundational text for English literary studies, Richards, pausing in the midst of an attempt to map a psychological theory of aesthetic value, reflected on the recent hullabaloo surrounding the psychoanalytic description of children:

> With the exception of some parents and nursemaids we have lately all been aghast at the value judgements of infants. Their impulses, their desires, their preferences, the things which they esteem, as displayed by the psycho-analysts, strike even those whose attitude towards humanity is not idealistic with some dismay. Even when the stories are duly discounted, enough which is verifiable remains for *infans polypervers* to present a truly impressive figure dominating all future psychological inquiry into value.[27]

In contrast to Freud's idyllic portrait of his eight-year-old son, the 'polymorphously perverse' infant, first described in Freud's *Three Essays on the Theory of Sexuality* (1905), appears as an affront – the unruly 'impulses', 'desires' and 'preferences' expressed in the infant's free-wheeling sexuality have left readers 'aghast' and 'dismay[ed]'. Richards's response to the '*infans polypervers*' exemplifies the 'panic' that Rose describes as a typical response to the Freudian infant – he is shocked, not merely at the idea of infantile sexuality, but also at the implications of this figure for mature aesthetic judgement.[28] And yet, Richards reluctantly concedes, this infant is nonetheless an ambivalently 'impressive figure', central to the question of how we – as adults – attribute value to art and to literature. The Freudian infant, whose sexuality is free to range equally over any number of different objects and aims, obtaining pleasure in all directions, lies at the core of the adult reader's aesthetic and literary 'preferences', threatening to undermine them.[29]

Despite Richards's anxiety at the untamed 'impulses' and 'desires' of the Freudian infant, the importance of this figure for the 'value judgements' of adult readers lies not so much in the scandalous 'perversity' of infantile sexuality as in the challenge that Freud's theory of infantile sexuality and the unconscious

---

[27] I. A. Richards, *Principles of Literary Criticism* (Abingdon: Routledge, 2001), p. 40.

[28] Rose, *The Case of Peter Pan*, p. 10.

[29] In *Practical Criticism*, Richards later observed that had he 'wished to plumb the depths' of his readers' 'Unconscious', where he was 'quite willing to agree the real motives of their likings and dislikings would be found', he 'should have devised something like a branch of psychoanalytic technique for the purpose'. I. A. Richards, *Practical Criticism: A Study of Literary Judgement*, ed. by John Constable (Abingdon: Routledge, 2001), p. 19. On Richards's hesitant relationship to psychoanalysis, see John Paul Russo, *I. A. Richards: His Life and Work*, 2nd edn (Abingdon: Routledge, 2015), p. 190, p. 280; Stonebridge, *The Destructive Element*, pp. 23–30.

presents, both to the prevailing fantasy of 'the child' and to the developmental account of modernism as a linear path to critical maturity. 'Psychoanalysis', Freud wrote in the *Three Essays*,

> considers that a choice of an object independently of its sex—freedom to range equally over male and female objects—as it is found in childhood, in primitive states of society and early periods of history, is the original basis from which, as a result of restriction in one direction or the other, both the normal and the inverted types develop.[30]

An 'aptitude' or 'disposition' to a 'polymorphously perverse' sexuality in childhood, Freud insisted, is a 'general and fundamental human characteristic' – an 'original basis' from which we all start out, and which persists unconsciously in spite of (and in conflict with) our painfully and precariously achieved adult sexual identities.[31] Childhood persists. A vestigial layer in the psyche, it endures as part of an unconscious life that tugs against linear accounts of development. The very fact of a pervasive 'infantile amnesia, which turns everyone's childhood into something like a prehistoric epoch and conceals from him the beginnings of his own sexual life', was, for Freud, evidence of a split, evidence of an unconscious part of our minds which another part of the mind stubbornly refuses to acknowledge.[32] In spite of this 'peculiar amnesia', it was clear to Freud that 'the very same impressions that we have forgotten have none the less left the deepest traces on our minds and have had a determining effect upon the whole of our later development'.[33]

Writing in 1915, Freud insisted that 'the development of the mind shows a peculiarity which is present in no other developmental process':

> When a village grows into a town or a child into a man, the village and the child become lost in the town and the man. [. . .] It is otherwise with the development of the mind. Here one can describe the state of affairs [. . .] only by saying that in this case every earlier stage of development persists alongside the later stage which has arisen from it; here succession also involves co-existence [. . .] The earlier mental state may not have manifested itself for years, but none the less it is so far present that

---

[30] Sigmund Freud, *Three Essays on the Theory of Sexuality* (1905), *Standard Edition*, VII, pp. 123–245 (pp. 144–5).

[31] Freud, *Three Essays*, p. 191, p. 144; see Arnold I. Davidson, 'How to Do the History of Psychoanalysis: A Reading of Freud's *Three Essays on the Theory of Sexuality*', *Critical Inquiry*, 13.2 (1987), 252–77 (pp. 264–4).

[32] Freud, *Three Essays*, pp. 174–6.

[33] Freud, *Three Essays*, pp. 174–5.

it may at any time again become the mode of expression of the forces in the mind, and indeed the only one, as though all later developments had been annulled or undone. This extraordinary plasticity [. . .] may be described as a special capacity for involution—for regression—since it may well happen that a later and higher stage of development, once abandoned, cannot be reached again. But the primitive stages can always be re-established; the primitive mind is, in the fullest meaning of the word, imperishable.[34]

The child, as Juliet Mitchell wrote in *Psychoanalysis and Feminism*, doesn't simply 'grow [. . .] out of' his or her polymorphous sexuality – the culture demands that the child reject their 'multifarious and multitudinous' desires, but at an unconscious level they remain.[35] Childhood, as Jacqueline Rose puts it, 'is something in which we continue to be implicated and which is never simply left behind'.[36]

Not only does childhood appear in Freud's writing as an 'imperishable', albeit unconscious, determining factor in adult life, childhood is also, as Freud discovered as early as his 1899 essay on 'Screen Memories', a crucial site of adult fantasies and projections, a terrain that we repeatedly return to and reshape according to later adult experiences, desires and fantasies. In the essay on 'Screen Memories', Freud found that vivid sensory recollections from childhood often turned out to be a kind of façade, not 'complete inventions', but 'false in the sense that they have shifted an event to a place where it did not occur [. . .] or that they have merged two people into one or substituted one for the other, or the scene as a whole gives signs of being combinations of two separate experiences'.[37] On 'close investigation', Freud found that 'these falsifications of memory are tendentious—that is, that they serve the purposes of the repression and replacement of objectionable or disagreeable impressions'.[38] These 'falsified memories' must, therefore, have 'originated at a period of life when it has become possible for conflicts of this kind [. . .] to have made a place for themselves in mental life' – 'far later', therefore, than the period of childhood to which their content apparently belongs.[39] Concluding that 'Our childhood

---

[34] Sigmund Freud, 'Thoughts for the Times on War and Death' (1915), *Standard Edition*, XIV, pp. 273–300 (pp. 285–6).

[35] Juliet Mitchell, *Psychoanalysis and Feminism* (London: Penguin, 1990), pp. 52–3.

[36] Rose, *The Case of Peter Pan*, p. 12. See also Carolyn Steedman, *Strange Dislocations: Childhood and the Idea of Human Interiority, 1780–1930* (Cambridge, MA: Harvard University Press, 1995).

[37] Sigmund Freud, 'Screen Memories' (1899), *Standard Edition*, III, pp. 299–322 (p. 322).

[38] Freud, 'Screen Memories', p. 322.

[39] Freud, 'Screen Memories', p. 322.

memories show us our earliest years not as they were but as they appeared at the later periods when the memories are aroused', Freud argued that 'It may indeed be questioned whether we have any memories at all *from* our childhood: memories *relating to* our childhood may be all that we possess'.[40]

Throughout Freud's writing, childhood scenes of reading appear at crucial moments in the development of his thinking about the relationship between childhood memory and fantasy. In his copy of *The Psychopathology of Everyday Life*, Freud noted the remark of one of his colleagues that 'fairy tales can be made use of as screen memories in the same way that empty shells are used as a home by the hermit crab'.[41] The 'screen memory', as Freud wrote in his 1899 essay, is a memory relating to childhood that 'owes its value as a memory not to its own content but to the relation existing between that content and some other, that has been suppressed'.[42] The screen memory masquerades as a strikingly vivid memory of an apparently 'everyday and indifferent' event, behind which lurks another, repressed memory, smuggled away, not only disguised by the screen of an apparently inconsequential scene from the past, but also often reshaped by the retrospective projection of later experiences, fantasies and desires.[43] Invoking the tendency of the mind to seek refuge in fictional forms, Freud's – or rather his colleague's – note about fairy tales as 'empty shells' for screen memories also hints at the ways that fiction gives shape, as well as shelter, to the amorphous and elusive qualities of human memory and desire.

In the case of the Wolf Man, Freud's famous case history recounting his analysis of a Russian aristocrat, Freud's account of the enigmatic relationship between childhood memory and fantasy hinged upon a crucial scene of childhood reading. In 1910, Sergei Pankejeff, who would become known to psychoanalytic history as the 'Wolf Man', came to Freud recounting a terrifying childhood dream: as a child of four, the patient recalled, he had dreamt that as he lay in bed, the window had suddenly opened, revealing six or seven white wolves sitting on a walnut tree, their big tails and pricked ears making them look more like foxes or sheep-dogs.[44] The patient had, Freud recounts, always connected the dream with his childhood fear 'of the picture of a wolf in a book of fairy-tales'.[45] Having ransacked the antiquarian bookshops of Vienna, the Wolf Man 'found the illustrated fairy-book of his childhood, and [. . .]

---

[40] Freud, 'Screen Memories', p. 322.
[41] Cited by John Fletcher, *Freud and the Scene of Trauma* (New York: Fordham University Press, 2013), p. 118.
[42] Freud, 'Screen Memories', p. 305.
[43] Freud, 'Screen Memories', p. 230.
[44] Sigmund Freud, *From the History of an Infantile Neurosis* (1918), *Standard Edition*, XVII, pp. 1–123 (p. 29).
[45] Freud, *An Infantile Neurosis*, p. 29.

recognized his bogy in an illustration to the story of "The Wolf and the Seven Little Goats"'.[46] Freud was, at first, insistent that the dream was rooted in an early childhood experience, during which the young man on his couch had, as an infant, witnessed the traumatic 'primal scene' of his parents during sexual intercourse. In his analysis of the dream, Freud interpreted the wolves in the walnut tree as a repressed figure of the Wolf Man's father mid-coitus – a figure that, Freud argues, had been retrospectively framed in the unconscious via the images of the wolf in the illustrated fairy tale (the wolf in the illustration is upright, just like the father in the marital bed). Freud argues that the little boy's phobia of wolves (both those illustrated in the fairy tales and those that appear in the dream) represented both a repressed desire for the father and a fear of the castration that the satisfaction of that desire would – according to the Oedipal logic introduced by the fairy tales – necessitate.

Over the course of the case study, Freud tends, as John Fletcher observes, to 'reduce' the 'retrospective action of later moments' such as the reading of fairy tales, painting a portrait in which there is a 'delayed "understanding" of a primal scene that carries its own meaning—castration—always already inscribed within it, and needing only to be "recognized" and "understood" and defended against'.[47] This, as Fletcher argues,

> undermines and puts at risk the more complex understanding of traumatic temporality (and its theoretical corollary, the thesis of overdetermination) that Freud developed, haltingly and unevenly, under the rubric of afterwardsness (Nachträglichkeit), with its double dimension of deferral and retroaction between the successive scenes that orchestrate the emergence and continuing afterlife of the trauma.[48]

But the case study is marked by hesitations and alterations, and, as Fletcher also highlights, despite Freud's use of conflicting terms, he also describes the dream as revealing a kind of 'deferred revision', whereby the little boy's investment in the parental scene is shaped by his childhood reading of fairy tales.[49] In this interpretation, the 'drama of castration' is not simply a biological destiny written into the primal scene and only waiting to be recognised: 'Neither a "comprehension" nor a "recognition", it is a fantasy deriving from the wolf stories as carriers of the idea of mutilation, loss, and punishment.'[50] The 'wolf stories' read in childhood make a crucial intervention in the psychic life of the

[46] Freud, *An Infantile Neurosis*, p. 39.
[47] Fletcher, *Freud and the Scene*, p. 258.
[48] Fletcher, *Freud and the Scene*, p. 252.
[49] Fletcher, *Freud and the Scene*, p. 255.
[50] Fletcher, *Freud and the Scene*, pp. 256–7.

Wolf Man, bringing retrospective meaning to the primal scene, and actively shaping both the fears and the fantasies that will come to dominate the child's, and the adult's, future life.

In his account of the Wolf Man, Freud underscores the crucial role played by fiction in the child's struggle to understand his designated place in a patriarchal world. Throughout the case study, Freud quarrels with himself, and with his readers, about the origins and status of the primal scene, shuttling between a narrative that insists on the actual historical occurrence of the scene, and a theory in which the primal scene functions as a fantasy rather than a historical event, shaped, in part, by the little boy's exposure to the fairy tales. Freud's discovery of the role of fantasy and his so-called 'abandonment' of the seduction theory has, of course, been viewed as one of the most controversial aspects of his writing.[51] And yet, as Jonathan Lear points out in response to Freud's critics, 'What is really at stake', in Freud's writing, is the discovery of what Freud called 'psychical reality', and what Lear calls 'the nature of the mind's own activity': 'Freud effectively discovered the mind is active and imaginative in the organization of its own experience.'[52] Ultimately, in the case of the Wolf Man, the question of the reality or otherwise of the primal scene is left undecided, but what Freud does make clear is the role that the childhood scene of reading plays in lending shape and significance to the reconstructed primal scene. In the story of the Wolf Man, the act of childhood reading opens up an account of the role that fantasy plays, not only in the individual life of the Wolf Man, but in all our lives as a form of vital fiction-making that serves to 'fill in the gaps' in our understanding of our own lives.[53] Writing on the peculiarly modernist features of Freud's celebrated case study, Peter Brooks observes:

> That the Wolfman's narrative and his very identity are bound up with the fictions he was told and read and dreamed as a child suggests a classic trope of the novelistic genre [. . .] What is radically modernist in Freud's narrative is that there is not and cannot be any disillusion: the self is bound in illusory relations, and the most one can hope for is some understanding of the order of relation itself, its uses as symbolic code. Freud's suggestion that the individual life history may open backward onto a phylogenetic masterplot is a further modernist gesture, an

[51] See Jeffrey Masson, *The Assault on Truth: Freud's Suppression of the Seduction Theory* (London: Faber, 1984).

[52] Jonathan Lear, *Open Minded: Working Out the Logic of the Soul* (Cambridge, MA: Harvard University Press, 1998), p. 20.

[53] Freud, *An Infantile Neurosis*, p. 97.

example of how we try to account for the insertion of the individual subject within political, biological, and cosmic history.[54]

In the case of the Wolf Man, Freud examined the role that fiction (whether an inherited 'phylogenetic masterplot', or an individual fantasy mediated by fairy stories) plays in shaping the individual reader's fantasy life. This is, as Brooks suggests, an interest that Freud shares with many modernist writers. But I also want to take this further, to suggest not only that Freud shares a modernist preoccupation with the role of fiction in shaping individual lives, but that the model of fantasy Freud developed, with its strange temporal shifts, its layering of multiple and overdetermined scenes, and its peculiar psychic reversals, also offers us a valuable set of insights into the modernist scene of reading.

In Freud's account of the Wolf Man, the childhood scene of reading is subject to the temporality of *Nachträglichkeit*, or 'afterwardsness', the phenomenon whereby, as Rita Felski summarises it, a traumatic event is only 'registered at a later date when the individual belatedly grasps its import'.[55] As Felski writes:

> Thanks to this time-lag between the occurrence of an event and its resonance, meaning is delayed, washed forward into the future rather than anchored in one defining moment. And even as fragments of past experience persist into the present, their meaning mutates under the pressure of new insight. Retrospection recreates the past even as it retrieves it, in a mutual contamination and commingling of different times.[56]

For Felski, Freud's account of 'afterwardsness' 'speaks directly to the enigmas of textual transmission' – to the fact that 'works bear the imprint of their historical moment, while also accounting for their potential to resonate across time'.[57] What I want to suggest here, however, is that Freud's account of 'afterwardsness' also 'speaks directly' to the 'enigmas', and to the strange temporalities, of the modernist scene of reading. In the writing of Woolf and Proust, the scene of childhood reading is rich with the associations of pleasure, intimacy

---

[54] Peter Brooks, *Reading for the Plot: Design and Intention in Narrative* (Oxford: Clarendon Press, 1984), p. 279. See also Steven Marcus, 'Freud and Dora: Story, History, Case History', in *Representations: Essays on Literature and Society* (New York: Random House, 1976), pp. 247–310 (pp. 263–4).

[55] Rita Felski, *The Uses of Literature* (Oxford: Blackwell, 2008), p. 119.

[56] Felski, *The Uses of Literature*, p. 119.

[57] Felski, *The Uses of Literature*, pp. 119–20. On the temporality of aesthetic experience, see also Griselda Pollock, *After-affects/After-images: Trauma and Aesthetic Transformation in the Virtual Feminist Museum* (Manchester: Manchester University Press, 2013).

and immediacy evoked in traditional representations of this scene. Like Freud, however, both Woolf and Proust also draw their reader's attention to the role that adult fantasy plays in shaping this scene, producing portraits of reading that, like Freud's account of the Wolf Man, reveal a more complex, enigmatic and shifting temporality at work in the childhood scene of reading. In these scenes, Woolf and Proust evoke the fantasy of childhood reading as a scene of unadulterated bliss, but they also present us with scenes of childhood reading that appear as striking models for the peculiar demands of reading modernism.

'WHY SHOULD THEY GROW UP, AND LOSE ALL THAT?': MRS RAMSAY'S BEDTIME STORIES

Taking out a penknife, Mr Bankes tapped the canvas with the bone handle. What did she wish to indicate by the triangular purple shape, 'just there?' he asked.

It was Mrs. Ramsay reading to James, she said. She knew his objection—that no one could tell it for a human shape. But she had made no attempt at likeness, she said. [. . .] Mr Bankes was interested. Mother and child then—objects of universal veneration—might be reduced, he pondered, to a purple shadow without irreverence.

But the picture was not of them, she said. Or, not in his sense. There were other senses, too, in which one might reverence them. By a shadow here and a light there, for instance. Her tribute took that form, if, as she vaguely supposed, a picture must be a tribute. A mother and child might be reduced to a shadow without irreverence. A light here required a shadow there. He considered. He was interested. He took it scientifically in complete good faith. The truth was that all his prejudices were on the other side, he explained. The largest picture in his drawing-room, which painters had praised, and valued at a higher price than he had given for it, was of the cherry trees in blossom on the banks of the Kennet. He had spent his honeymoon on the banks of the Kennet, he said.[58]

Writing about Grimm's fairy tales alongside other children's classics in a 1925 essay in the *Nation and Athenaeum*, Virginia Woolf insisted that nobody ever remembers reading such books for the first time – a kind of amnesia descends over the scene, because, Woolf claims, these are 'not books, but stories communicated by word of mouth in those tender years when fact and fiction merge, and thus belong to the memories and myths of life, and not to its aesthetic experience'.[59] In the following edition of the paper, one of the columnists took issue with Woolf's essay, claiming: 'My own record [of reading *David Copperfield*] is four

[58] Woolf, *To the Lighthouse*, p. 45.
[59] Virginia Woolf, 'David Copperfield' (1925), in *Essays*, IV, pp. 284–9 (p. 285).

readings, two of them aloud without the skipping of a word.'[60] 'Each reading', he insisted, 'is an entirely clear memory.'[61] Woolf wrote back, insisting that her claim that 'nobody can remember reading "David Copperfield" for the first time' was not a dismissal of *David Copperfield*, or a claim, 'as he infers, that it slips off the mind unremembered', but rather

> that 'David Copperfield' takes such rank among our classics, and is a book of such astonishing vividness, that parents will read it aloud to their children before they can quite distinguish fact from fiction, and they will never in later life be able to recall the first time they read it. Grimm's 'Fairy Tales' and 'Robinson Crusoe' are for many people in the same case.[62]

The childhood scene of reading, Woolf argues, takes on a mythical quality in the child's mind that eludes conscious recall. Childhood stories, Woolf argues, read aloud by parents to their children 'before they can quite distinguish fact from fiction', become bound up in the child's imaginative life.

Woolf writes, in her essay on *David Copperfield*, of the invisible hold these stories have over the childish imagination, but, as her portrait of Mrs Ramsay reading to James testifies, she was also, like Freud, alert to the fantasy or 'myth' of childhood at work in our adult tendency to romanticise this scene. In *To the Lighthouse*, Woolf's portrait of Mrs Ramsay reading to James evokes the rich fantasy life, the pleasures and consolations of childhood reading, and conjures its lingering significance within the mind of both the child and the adult. In this novel too, though, Woolf is also mindful of, and asks her readers to attend to, the adult fantasies about childhood and childhood reading that are attached to this scene. The extended opening scene of *To the Lighthouse* is framed by a series of reflections on the fantasies that underpin both the child's and the adult's investment in this powerfully freighted scene. In this 'Madonna-like tableau' (to borrow Maud Ellmann's apt description), James jealously guards the scene of reading as a site of intimacy with his mother, 'looking fixedly at the page' and 'pointing his finger' at the words of the fairy tale, in a desperate attempt 'to recall his mother's attention, which, he knew angrily, wavered instantly his father stopped':

> Mrs. Ramsay, who had been sitting loosely, holding her son in her arm, braced herself, and, half turning, seemed to raise herself with an effort, and at once to pour erect into the air a rain of energy, a column of spray

---

[60] Kappa, 'Life and Politics', *Nation and Athenaeum*, 37.23 (5 September 1925), 672.
[61] Kappa, 'Life and Politics', p. 672.
[62] Virginia Woolf, 'Letters', *Nation and Athenaeum*, 37.24 (12 September 1925), 699.

[. . .] and into this delicious fecundity, this fountain and spray of life, the fatal sterility of the male plunged itself, like a beak of brass, barren and bare. He wanted sympathy [. . .] Standing between her knees, very stiff, James felt all her strength flaring up to be drunk and quenched by the beak of brass, the arid scimitar of the male, which smote mercilessly, again and again, demanding sympathy.[63]

Intruding on the intimacy of mother and child reading, Mr Ramsay demands sympathy from his wife, who reassures him 'as a nurse carrying a light across a dark room assures a fractious child' until he is 'Filled with her words, like a child who drops off satisfied'.[64] While Mr Ramsay and James both seek comfort in the figure of Mrs Ramsay, she too seeks out her own forms of solace. Sitting with James, Mrs Ramsay listens to the

monotonous fall of the waves on the beach, which for the most part beat a measured and soothing tattoo to her thoughts and seemed consolingly to repeat over and over again as she sat with the children the words of some old cradle song, murmured by nature, 'I am guarding you—I am your support' [. . .][65]

But the comfort afforded to Mrs Ramsay (and implicitly to us as readers of Woolf's own lusciously rhythmic prose) is fragile: in the same sentence, Woolf describes how, 'at other times suddenly and unexpectedly', the sound of the waves 'had no such kindly meaning, but like a ghostly roll of drums remorselessly beat the measure of life', thundering 'hollow in her ears' and making Mrs Ramsay 'look up with an impulse of terror'.[66]

As she reads to James, Mrs Ramsay determines to 'devote her mind to the story of the Fisherman and his Wife and so pacify that bundle of sensitiveness [. . .] her son James', but, despite this characterisation of maternal devotion, Woolf also gestures to the way that Mrs Ramsay uses the fantasy of the child to keep her own anxieties at bay.[67] As she reads, Mrs Ramsay free associates, 'reading and thinking, quite easily, both at the same time', her thoughts punctuated with the 'turn of the page' and snippets of dialogue from the story.[68]

[63] Woolf, *To the Lighthouse*, pp. 33–4. Maud Ellmann, *The Nets of Modernism: Henry James, Virginia Woolf, James Joyce, and Sigmund Freud* (Cambridge: Cambridge University Press, 2010), pp. 82–4.

[64] Woolf, *To the Lighthouse*, p. 34.

[65] Woolf, *To the Lighthouse*, pp. 16–17.

[66] Woolf, *To the Lighthouse*, p. 17.

[67] Woolf, *To the Lighthouse*, p. 37.

[68] Woolf, *To the Lighthouse*, pp. 47–8.

Allowing her attention to wander from the fisherman's wife's desire to be king, to her own fear of being considered 'domineering' and 'tyrannical', Mrs Ramsay admits her own desire to keep her children 'for ever just as they were':

> Oh, but she never wanted James to grow a day older or Cam either. These two she would have liked to keep for ever just as they were [. . .] Nothing made up for the loss. When she read just now to James, 'and there were numbers of soldiers with kettle-drums and trumpets,' and his eyes darkened, she thought, why should they grow up, and lose all that? He was [. . .] the most sensitive of her children. [. . .] Why, she asked, pressing her chin on James's head, should they grow up so fast? [. . .] She would have liked always to have had a baby. She was happiest carrying one in her arms. Then people might say she was tyrannical, domineering, masterful, if they chose [. . .] And, touching his hair with her lips, she thought he will never be so happy again [. . .][69]

Mrs Ramsay's mournful longing to keep her children as children forever, repeated as a refrain over the next few pages – 'Why must they grow up and lose it all?' – echoes Mrs Darling's exclamation at the beginning of J. M. Barrie's *Peter and Wendy* (1911): 'Oh, why can't you remain like this forever!'[70] Underscoring the 'tyrannical' strain in Mrs Ramsay's desire to keep her children in an idyllic never never land, and pointing to the ways in which Mrs Ramsay's own desires are invested in, and served by, this image of the contented child, Woolf hints, in this passage, not only at the way that the adult uses the fantasy of the child as a means of keeping her own worries at bay, but also at the way in which the mother reading to the child is also a tool of power. As Juliet Dusinberre has noted, in the draft of *To the Lighthouse*, Mrs Ramsay reads Grimm's story of 'The Three Dwarfs' and Woolf has added a pencilled note: '(the strain of having told lies)'.[71] In the final text, Mrs Ramsay reads the story of 'The Fisherman and his Wife', in which a poor fisherman catches and releases a golden flounder who is a prince in disguise: the fisherman's wife insists he ask the flounder to grant a succession of wishes – first she wishes for a home, then a palace, before demanding to be king, emperor and Pope. When the wife asks to be God the couple are undone by her greed and sent back to their 'dirty hovel'. Both stories, as Dusinberre notes, 'underline Mrs Ramsay's role as an inventor of plots for other people's lives' and underscore 'Mrs Ramsay's lust for power'.[72] In this scene, Mrs Ramsay laments

---

[69] Woolf, *To the Lighthouse*, pp. 49–50.

[70] Woolf, *To the Lighthouse*, p. 50; J. M. Barrie, *Peter Pan*, ed. by Jack Zipes (London: Penguin, 2004), p. 5.

[71] Juliet Dusinberre, *Alice to the Lighthouse: Children's Books and Radical Experiments in Art* (Basingstoke: Macmillan, 1987), p. 145.

[72] Dusinberre, *Alice*, p. 145.

that James will 'grow up, and lose all that' at precisely the moment when his eyes 'darken' as she reads a line from the fairy tale describing 'numbers of soldiers with kettle-drums and trumpets'.[73] By portraying Mrs Ramsay's longing to preserve her son's responsiveness to an image of 'soldiers with kettle-drums and trumpets', Woolf gestures to the idea of childhood as a site of ideological manipulation. There is a quietly sinister aspect to Mrs Ramsay's longing to preserve the malleability of the child reader, in a novel that is itself scarred by the losses of the First World War. Although Woolf conveys the powerful seductions and consolations of this scene of maternal devotion, she also foregrounds the adult longings that underpin our conventional representations of this scene, revealing that the image of seductive childhood reading might also serve to screen adult fears, fantasies and desires from view.

For both James Ramsay and the Wolf Man, the childhood scene of reading fairy tales encodes a knotted web of conflicting Oedipal longings and desires in relationship to the child's parents. In Freud's case study of the Wolf Man, the fairy stories read as a child inspire the childhood dream about the wolves in the walnut tree as an instance of 'deferred revision', a fantasy that retrospectively recreates the primal scene (whether actually witnessed, or a fantasy). The fairy stories also linger into the Wolf Man's future, where the meaning of both the dream and the stories shifts and mutates under the pressure of new experiences, desires, fears and insights. The stories sit at the centre of a complex web of memories, desires, fears and fantasies, encompassing a layered set of references to the primal scene, the little boy's attempted seduction of his nursemaid, Gruscha, and her responding threat of castration, the boy's seduction by his sister, the threat of castration from his Nanya, and a story told to him by his grandfather about a tailor and a wolf. For James, in *To the Lighthouse*, the childhood scene of reading functions in a similar way, the scene itself resurfacing in 'The Lighthouse' as a buried memory that carries with it a host of memories, desires and family grievances. Sitting in the boat on the way to the lighthouse, accompanied by his sister, Cam, and their grieving father, James experiences a form of Proustian *mémoire involontaire* – he remembers 'a flash of blue [. . .] and then somebody sitting with him laughed, surrendered, and he was very angry. It must have been his mother, he thought, sitting on a low chair, with his father standing over her.'[74] Inspired by this flash of memory, James begins to search among

> the infinite series of impressions which time had laid down, leaf upon leaf, fold upon fold softly, incessantly upon his brain; among scents, sounds; voices, harsh, hollow, sweet; and lights passing, and brooms

[73] Woolf, *To the Lighthouse*, p. 49.
[74] Woolf, *To the Lighthouse*, p. 139.

tapping; and the wash and hush of the sea, how a man had marched up and down and stopped dead, upright, over them.[75]

As in Freud's account of screen memories, the repressed memory of James's father's intrusion on to the maternal scene of reading, conjured so evocatively in 'The Window', lies buried beneath layers of sensory impressions. The 'old symbol of taking a knife and striking his father to the heart' remains as a powerful and enduring symbol for James, a kind of screen memory that contains within it all of the intensity of James's childhood feelings about his father and his mother:

> Only now, as he grew older, and sat staring at his father in an impotent rage, it was not him, that old man reading, whom he wanted to kill, but it was the thing that descended on him—without his knowing it perhaps: that fierce sudden black-winged harpy, with its talons and its beak all cold and hard, that struck and struck at you (he could feel the beak on his bare legs where it had struck when he was a child) and then made off, and there he was again, an old man, very sad, reading his book.[76]

Although, for James, the content of the fairy story from childhood (the story of 'The Fisherman and his Wife') does not itself contribute to the shaping of this scene, the scene of childhood reading itself persists, lurking under the guise of the fantastic fairy-tale-like figure of the 'black-winged harpy', taking on new meanings, even as it continues to shape James's own shifting relationship to the earlier scene.

On completing *To the Lighthouse*, Woolf wrote to her friend Roger Fry, insisting that 'I meant *nothing* by The Lighthouse':

> One has to have a central line down the middle of the book to hold the design together. I saw that all sorts of feelings would accrue to this, but I refused to think them out, and trusted that people would make it the deposit for their own emotions – which they have done, one thinking it means one thing, another another. I can't manage Symbolism except in this vague, generalised way. Whether its right or wrong I don't know, but directly I'm told what a thing means, it becomes hateful to me.[77]

In her depiction of Mrs Ramsay reading to James, Woolf repeatedly draws her own reader's attention to the many feelings that might 'accrue', like a 'deposit',

[75] Woolf, *To the Lighthouse*, p. 139.
[76] Woolf, *To The Lighthouse*, pp. 150–1.
[77] Woolf, *Letters*, III, p. 385.

to this richly laden image. In Lily Briscoe's portrait of Mrs Ramsay and James, she too draws on a fantasy of childhood reading as a seductive scene of pleasure and consolation, but as her conversation with Mr Bankes reveals, Lily also departs from the traditional portrayal of this scene. In *To the Lighthouse*, Lily's painting of Mrs Ramsay reading Grimm's fairy tale to James invokes a 'subject which', as Lily and Mr Bankes agree, 'Raphael had treated divinely'.[78] Like Vanessa Bell's 1923 copy of Raphael's *Colonna Madonna*, 'this picture of mother and child' (as Woolf described it) invokes Raphael's sacred images of the Madonna and child with a book, as well as the Victorian and Edwardian reverence for reading as an act of maternal nourishment, and Woolf's aunt Julia Margaret Cameron's evocative photographs of the mother and child.[79] But, although Lily's painting gestures to this reverential tradition, at the same time, Woolf draws our attention to the ways in which both she and Lily depart from the traditional representation of this scene.

Looking at Lily's painting, Mr Bankes is perplexed: tapping the canvas with his penknife, he demands to know what it is that Lily wishes 'to indicate by the triangular purple shape, "just there?"'[80] Lily is familiar with 'his objection—that no one could tell it for a human shape', but Mr Bankes's curiosity is piqued: he contemplates the idea that 'Mother and child [. . .] objects of universal veneration' can be 'reduced' to a 'purple shadow without irreverence'.[81] Like the ceramic sculpture *Madonna and Child*, designed and decorated by Vanessa Bell around 1915 (Figure 1.1), both Lily's portrait and Woolf's novel depart from traditional and mimetic representations of mother and child. Bell's sculpture is titled *Madonna and Child*, but verges on the edge of abstraction: a blue triangular, or pyramidal, shape fringed with gold signifies the Madonna's gown, enfolding two shaded elliptical shapes designating mother and child, but the overall effect is closer to Woolf's ambivalent description of Mrs Ramsay as a 'wedge-shaped core of darkness' than to any realist or straightforwardly reverent celebration of maternal devotion.[82] Lily's painting presents the mother and child reading as an abstract 'triangular purple shape', while Woolf herself famously imagined *To the Lighthouse* by drawing the abstract image of 'Two blocks joined by a corridor'.[83] Woolf represented the novel as a sideways 'I' or

---

[78] Woolf, *To the Lighthouse*, p. 145.

[79] See Vanessa Bell, *Colonna Madonna* (c. 1923), Collections of the Charleston Trust, https://artuk.org/discover/artworks/colonna-madonna-73753 (accessed 31 October 2023). On the Victorian and Edwardian reverence for mother and child reading, see Kate Flint, *The Woman Reader 1837–1914* (Oxford: Oxford University Press, 1993), p. 42. For an example of Julia Margaret Cameron's photographs, see *Madonna with Children*, c. 1864, MoMA, https://www.moma.org/collection/works/50906 (accessed 31 October 2023).

[80] Woolf, *To the Lighthouse*, p. 45.

[81] Woolf, *To the Lighthouse*, p. 45.

[82] Woolf, *To the Lighthouse*, p. 52.

Figure 1.1 Vanessa Bell, *Madonna and Child*, c. 1915. Collections of the Charleston Trust, © Estate of Vanessa Bell. All rights reserved, DACS 2023.

'H' shape, 'The Window' and 'The Lighthouse' connected by 'Time Passes' – 'this impersonal thing', 'the flight of time [. . .] all eyeless & featureless with nothing to cling to'.[84] Lily's painting is, in Jane Goldman's words, 'a coterminal analogue of the very text in which it is made', her conversation with Mr Bankes highlighting not only the 'shock' that Lily's post-impressionist painting provokes in a spectator like Mr Bankes (whose 'prejudices' are, he notes, on the side of sentimental and monetary value, rather than post-impressionist significant form), but also serving to draw Woolf's own readers' attention to the impact of Woolf's experimental use of form on their experience of reading this modernist novel.[85] Reflecting, in 'The Lighthouse', on her conversation with Mr Bankes

---

[83] Virginia Woolf, 'Notes for Writing', Holograph Notebook, Appendix A/11, 1926, http://www.woolfonline.com/?node=content/image/gallery&project=1&parent=6&taxa=16&content=732 (accessed 31 October 2023). Virginia Woolf Collection of Papers, Henry W. and Albert A. Berg Collection of English and American Literature, New York Public Library, Astor, Lenox and Tilden Foundations.

[84] Woolf, *Diary*, III, p. 36, p. 76.

[85] Jane Goldman, '*To the Lighthouse*'s Use of Form', in *The Cambridge Companion to To the Lighthouse*, ed. by Allison Pease (Cambridge: Cambridge University Press, 2015), pp. 30–46 (p. 36).

about her departure from the conventions of representational art, Lily recalls his 'wise child's eyes', 'shocked' by her 'neglect of the significance of mother and son'.[86] By framing both Lily's and her own portraits of childhood reading with these meta-reflections on modernist forms of representation, Woolf draws her reader's attention to her own departure from the conventional representation of childhood reading. In this extended portrait of Mrs Ramsay reading to James, Woolf solicits her own readers to participate in an experience of reading that is deeply absorbing and yet challenges the adult fantasies attached to the conventional portrait of the mother and child reading, refusing any of the easy consolations associated with that scene.

Rhoda and the Russian Empress

'Now I will go to the bathroom and take off my shoes and wash; but as I wash, as I bend my head down over the basin, I will let the Russian Empress's veil flow about my shoulders. The diamonds of the Imperial crown blaze on my forehead. I hear the roar of the hostile mob as I step out on to the balcony. Now I dry my hands, vigorously, so that Miss, whose name I forget, cannot suspect that I am waving my fist at an infuriated mob. "I am your Empress, people." My attitude is one of defiance. I am fearless, I conquer.

'But this is a thin dream. This is a papery tree. Miss Lambert blows it down. Even the sight of her vanishing down the corridor blows it to atoms. It is not solid; it gives me no satisfaction—this Empress dream. It leaves me, now that it has fallen, here in the passage rather shivering. Things seem paler. I will go now into the library and take out some book, and read and look; and read again and look. Here is a poem about a hedge. I will wander down it and pick flowers, green cowbind and the moonlight-coloured May, wild roses and ivy serpentine. I will clasp them in my hands and lay them on the desk's shiny surface. I will sit by the river's trembling edge and look at the water-lilies, broad and bright, which lit the oak that overhung the hedge with moonlight beams of their own watery light. I will pick flowers; I will bind flowers in one garland and clasp them and present them – Oh! to whom? There is some check in the flow of my being; a deep stream presses on some obstacle; it jerks; it tugs; some knot in the centre resists. Oh, this is pain, this is anguish! I faint, I fail. Now my body thaws; I am unsealed, I am incandescent. Now the stream pours in a deep tide fertilising, opening the shut, forcing the tight-folded, flooding free. To whom shall I give all that now flows

---

[86] Woolf, *To the Lighthouse*, p. 145.

through me, from my warm, my porous body? I will gather my flowers and present them – Oh! to whom?'[87]

In Woolf's 1931 novel *The Waves*, a boarding school bathroom is transformed into an imperial balcony, as Rhoda daydreams that she is a Russian Empress, waving her fist at an infuriated mob. Imagining herself as the Tsarina Alexandra Feodorovna, empress consort of Tsar Nicholas II, with the Russian Revolution of 1905, and, as David Bradshaw points out, 'especially the events of "Bloody Sunday" in January that year, going on around her', Rhoda takes up a striking position of imperial power.[88] Echoing similar scenes earlier in *The Waves*, where Rhoda imagines the petals floating in a bowl of water as ships in the Spanish Armada, and anticipating the dramatic portrayal of Rose Pargiter's imperialist childhood games in *The Years*, this scene reveals childhood as a site of vivid imperial fantasy.[89] And yet, despite the strikingly evoked childhood fantasy of imperial domination, Rhoda's 'thin dream' is blown 'to atoms', and she turns instead to 'some book' – in fact, she turns to Percy Bysshe Shelley's poem 'The Question' – in quest of a more 'solid' and satisfying imaginative experience.[90]

In the early drafts of *The Waves*, which were written before Woolf had taken the decision to employ the first-person monologues that appear in the published novel, this scene appears in the third person, and Shelley is named directly as the author of the book that Rhoda reads:

> Putting her hand to her head (she was bending over the lavatory basin washing after gymnasium) Rhoda felt [. . .] the veil of the Czarina [. . .] about her shoulders. There are diamonds on my brow, she felt. & going into the library (she took down the works of Shelley in one volume;&) read [. . .] about the floating water-lilies broad & bright, to which lit the oak that overhung the hedge [. . .] with moonlight beams of their own watery light, & she hastened ~~to the spot whence I had come~~, with her ~~garland~~ That I might there present it—O! to whom? O to whom? she asked.[91]

---

[87] Woolf, *The Waves*, p. 44.

[88] David Bradshaw, 'Explanatory Notes', in Virginia Woolf, *The Waves*, ed. by David Bradshaw (Oxford: Oxford University Press, 2015), pp. 169–203 (p. 182, n. 32).

[89] Woolf, *The Waves*, p. 20; Virginia Woolf, *The Years*, ed. by Anna Snaith (Cambridge: Cambridge University Press, 2012), p. 24.

[90] Percy Bysshe Shelley, 'The Question', in *The Complete Poetical Works of Percy Bysshe Shelley*, ed. by Thomas Hutchinson, cor. by G. M. Matthews (Oxford: Oxford University Press, 1970), pp. 614–15.

[91] Woolf, *The Waves: The Two Holograph Drafts*, p. 38.

In a later draft, Woolf continued to emphasise the continuity between Rhoda's imperialist daydream and the scene of reading: 'walking very slowly, so as not to disarrange the diadem, she went into the library, this hot spring afternoon, & took down the double columned Shelley that stood there with the round label, C. 48.'[92] In this (still third-person) version of the scene, the lines from the poem are indented on the page, replicating Rhoda's visual experience of looking at the words on a page for Woolf's own reader:

> Leaning her arms on the desk, with the veil flowing over her shoulders,
> she read about the floating water lilies, broad & bright
> > which lit the oak that overhangs the hedge
> > > With moonlightbeams of their own watery light
> & she gathered flower after flower, as she read, & made a nosegay &
> hastened to present it
> > O! to whom?[93]

In the published text of *The Waves*, the lines of the poem are re-incorporated into Rhoda's first-person monologue, and the explicit reference to 'the double columned' Shelley has been deleted. This not only creates a stronger sense of the way that the lines of the poem become bound up inside Rhoda's mind as she reads, but the shift to first-person monologue also offers a more direct solicitation to Woolf's own reader to identify with Rhoda, offering us a more intimate insight into Rhoda's reading experience. In these earlier versions of the scene, Rhoda moves seamlessly from imperial daydream in the bathroom to reading poetry in the library, taking care not to dislodge her crown as she walks from one room to another. Rhoda reads Shelley with the Empress's veil 'flowing over her shoulders'. But in the final text, this apparently smooth transition – from a child's fantasy of defiant imperial domination, to the scene of reading Romantic poetry – is ruptured. Rhoda's imperial daydream is shattered, and the fantasy of defiant dominion collapses.

Turning from her 'thin dream', now blown to atoms, to Shelley's poem, Rhoda appears to demonstrate what Elaine Scarry has described as the difference between daydreaming and 'imagining-under-authorial-instruction'.[94] For Scarry this is the difference, in sensory and perceptual terms, between the frailty of mere daydream and the comparatively rich, solid and vivid experience of imagining within a poem or a novel. Discussing the sensory impoverishment

---

[92] Woolf, *The Waves: The Two Holograph Drafts*, p. 127.

[93] Woolf, *The Waves: The Two Holograph Drafts*, p. 128.

[94] Elaine Scarry, 'On Vivacity: The Difference between Daydreaming and Imagining-Under-Authorial-Instruction', *Representations*, 52 (Autumn 1995), 1–26; Elaine Scarry, *Dreaming by the Book* (Princeton: Princeton University Press, 2001), pp. 1–39.

of daydream, Scarry argues that, in contrast, writers create a 'perceptual mimesis', which, by an evocation of solidity within the literary work, allows the reading experience to approach the perceptual experience of solidity in the sensory world.[95] Fictional walls, such as those of Proust's bedroom at Combray, provide a solid base for the reader's imagination: 'The idea of the solid wall [. . .] prevents our further *sinking inward*. It provides the *vertical floor* of all subsequent imaginings that lets us perform, without vertigo or alarm, the projective act, and thereby lifts the inhibitions on mental vivacity ordinarily in place as protections.'[96] Throughout *The Waves*, Rhoda gives herself over to daydreams, but then has to protect against the vertiginous perils of self-dissolution by hanging on to solid objects: 'I will assure myself, touching the rail, of something hard. Now I cannot sink; cannot altogether fall through the thin sheet now.'[97] When she reads Shelley's poem 'The Question', Rhoda describes a dramatic form of self-projection into the landscape of the poem. In 'The Question', the speaker recounts a dream, in which he walks by a stream and a hedge with 'Green cowbind and the moonlight-coloured may', 'wild roses, and ivy serpentine'.[98] Rhoda, treating words as objects, anticipates 'pick[ing]' these flowers out of the poem, 'clasp[ing]' them in her hands, and laying them on her desk, before imagining herself sitting by the 'river's trembling edge' (another line that Rhoda cites directly from Shelley's poem), and looking at the 'water-lilies, broad and bright'.[99] In this scene, Rhoda's first-person account of reading Shelley vividly evokes the intense sensory qualities of her imaginative universe, recreating for Woolf's own reader a striking sense of Rhoda's capacity to conjure solid objects from the written words on the page. Rhoda's habit of plucking lines from Shelley's poem like objects that she places on the desk in front of her conveys the intense perceptual experience of reading poetry, an experience that, for Rhoda, approaches the sensory experience of the tactile world. But Rhoda's reading of Shelley is at odds with Scarry's claim that 'a fiction's *vertical floor* [. . .], by promising to stop our inward fall, permits us to enter capaciously into the projective space with fearlessness and with the lifting of inhibitions on vivacity that permits'.[100] For projection is both a perceptual and a psychic act – while Scarry writes of the perceptual projection of visual images that coalesce into a mimesis of solidity, her language also hints at the projection of a psyche liberated from mental inhibition. Rhoda's reading

---

[95] Scarry, 'On Vivacity', pp. 1–3.
[96] Scarry, 'On Vivacity', p. 6, Scarry's emphasis; see also Jacobus, *Psychoanalysis*, pp. 41–3.
[97] Woolf, *The Waves*, p. 19.
[98] Shelley, 'The Question', ll. 17–18, l. 21.
[99] Shelley, 'The Question', l. 25, l. 28.
[100] Scarry, 'On Vivacity', p. 8, Scarry's emphasis.

experience involves a dramatic projective act in both of these senses, but the projective space is by no means entered into with 'fearlessness'.

There is a movement in Woolf's writing from the description of the phenomenological, sensory and perceptual qualities of reading (reading as hallucination, or magic, almost) to the evocation of psychic and emotional engagement and disturbance. Overcoming mental inhibitions – the internal 'obstacle', the 'check in the flow of my being', that which 'jerks', 'tugs', 'resists' – is, for Rhoda, an experience of 'pain' and 'anguish'. In an attempt to describe the experience, Rhoda quotes a line from another Shelley poem: 'I faint, I fail.'[101] As, painfully, these inhibitions are lifted, Rhoda describes a form of intimate bodily and psychical communion with the poem: the tense shifts from the prospective 'I *will* pick flowers' to the present tense, 'There *is* some check', 'this *is* pain', 'I *am* unsealed'. Rhoda moves from an imaginary identification with the speaker of the poem, to a description of her own body as a kind of vessel for the flooding waters. Like Lily Briscoe, who longs for 'a device for becoming, like waters poured into one jar, inextricably the same, one with the object one adored', Rhoda longs for, and in fact seems to achieve, an intimacy with the poem that is also a kind of mimetic identity with the poem itself.[102]

In earlier drafts of this scene, the sense of physical bodily intimacy is heightened and the description more explicitly erotic, following an account of Rhoda's love for another schoolgirl, Alice. By day, Rhoda steals glances at Alice 'so as to gather another supply of that wonderful material, from which to build [. . .] sitting over a book, or in bed at night, those pagodas, those dreams'.[103] At night, she dreams up 'the wonderful story of Alice & herself', 'but always as she was about to kiss ~~her~~, the lips faded'.[104]

> O to whom, she repeated [. . .] & feeling the soft ~~damp wet~~ white flowers, laid beside her in sheafs [. . .] her body felt like them [. . .] heavy with some ~~sxtraordinary~~ sweeping ~~desire, which~~ was painful & burdensome, yet extremely luxurious; & she was fretful [. . .] & felt [. . .] indifference, & her sense of the overpowering sweetness of life, & its terror, in her thighs, which seemed full, [. . .] laden like a bees with honey, & there was some burden in them to [. . .] let flow, along with all the [. . .] sweet waters, with white lilies floating on them. Her body felt porous, infinitely susceptible, made of some O to whom she repeated, looking out of the window at the distant couples [. . .] She seemed to think to feel all over her [. . .] not sharply & separately, but in a broad stream

101 Shelley, 'The Indian Serenade', l. 18, in *Complete Poetical Works*, p. 580.
102 Woolf, *To The Lighthouse*, p. 44.
103 Woolf, *The Waves: The Two Holograph Drafts*, p. 123.
104 Woolf, *The Waves: The Two Holograph Drafts*, p. 123.

[. . .] as if from her whole body, become porous and illumined. [. . .] The sweet stream, that was yet full of irregularity & thus of pain, as if the flow [. . .] were [. . .] checked here in her back or thigh, had to surmount opposition, to feel its way round some obstacle, went flowing out in a ~~delicious~~ deep tide, fertilising & thick & sweet, leaving her ~~moist~~, white in the pale—languid exhausted, but relieved of some oppression [. . .][105]

This exhilarating description of uninhibited queer intimacy is, however, in the final version of the text, shot through with a deep ambivalence and melancholy, an anxiety and alarm concerning a potentially abyssal projection into the absent other marked by the exclamation, 'Oh! to whom?' Reading might beat day-dreaming in terms of its superior evocation of perceptual solidity, but in Rhoda's monologue her ecstatic account of intimate identification with the poem is also characterised by a pervasive ambivalence about the psychic leaps required in this act of reading. Woolf described Shelley as one of the 'priests who take you by the hand and lead you straight up to the mystery', who 'give us text after text to be hung upon the wall, saying after saying to be laid upon the heart like an amulet against disaster'.[106] 'I faint, I fail' appears, in *The Waves*, as one of Rhoda's poetic 'amulet[s]'. But it appears, in this scene, as a complex symbol for this portrait of reading: on the one hand, poetry does appear as an 'amulet against disaster' for Rhoda, holding out a promise of literary enchantment, rep-aration and (in the drafts) wish-fulfilment. And yet, on the other hand, the line 'I faint, I fail' seems to emblematise the way that reading is, for Rhoda, bound up with an intense fearfulness regarding the psychic perils of self-projection.

PROUST'S MADELEINES AND MADONNAS

Marcel Proust might seem at first to offer a more idealised depiction of child-hood reading. That epiphanic moment when the narrator tastes the warm moist madeleine that will unlock his childhood memories of Combray is inti-mately connected to the paradise of his mother's bedtime stories. Amongst the multitude of figures (mothers, lovers, the sacred and the sweet, patisseries and books) that Julia Kristeva discovers lurking behind Proust's madeleine lies one Madeleine Blanchet, the miller's wife who becomes the adoptive mother, lover and then wife of François, hero of George Sand's *François le Champi*. This is the novel that the narrator's mother reads to him as a child in his bedroom at Combray – a novel implicitly yoked together with the lighter reading that his grandmother considers to be 'as unwholesome as sweets and cakes'.[107] 'The

---

[105] Woolf, *The Waves: The Two Holograph Drafts*, pp. 128–9.
[106] Woolf, 'The Pastons and Chaucer' (1925), in *Essays*, IV, pp. 20–38 (p. 31).
[107] Marcel Proust, *Swann's Way* (1913), trans. by C. K. Scott Moncrieff and Terence Kilmartin, rev. by D. J. Enright (London: Vintage, 2005), p. 45.

madeleines', writes Kristeva, 'are what preserve both the underwater memories and the vestiges of shells and aquatic moulds that emerge from this liquid and maternal world of *reading*.'[108]

The association of madeleines, mothers, madonnas, communion, sweet pastries and childhood reading is also at work in Proust's description of clandestine childhood reading in his essay 'On Reading'. In this essay Proust claimed that 'There are perhaps no days of our childhood that we lived as fully as the days we think we left behind without living at all: the days we spent with a favourite book'.[109] Describing the 'sorcery' of that 'enchanting childhood reading whose memory must remain sacred to us all', he recalls reading in a secret 'bower', or 'shelter[ing]' late at night in bed, surreptitiously finishing a book.[110] 'On Reading' moves seamlessly from the child's irresistible urge to continue reading late into the night, to the narrator's memory of the church overlooking his childhood bedroom, to its 'consecrated bread' and the 'feast days' on which ladies would go from the church to the patisserie and buy 'one of those cakes in the shape of a tower [. . .] "manqués", "Saint-Honorés", "Genoese"—cakes whose leisurely, sugary scent remains mixed in my mind with the bells of high mass and the happiness of Sundays'.[111]

For Proust's narrator the sweet, dulcet tones of his mother's reading make up for the painful denial of her bedtime kiss, that longed-for moment in which she would hold out her face 'like a host for an act of peace-giving communion in which my lips might imbibe her real presence'.[112] The scene of reading in *Swann's Way* can, as Adam Watt argues, be read as a 'primal scene' of reading, which guarantees the lingering psychic significance of childhood reading for Proust's narrator.[113] As the narrator's mother recites her bedtime story, her language, like Mrs Ramsay's, takes on a consoling and restorative rhythm, her words are a liquid current, a tide running in and out, soothing the fractious child. From the maternal kiss as communion, to the mother reading as sweet nourishment for the aching soul, to a scene in adulthood where the mother proffers a 'little scallop-shell of pastry' which, 'so richly sensual under its

---

[108] Julia Kristeva, *Time and Sense: Proust and the Experience of Literature*, trans. by Ross Guberman (New York: Columbia University Press, 1996), pp. 5–9. On *François le Champi* as 'the foundation myth [. . .] for the entire Oedipal dimension of Proust's book', see Malcolm Bowie, *Proust Among the Stars* (London: HarperCollins, 1998), pp. 93–5.

[109] Proust, 'On Reading', p. 3.

[110] Proust, 'On Reading', p. 18, pp. 14–15.

[111] Proust, 'On Reading', p. 15.

[112] Proust, *Swann's Way*, p. 13.

[113] Adam Watt, *Reading in Proust's À la recherche: 'le délire de la lecture'* (Oxford: Clarendon Press, 2009), p. 17, pp. 26–7.

severe, religious folds', will recapture lost time, Proust evokes an idyllic scene of reading as a form of maternal nourishment and enchantment.[114]

And yet, even as, like Woolf, Proust gestures to the idealised image of mother and child reading, À la recherche also produces an account of the child reader that is more complex than simply unadulterated nostalgia for the enchantment of childhood reading.[115] In Time Regained, when the narrator finds himself alone in the library of the Prince de Guermantes, Proust adds another dimension to the memory of this childhood scene of reading. Enclosed in the Prince de Guermantes' library, the narrator finds himself dwelling (not for the first time) on 'the subjective element in [. . .] love'.[116] Insisting that love operates as a form of projection (that 'love places in a person who is loved what exists only in the person who loves'), the narrator goes on to transfer this insight concerning the subjective nature of human relationships on to the realm of nationalist feeling.[117] Contemplating the irrational features of wartime French nationalism and 'Germanophobia', Proust writes:

> Finally, to a certain extent, the Germanophilia of M. de Charlus [. . .] had helped me to free myself for a moment, if not from my Germanophobia, at least from my belief in the pure objectivity of this feeling, had helped to make me think that perhaps what applied to love applied also to hate and that, in the terrible judgement which at this time France passed on Germany—that she was a nation outside the pale of humanity—the most important element was an objectification of feelings as subjective as those which had caused Rachel and Albertine to appear so precious, the one to Saint-Loup and the other to me. What, in fact, made it possible that this perversity was not entirely intrinsic to Germany was that, just as I as an individual had had successive loves and at the end of each one its object had appeared to me valueless, so I had already seen in my country successive hates which had, for example, at one time condemned as traitors—a thousand times worse than the Germans into whose hands they were delivering France—those very Dreyfusards such as Reinach with whom today patriotic Frenchmen were collaborating against a race whose every member was of necessity a liar, a savage beast, a madman, excepting only

---

[114] Proust, Swann's Way, p. 54.

[115] On Proust and the child, see Carol Mavor, Reading Boyishly: Roland Barthes, J. M. Barrie, Jacques Henri Lartigue, Marcel Proust, and D. W. Winnicott (Durham, NC: Duke University Press, 2007).

[116] Marcel Proust, Time Regained, trans. by Andreas Mayor and Terence Kilmartin, rev. by D. J. Enright (London: Vintage, 2000), p. 274.

[117] Proust, Time Regained, p. 275.

those Germans who, like the King of Romania, the King of the Belgians, or the Empress of Russia, had embraced the French cause.[118]

Reiterating an argument he has made earlier that the 'logic that governs' nations is 'an inner logic, wrought and perpetually re-wrought by passions, like that of men and women at grips with one another in an amorous or domestic quarrel', Proust points to the irrational dimensions of nationalist feeling.[119] He cites as an example the behaviour of the anti-Dreyfusards, who, over the period of European history stretching from the Dreyfus affair to the First World War, had shifted from virulent antisemitic condemnation of Jewish Dreyfusards like Joseph Reinach, to collaborating with the very same Dreyfusards in vocalising a violent anti-German French nationalism. This 'subjective element', Proust argues, 'struck one forcibly', not only in the tendency of French nationalists to decry every German as 'a liar, a savage beast, a madman', but also in conversation with the 'pro-Germans', who had 'the faculty of ceasing for a moment to understand and even to listen when one spoke to them about the German atrocities in Belgium'.[120] 'And yet', Proust adds in a crucial parenthesis, 'they were real, these atrocities: the subjective element that I had observed to exist in hatred as in vision itself did not imply that an object could not possess real qualities or defects and in no way tended to make reality vanish into pure relativism.'[121] The delusory components of nationalist feeling and racial prejudice, Proust insists, coexist, sometimes in stark conflict, with the stubborn 'reality' of wartime 'atrocities'. On both sides of the trenches, the 'subjective element' drives racist hatred, as well as, in the case of the 'pro-Germans', a dangerously blind disavowal of historical reality.

It is at this point, in the midst of this extended analysis of the psycho-politics of nationalism, that Proust turns, once more, to his all-important childhood scene of reading, tracing his awareness of this 'internal influence' in the realm of nationalist feeling back to his childhood reading in the garden at Combray:

And if, after so many years had slipped away and so much time had been lost, I felt this internal influence [*cette influence capitale du lac interne*] to be dominant even in the sphere of international relations, had I not already some notion of its existence right at the beginning of my life, when I was reading in the garden at Combray one of those novels by Bergotte which, even today, if I chance to turn over a few of its forgotten

---

[118] Proust, *Time Regained*, pp. 275–6.

[119] Proust, *Time Regained*, p. 102. See Jacqueline Rose, *Proust among the Nations: From Dreyfus to the Middle East* (London: University of Chicago Press, 2011).

[120] Proust, *Time Regained*, pp. 276–7.

[121] Proust, *Time Regained*, p. 277.

pages where I see the wiles of some villain described, I cannot put down until I have assured myself, by skipping a hundred pages, that towards the end this same villain is humiliated as he deserves to be and lives long enough to see that his sinister schemes have failed?[122]

In this passage, the narrator traces his adult awareness of the fantasy dimensions governing racial prejudice and nationalist feeling back to his own (still compelling) childish passion for pursuing fictional 'villains' to punishment and humiliation at the end of novels by Bergotte. There is an element of sadistic pleasure in the child (and the adult) reader's desire to witness the humiliation of the fictional villain. But Proust suggests that it is his (or his narrator's) own self-awareness of this pleasure, and its inner logic, that facilitates the narrator's adult insight into the 'sphere of international relations'.

This Proustian portrait of the child reader, who pursues questions of justice and retribution in terms of melodramatic fiction, troubles the idea that empathetic reading is necessarily ethically or morally improving. And yet, even as this portrait invokes a familiar anxiety about the child's vulnerability to uncritical forms of identification, it does, at the same time, suggest that a self-reflexive analysis of such a process of reading might be one way of unpicking, or at least remaining alert to, the complex fantasy elements underpinning hatred and war. It is precisely the adult narrator's capacity to analyse the power of his childish identification with books that allows him, as an adult, to isolate the 'subjective' element in the 'sphere of international relations'.

Despite the lusciously seductive account of maternal reading in *Swann's Way*, there is also something darker that underlies Proust's evocation of the child's unbridled communion with the world of books. In the opening scene of reading, on the very first page of *À la recherche*, the narrator dreams not, like Freud's eight-year-old boy, that he becomes the hero of his book – François I or Charles V, say – but that he is 'a church, a quartet, *the rivalry between* François I and Charles V':

I would make as if to put away the book which I imagined was still in my hands, and to blow out the light; I had not stopped, while sleeping, from reflecting upon that which I had just been reading, but these thoughts had taken a rather peculiar turn; it seemed to me that I myself was the immediate subject of my book [*ce dont parlait l'ouvrage*]: a church, a quartet, the rivalry between François I and Charles V. This belief would persist for some moments after I awoke; it did not shock [*choquait*] my

---

[122] Proust, *Time Regained*, p. 277; translation modified in places, with reference to Marcel Proust, *À la recherche du temps perdu*, ed. by Jean-Yves Tadié et al., 4 vols (Paris: Gallimard, 1987–89).

reason, but weighed like scales upon my eyes and prevented them from registering the fact that the candle was no longer burning. Then it would begin to seem unintelligible, as, after metempsychosis, the thoughts of a previous existence must seem [*comme après la métempsycose les pensées d'une existence antérieure*]; the subject of my book would separate itself from me, leaving me free to apply myself to it or not; and at the same time my sight would return and I would be astonished to find myself in a state of darkness, pleasant and restful enough for my eyes, but even more, perhaps, for my mind, to which it appeared incomprehensible, without a cause, something dark indeed [*comme une chose vraiment obscure*].[123]

In this scene, Proust describes a strange form of impersonal identification: the reader, while dreaming, becomes a religious building, a piece of music, a rivalry between ancient monarchs. As, upon waking, this dream becomes unintelligible, Proust compares it to a form of previous existence – the reader's dream-like identifications are pushed back into the earlier migrations of the soul in metempsychosis, while the narrator is thrust forward into a realm of obscurity and self-estrangement. It is, in fact, almost impossible to be certain whether this opening passage describes the narrator as an adult or as a child; the opening section of *Swann's Way*, a form of writing that seems to occupy the very borderlands of sleep, unsettles our sense of temporal certainty, insisting, as in this opening paragraph, on the mind's capacity to become dislocated from itself, to travel backwards in both individual and historical time. Reading and falling in and out of sleep conspire in these pages to send the narrator back 'to an earlier stage in my life', leaving him to wake up 'under the thrall of one of my childish terrors', or waiting for his mother's goodnight kiss.[124]

In the final volume, in the library scene, the adult narrator undergoes a similarly strange experience. Opening a volume of *François le Champi* – the novel that his mother read to him as a child – he feels himself troubled by a 'stranger':

I felt myself unpleasantly struck by an impression [. . .] This was a very deeply buried impression [. . .] in which memories of childhood and family were tenderly intermingled [. . .] My first reaction had been to ask myself, angrily, who this stranger was who was coming to trouble me. The stranger was none other than myself, the child I had been at that time, brought to life within me by the book, which knowing nothing of me except this child had instantly summoned him to its presence, wanting to be seen only by his eyes, to be loved only by his heart, to speak only to him.[125]

---

[123] Proust, *Swann's Way*, p. 1; translation modified in places.
[124] Proust, *Swann's Way*, p. 2, p. 5.
[125] Proust, *Time Regained*, pp. 239–40.

Although the narrator comes to recognise that the 'stranger' was 'none other than myself', 'myself' is still described in the past tense and the third person as 'the child I had been at that time' (*'c'était l'enfant que j'étais alors'*).[126] The book 'summoned *him* to its presence, wanting to be seen only by *his* eyes, to be loved only by *his* heart, to speak only to *him*' (*'c'est cet enfant que le livre avait appelé [. . .] ne voulant être regardé que par ses yeux, aimé que par son cœur, et ne parler qu'à lui'*).[127] There's something in this stress on the child as a third person – a stranger from the past – that conveys a sense of self-estrangement. The '"pen" of George Sand' is figured, like the famous madeleine, as a source of involuntary memory:

> a pen which, unintentionally, [. . .] I had charged with electricity, and now a thousand trifling details of Combray which for years had not entered my mind came lightly and spontaneously leaping [. . .] to suspend themselves from the magnetised nib in an interminable and trembling chain of memories.[128]

But the resurrection from 'within me' of 'a child who takes my place, who alone has the right to spell out the title *François le Champi*, and who reads it as he read it once before' provokes the comparison of 'my personality today' with 'an abandoned quarry'.[129] There is something dark and disquieting inscribed within the psychic and temporal leaps of reading for Proust – an experience with which we too are encouraged to identify as we navigate the twists and turns of the Proustian sentence. Invited to identify as the child reader inscribed within the modernist text, the reader is solicited to undergo a similarly uncanny experience of psychic and temporal dislocation.

*   *   *

For the Leavises, with whom I began this chapter, modernist literature served as a kind of initiation into critical 'maturity', an inoculation against the regressive perils of popular culture. I. A. Richards may have betrayed an unmistakable anxiety concerning the implications of Freud's 'discoveries' about childhood, but this anxiety would be forthrightly set aside, and disavowed, by the Leavis-ite literary criticism that would put the maturity of modernism at the heart of an emergent institutionalised literary study in Britain and beyond. Although modernist difficulty might at first feel infantilising, this was interpreted as a

---

[126] Proust, *À la recherche*, IV, p. 463.
[127] Proust, *À la recherche*, IV, p. 463, my emphasis.
[128] Proust, *Time Regained*, pp. 240–1.
[129] Proust, *Time Regained*, p. 242.

reflection of the true infantilism wrought upon modern readers by the pervasive influence of a regressive mass culture. Modernist literature issued its readers with a demand to grow up, to confront this feeling of infantilism and, crucially, to master it – such readers would become, in the process, 'mature' readers, members of that 'very small minority', the 'critically *adult* public'.[130] Modernist difficulty, in this account, echoed Q. D. Leavis's exhortation to the reader to 'respond as an adult', or it condemned his or her failure to do so, consigning the reader to a perpetual, 'Peter-Pan-like' infancy.[131]

And yet, as we have seen throughout this chapter, modernist writers and psychoanalysts were fascinated by the figure of the child reader, producing accounts of childhood reading that disrupt and complicate the Scrutineers' account of modernism as a path to rational critical maturity. The Freudian infant, lurking in one of the foundational texts of institutionalised twentieth-century literary criticism, challenges the notion that childhood can be consigned to an infancy conceived of as a developmental stage, a period of time, to be outgrown and left behind, banished safely to the past, on the onward march to adulthood. In this psychoanalytic account, childhood persists within the mind of the adult reader, always threatening to re-emerge, thwarting the linear account of modernism as a path towards maturity.

In the writing of Freud, Woolf and Proust, the scenes of childhood reading do frequently invoke pleasure, immediacy and consolation, suggesting a nostalgic longing for a lost world of childhood enchantment. But all three writers also draw their readers' attention to the adult fantasies at work in shaping this scene. For Freud, although an individual's childhood operates as a powerful presence in the adult unconscious, it also remains stubbornly concealed, shaped and moulded by adult projections, desires and cultural fantasies about 'the child'. In both Woolf's and Proust's writing, the scenes of childhood reading do evoke pleasure, consolation and intimacy, but these scenes also show us a stranger account of childhood reading. Rhoda's description of self-projection into the landscape of the poem, like Proust's narrator's description of reading as entering a strangely disorientating childhood dreamscape, disrupts more conventional images of the child as experiencing a blissful immersion inside the covers of the book.

In the scenes that I've examined in this chapter, the child readers depicted in *The Waves* and *À la recherche* appear as the projected readers of modernism, modelling the peculiar forms of immersion, the strange psychic leaps and the temporal shifts solicited in the readers of Woolf's and Proust's modernist prose. In Freud's writing on dreams, an eight-year-old boy becomes the hero of his book, whereas in *À la recherche* the narrator dreams that he is a religious building, a piece of music, a rivalry between ancient monarchs. Rhoda, similarly,

---

[130] Leavis, 'Mass Civilization and Minority Culture', p. 159, my emphasis.
[131] Leavis, *Fiction*, p. 235; Knights, 'Reading as a Man', p. 79.

identifies not only with the speaker of Shelley's poem, but with the poem itself, experiencing a kind of intimacy with the poem that is at once exhilarating and anxious. In soliciting the adult reader of the modernist text to identify as a child (both the child in the text, but also one's own inner child), these scenes of reading ask the reader to share Proust's narrator's self-estranging adult encounter with his own unconscious childhood self, which he finds smuggled away in a childhood classic, and to share Rhoda's anxious identification with a poem by Shelley. As such, these scenes not only represent the strangeness of the childhood scene of reading, they also ask their readers to enact it. Reading, in these passages, makes children of us all.

These portraits of childhood reading in *To the Lighthouse*, *The Waves* and *À la recherche* encourage us, as adult readers, to reflect not only on the processes of the act of reading in which we, as readers, are engaged, but also on the social and political meanings of this experience of reading. For Proust, his narrator's childhood compulsion to pursue fictional villains to their punishment is, he claims, the source of his insight into the fantasy components of nationalist feeling. As we've seen in this chapter, although Proust invokes the familiar portrait of the child's capacity for powerful forms of literary identification, he also rejects the tendency either to celebrate the scene of reading as a form of sentimental education or to condemn the child's vulnerability to ideological manipulation, instead suggesting that his capacity to reflect on the subjective motivations in childhood reading is itself the source of his adult insight into the role of the passions in political life. Both Woolf and Proust present scenes of childhood reading that, in their very strangeness, seem to puncture the familiar narratives of the child either as the subject of sentimental education or as vulnerable to ideological manipulation, presenting childhood reading as an altogether more complex and nuanced experience. And yet, for Woolf in particular, the figure of the child reader seems both to celebrate the child's capacity for uninhibited and rapturous identification and, at the same time, to worry about the potentially negative consequences of this lack of inhibition. In *The Waves*, the portrait of Rhoda reading Shelley appears in a novel that seems both to celebrate the scene of reading as a scene of unbridled communion and, as we shall see in Chapter 3, to worry about the potentially undemocratic nature of such forms of literary communion. There is a fragile border, in this 1930s novel, between reading as a form of rapturous self-projection into the literary text, and a more ambivalent portrayal of the erasure of the boundaries of the individual mind. As we shall see in later chapters, an uncertainty about self-surrender to the literary text came increasingly to dominate modernist writing in the 1930s, as writers became wary of the resemblance between aesthetic self-abandonment and the troubling mass politics of the 1930s.

2

STRANGE TABOOS AND DETRIMENTAL DIETS: READING ETHEL M. DELL

In his 1924 essay *The Artist and Psycho-Analysis*, Roger Fry cited a lengthy passage from Freud's *Introductory Lectures on Psycho-Analysis*. The artist, wrote Freud, is 'urged on by instinctive needs which are too clamorous':

> So, like any other with an unsatisfied longing, he turns away from reality and transfers all his interest, and all his Libido, too, on to the creation of his wishes in life. [. . .] [T]he intermediate world of phantasy is sanctioned by general human consent, and every hungry soul looks to it for comfort and consolation. But to those who are not artists the gratification that can be drawn from the springs of phantasy is very limited; their inexorable repressions prevent the enjoyment of all but the meagre day-dreams which can become conscious. A true artist has more at his disposal. First of all he understands how to elaborate his day-dreams, so that they lose that personal note which grates upon strange ears and becomes enjoyable to others; he knows too how to modify them sufficiently so that their origin in prohibited sources is not easily detected. Further, he possesses the mysterious ability to mould his particular material until it expresses the idea of his phantasy faithfully; and then he knows how to attach to this reflection of his phantasy-life so strong a stream of pleasure that, for a time at least, the repressions are out-balanced and dispelled by it. When he can do all this, he opens out to others the way back to the comfort and consolation of their own unconscious sources of pleasure, and

so reaps their gratitude and admiration; then he has won—through his phantasy—what before he could only win in phantasy, honour, power, and the love of women.[1]

The artist, Freud claims, dissatisfied by a reality which 'leaves him starving', projects his fantasy life into the artwork, and, by virtue of his superior powers of sublimation, modifies the 'personal note' of his capricious fantasies so that they can be devoured by those 'hungry soul[s]' who, failed by their own 'meagre day-dreams', turn to art 'for comfort and consolation'.[2]

For Fry, Freud offered the perfect description of what he called the 'impure artist', who caters for 'hungry girl clerks and housemaids'.[3] 'It is quite true', Fry observed, 'that this explains nearly all contemporary artistic creation':

> You have only to think of the average novel, especially the feuilleton of papers like the *Daily Mail* and the *Daily Mirror*, and others, which supply every day their pittance of imagined romantic love to hungry girl clerks and housemaids. In fact I believe the most successful and widely read of these (mostly lady) novelists do really day-dream in print, as it were; nothing else would account for their astounding productivity. These people have the fortunate gift of dreaming the average person's day-dream so that the wish-fulfilment which comes natural to them coincides precisely with the wish-fulfilment of a vast number of the population.[4]

In 'best-sellers' and at the cinema, Fry claims, 'wish-fulfilment reigns supreme': 'By a process which is mere child's play in the dream life we instantly identify ourselves with the hero, and then what satisfaction we attain!'[5] But 'None of these conditions', according to Fry, 'apply to the first-rate novel' – on the contrary, such novels depend 'upon a peculiar detachment from the instinctive life': 'no one who hoped to get an ideal wish-fulfilment would go to *Mme. Bovary* or *Anna Karenina* or even *Vanity Fair*.'[6] For Fry, there is 'an art which corresponds to the dream life, an art in which the phantasy-making power of the libido is at work to produce a wish-fulfilment', but 'there is also an art which

---

[1] Sigmund Freud, *Introductory Lectures on Psycho-Analysis: A Course of Twenty-Eight Lectures Delivered at the University of Vienna*, trans. by Joan Riviere (London: George Allen & Unwin and International Psycho-Analytical Institute, 1922), pp. 314–15, cited by Fry, *The Artist*, p. 10.

[2] Freud, *Introductory Lectures*, p. 311, pp. 314–15.

[3] Fry, *The Artist*, p. 11.

[4] Fry, *The Artist*, pp. 11–12.

[5] Fry, *The Artist*, p. 12.

[6] Fry, *The Artist*, p. 12.

has withdrawn itself from the dream', an art 'which is pre-eminently *objective* and *dis-interested*'.[7]

Citing the same passage from Freud's *Introductory Lectures* in his 1924 article 'Dr. Freud on Art', Clive Bell relentlessly mocked Freud's model of reading as a means of gratifying unfulfilled wishes, comparing Freud's taste in literature to that of one of Fry's 'hungry [. . .] housemaids':

> Now this, I dare say, is a pretty good account of what housemaids, and Dr. Freud presumably, take for art. Indeed, the novelette is the perfect example of 'wish fulfilment in the world of phantasy.' The housemaid dreams of becoming a great actress and being loved by a handsome earl; Dr. Freud dreams of having been born a handsome earl and loving a great actress. And for fifteen delirious minutes, while the story lasts, the dream comes true. But this has nothing to do with art.[8]

For these neo-Kantian modernists, 'Dr. Freud's' account of the reader's 'hungry soul' might offer an insight into the impure desires of 'hungry girl clerks and housemaids', but Freud's theory of art as gratification bore no resemblance to the '*dis-interested*' and 'pure' 'aesthetic emotion' inspired by the formal features of high art.[9]

Despite his best attempts to distinguish between the 'pure' and the 'impure' emotions provoked by art, by the end of his paper, Fry admits 'the great probability, to me almost a certainty, that all psychic energy is derived ultimately from the instinctive life and has its source in the satisfaction, at however distant a remove, of some instinctive need or desire'.[10] Fry describes the pleasure obtained in the 'recognition of order', but admits that he is not satisfied with the notion that aesthetic pleasure comes from the disinterested perception of formal 'order and inter-relation' alone.[11] Every 'part', Fry argues, 'as well as the whole, becomes suffused with an emotional tone':

> The emotional tone is not due to any recognizable reminiscence or suggestion of the emotional experiences of life; but I do sometimes wonder

---

[7] Fry, *The Artist*, p. 18, Fry's emphasis.

[8] Clive Bell, 'Dr. Freud on Art', *Nation and Athenaeum*, 35.23 (6 September 1924), 690–1 (p. 690).

[9] Fry, *The Artist*, p. 18, Fry's emphasis. On Fry's and Bell's neo-Kantianism, see Christine Froula, *Virginia Woolf and the Bloomsbury Avant-Garde: War, Civilization, Modernity* (New York: Columbia University Press, 2005), pp. 12–16. On the Kantian roots of a pervasive modernist 'scorn for culinary art', see Alys Moody, *The Art of Hunger: Aesthetic Autonomy and the Afterlives of Modernism* (Oxford: Oxford University Press, 2018), pp. 8–16. See also Ngai, *Our Aesthetic Categories*, pp. 90–3.

[10] Fry, *The Artist*, pp. 18–19.

[11] Fry, *The Artist*, p. 19.

if it nevertheless does not get its force from arousing some very deep, very vague, and immensely generalized reminiscences. It looks as though art had got access to the substratum of all the emotional colours of life, to something which underlies all the particular and specialized emotions of actual life.[12]

Discussing Fry's essay, Lyndsey Stonebridge notes that 'as Fry struggles to discriminate between the more brute primary pleasures of the masses and the aesthetic emotions of pure art, primary and instinctive gratifications continually re-emerge in his attempt to protect the autonomy of art'.[13] As Stonebridge adds:

While Fry continues to fetishize the autonomous realm of the visual at the expense of the drive-invested body, what looks like a straightforward denial in his writing can also be read as a disavowal: Fry knows the aesthetic realm cannot be autonomous, but all the same he will continue to promote it as such.[14]

Fry's attempt to secure high art from psychoanalysis is less a denial that psychoanalysis can be put into profitable dialogue with theories of artistic production and reception, than a deep-rooted class- and gender-based anxiety about the failure of aesthetic theory to set out a convincing difference between high and low, pure and popular forms of, and tastes in, art. The desire to secure high art from psychoanalysis is in fact nothing of the sort: it is an attempt to secure it from the crude passions of the common woman reader. For these Bloomsbury art critics, Freud's psychoanalytic account of art and its pleasures was complicit with a degraded and feminised form of popular culture, in which 'hungry girl clerks and housemaids' found themselves enslaved to the gratifications afforded by popular novels and the cinema.

For many modernist writers and critics, the spurned figure of the 'hungry [. . .] housemaid', or the gluttonous romance reader, found one of her fullest articulations in the typically outraged modernist portraits of the popular novelist Ethel M. Dell and her readers. Dell's first novel, *The Way of an Eagle*, was turned down by eight publishers before T. Fisher Unwin agreed to publish it in January 1912; by 1915, having gone through twenty-seven printings, the novel accounted for over half of the publisher's profits.[15] Dell went on to publish a further thirty-two novels, eight volumes of short stories, and a book of poetry

[12] Fry, *The Artist*, p. 19.

[13] Stonebridge, *The Destructive Element*, p. 51.

[14] Stonebridge, *The Destructive Element*, pp. 51–2.

[15] Clive Bloom, *Bestsellers: Popular Fiction Since 1900*, 2nd edn (Basingstoke: Palgrave Macmillan, 2008), pp. 193–4; Penelope Dell, *Nettie and Sissie: The Biography of Ethel M. Dell and her Sister Ella* (London: Hamish Hamilton, 1977), p. 34.

before her death in 1939. Dell was thirty-one and unmarried when *The Way of an Eagle* was first published. Born on 2 August 1881, Dell had grown up in a comfortable, though not wealthy, middle-class family in South London. Up until 1922 – when, at the age of forty, she married Lieutenant-Colonel Gerald Tahourdin Savage – Dell lived quietly with her sister, refusing to allow her photograph to be published by the prying press, although assiduously replying to her fan mail and, according to her niece and biographer, becoming good friends with a number of her 'spinster' readers.[16] In this period, which also saw the emergence of Mills & Boon as the leading publishers of romance fiction, Dell became one of the most successful romance authors of the early twentieth century. For historians of mass-produced twentieth-century romance fiction, *The Way of an Eagle* – alongside *Three Weeks* (1907) by Elinor Glyn, and *The Sheik* (1919) by E. M. Hull – is one of the pioneering prototypes of the genre. While Catherine Cookson cited Dell as a major influence on her own romantic fiction, Barbara Cartland, who produced 'condensed' editions of Dell's novels as part of her 'Library of Love' in the 1970s and 1980s, claimed to have 'copied' Dell's 'formula' all of her life.[17] In 1918, G. B. Samuelson's film of *The Way of an Eagle* 'broke all records up and down the country', and between 1919 and 1924 the Stoll Film Company produced eighteen films based on Ethel M. Dell's work as part of their 'Eminent British Authors' series; Dell was the most regularly adapted author in this series, which also included films based on writing by H. G. Wells, Arthur Conan Doyle and Edgar Wallace.[18] In an article titled 'The Feminine Interest', Stoll's publicist described Dell as author of the 'sort of film story that appeals to women and girls by the thousand', the sort of film that 'fills' the exhibitor's 'picture-palace and his cash-box'.[19] Maurice Elvey, who directed

---

[16] Dell, *Nettie and Sissie*, p. 36, pp. 41–2; Harriet Harvey Wood, 'Dell, Ethel Mary (1881–1939)', in *Oxford Dictionary of National Biography* (Oxford: Oxford University Press, 2004).

[17] Joseph McAleer, *Popular Reading and Publishing in Britain 1914–1950* (Oxford: Clarendon Press, 1992), pp. 100–32 (p. 101, pp. 102–3); Joseph McAleer, *Passion's Fortune: The Story of Mills & Boon* (Oxford: Oxford University Press, 1999), pp. 11–34; jay [sic] Dixon, *The Romance Fiction of Mills & Boon 1909–1990s* (London: UCL Press, 1999), pp. 13–25; Carol Dyhouse, *Heartthrobs: A History of Women and Desire* (Oxford: Oxford University Press, 2017), pp. 22–4; Henry Cloud, *Barbara Cartland: Crusader in Pink* (London: Weidenfeld & Nicolson, 1979), pp. 23–4, cited by McAleer, *Popular Reading*, pp. 34–5; Bloom, *Bestsellers*, p. 259.

[18] Ed Harris, *Britain's Forgotten Film Factory: The Story of Isleworth Film Studios* (Stroud: Amberley Publishing, 2012), p. 36; Nathalie Morris, 'Pictures, Romance and Luxury: Women and British Cinema in the 1910s and 1920s', in *British Women's Cinema*, ed. by Melanie Bell and Melanie Williams (Abingdon: Routledge, 2010), pp. 19–33 (pp. 23–4).

[19] Pearkes Withers, 'The Feminine Interest', *Stoll's Editorial News*, 16 September, 15–16 (p. 15), cited by Morris, 'Pictures, Romance and Luxury', p. 24.

a number of these films, claimed that 'The name of Ethel M. Dell was enough to sell millions of copies of anything she wrote'.[20] Recounting Dell's desire to hold 'some authority over the script', Elvey described the incongruity of Dell, 'the most ordinary, quiet, gentle little creature', and her 'quiet and spinsterlike life', when juxtaposed with the 'worldly' and 'for those days risqué themes' of her books.[21] Summing up the novels and films as 'harmless romantic tales', Elvey nonetheless hints at what Dell's biographer and niece Penelope Dell describes as 'Ethel's heavenly "pegs"'.[22] These allowed Dell to package sometimes violent eroticism as harmless romance and, without being 'pornographic', to tell 'so deliciously and explicitly, of the very things which are taboo'. According to her niece, Dell 'found a mixture that could be swallowed undiluted, enjoyed, and yet still perform its duty'.[23]

The name Ethel M. Dell may have filled the cash-boxes of picture palaces up and down the country, but this name alone also provoked scorn amongst the intelligentsia. For her critics – of whom there were many – Dell's writing epitomised an addictive form of mass culture that was served up to satisfy the voracious gluttony of compulsive female readers. For George Orwell, Dell represented a particularly revolting form of feminised and indulgent consumerist culture, evoking 'wistful spinsters and the fat wives of tobacconists'.[24] In the opening scene of Orwell's 1936 novel *Keep the Aspidistra Flying*, Gordon Comstock imagines Dell's novels on the shelves of the 'twopenny no-deposit library' as part of a tomb of 'soggy, half-baked trash massed together in one place': 'Pudding, suet pudding. Eight hundred slabs of pudding walling him in—a vault of puddingstone.'[25] For Orwell, whose response to Dell is tinged with misogyny, Dell represented a feminised form of indulgent, gluttonous and repetitive reading of novels that were, in Orwell's eyes, reducible to half-baked, stodgy suet pudding, 'trash' and, as he put it more explicitly in one essay, 'tripe'.[26]

---

[20] Dennis Gifford, 'The Early Memoirs of Maurice Elvey', *Griffithiana*, 60/61 (1997), 76–125 (pp. 117–18).

[21] Gifford, 'The Early Memoirs of Maurice Elvey', pp. 117–18.

[22] Gifford, 'The Early Memoirs of Maurice Elvey', pp. 117–18; Dell, *Nettie and Sissie*, p. xiv.

[23] Dell, *Nettie and Sissie*, p. xiv.

[24] Orwell, 'Bookshop Memories', p. 275.

[25] George Orwell, *Keep the Aspidistra Flying* (London: Penguin, 2000), pp. 2–3, pp. 9–10.

[26] Orwell, 'In Defence of the Novel' (1936), in *Collected Essays*, I, pp. 281–7 (p. 284, p. 282); George Orwell, 'Inside the Whale' (1940), in *Collected Essays*, I, pp. 540–78 (p. 570); George Orwell, 'The Cost of Letters' (1946), in *Collected Essays*, IV, pp. 236–8 (p. 237). See also Nicola Beauman, *A Very Great Profession: The Woman's Novel 1914–39*, 2nd edn (London: Persephone, 2008), pp. 250–1.

For Q. D. Leavis, the mechanisms of popular romantic fiction had been captured powerfully in James Joyce's portrait of Gerty MacDowell. 'For Gerty MacDowell', wrote Leavis,

> Every situation has a prescribed attitude provided by memories of slightly similar situations in cheap fiction, she thinks in terms of clichés drawn from the same sources, and is completely out of touch with reality.[27]

'Such a life', Leavis argued, 'is not only crude, impoverished, and narrow, it is dangerous.'[28] For Elizabeth Bowen, too, this passage of *Ulysses* appeared as 'Ethel M. Dell-ese', while a number of other early critics drew the same comparison, one insisting that 'Gerty MacDowell's cheap little flirtation is perfectly described in terms borrowed from an Ethel M. Dell novel'.[29] For Leavis, who echoes Mary Wollstonecraft's worry that excessive novel reading might propel readers to 'plump into actual vice', novelists like Ethel M. Dell and E. M. Hull represented a 'detrimental diet [. . .] in so far as a habit of fantasying will lead to maladjustment in actual life'.[30]

Allusions to Dell in early-twentieth-century culture often appear as little more than passing allusions or jibes, made frequently no doubt by authors who had perhaps not read much more than a page of Dell's writing. And yet, taken collectively, these references to Dell and her readers – which appear in the work of writers and critics including Orwell, Leavis, I. A. Richards, Elizabeth Bowen, Rebecca West, Virginia Woolf and James Strachey – nonetheless testify to the powerful grip that this writer and her readers held on the early-twentieth-century literary imagination.[31] In *Fiction and the Reading Public*, Leavis observed that while the

---

[27] Leavis, *Fiction*, p. 245.

[28] Leavis, *Fiction*, p. 245.

[29] Elizabeth Bowen, 'James Joyce' (1941), in *People, Places, Things: Essays by Elizabeth Bowen*, ed. by Allan Hepburn (Edinburgh: Edinburgh University Press, 2008), pp. 239–47 (p. 246); S. Foster Damon, 'The Odyssey in Dublin', in *James Joyce: Two Decades of Criticism*, ed. by Seon Givens (New York: Vanguard Press, 1948), pp. 203–42 (p. 217); Edward Wagenknecht, *Cavalcade of the English Novel: From Elizabeth to George VI* (New York: H. Holt and Co., 1943), p. 519.

[30] Mary Wollstonecraft, *A Vindication of the Rights of Woman* (1792), ed. by Janet Todd (Oxford: Oxford University Press, 1993), p. 271; Leavis, *Fiction*, pp. 53–4.

[31] Arguing that the 'all-pervasive' 'educational influence of the arts' could be demonstrated through the pervasive detrimental influence of 'bad art', I. A. Richards insisted that, if the reader is not 'fully "vigilant"', the 'enjoyment of Miss Dell' 'is likely to have as a consequence not only an acceptance of the mediocre in ordinary life, but a blurring and confusion of impulses and a very widespread loss of value'. Following a visit to Margaret Llewelyn Davies in May 1925, Virginia Woolf commented that she 'takes Ethel M. Dell and Dickens' as an antidote for her worries. Richards, *Principles of Literary Criticism*, pp. 215–17; Woolf, *Diary*, III, p. 23.

'lowbrow public' were entirely ignorant of the 'work and even of the names of the highbrow writers, for the highbrow public "Ethel M. Dell"' appeared (alongside *Tarzan*) as a 'convenient symbol' of lowbrow taste, 'drawn from hearsay rather than first-hand knowledge'.[32] A recurrent figure in early-twentieth-century criticism, Ethel M. Dell functions repeatedly as just such a 'convenient symbol', or fantasy, of lowbrow taste; she is filled out, fattened almost to bursting point, with fantasies of what the reader of popular romances is up to when she reads.

Turning to Ethel M. Dell's writing, however, I want to suggest that although these novels do uphold a deeply conservative and patriarchal vision of femininity, they also, at the same time, both internalise and challenge the characteristic tropes of the romance reader as a glutton and an addict. For her critics, Ethel M. Dell represented an addictive form of popular fiction that was served up to satisfy the voracious gluttony of a passive, greedy and compulsive type of female reader. Figured as 'detrimental diet', 'suet pudding', a 'mind opiate' to be 'suck[ed] down' passively and unreflectingly by naïve and unthinking female readers, Dell's first, and most famous, novel *The Way of an Eagle* takes up a position in early-twentieth-century culture in which it is repeatedly defined as the other of a masculine, disinterested and abstemious form of modernism.[33] And yet, as we shall see, in the opening pages of *The Way of an Eagle*, we are confronted with a troubling scene of violent forcible drugging that immediately complicates critical accounts of Dell as a 'mind opiate' for addicted gluttons.[34] Consciously or not, I want to argue, *The Way of an Eagle* internalises the language of compulsion, addiction and masochism that has surrounded the reader of romances from Mary Wollstonecraft, through *Madame Bovary*, and into the modernist period and after – thereby rendering any such simplistic reading of its readers impossible. In her novels, Dell stages scenes of consumption and scenes of reading that complicate the criticisms of her novels as 'detrimental diet', drawing attention to a deep-rooted set of cultural anxieties about women's agency and about the nature of women's hungers and desires.

THE WAY OF AN EAGLE (1912) AND FORCIBLE FEEDING

The Way of an Eagle begins in an uneasy imperial India. Muriel Roscoe, daughter of a brigadier in the British army, lies at the heart of a frontier fort under siege from a 'storm of rebellion'.[35] General Roscoe, 'on a tour of inspection and also, to a very mild degree, of intimidation', has been betrayed by 'traitors' amongst his 'native soldiers'; running low on food, the remaining

---

[32] Leavis, *Fiction*, p. 20, p. 35.

[33] Leavis, *Fiction*, pp. 53–4; Orwell, *Keep the Aspidistra*, p. 3; Leavis, *Fiction*, p. 56; Strachey, 'Some Unconscious Factors', p. 326.

[34] Leavis, *Fiction*, p. 56.

[35] Ethel M. Dell, *The Way of an Eagle* (London: Virago, 1996), p. 13.

British soldiers are powerless against 'the rising flood of rebellion'.[36] Muriel, the 'only white woman in the garrison', is confined to a chamber at the centre of the fort, 'narrow as a prison cell'.[37] In the 'midst of nerve-shattering tumult', 'lying through many sleepless nights with nerves strung to a pitch of torture', her 'vivid imagination ever at work upon pictures more ghastly than even the ghastly reality which she was not allowed to see', Muriel is 'driven to extremity': she seeks 'relief in a remedy from which in her normal senses she would have turned in disgust' – she finds relief in opium.[38] Summoning three officers to his room, the brigadier (who announces that they are the only remaining 'four white men among a host of dark', and 'bordering on starvation') asks which of them will undertake to look after Muriel – which of them is prepared 'to shoot her' rather than leave her to be killed, or worse, it is implied, by the rebels.[39] Entrusted by her father to the care of Nick Ratcliffe, Muriel finds herself at the mercy of a man she detests, a man who, with a 'rigidity of defiance', she is determined 'to resist'.[40]

In this, the first scene between hero and heroine, a servant brings Muriel a full glass of opium, saying that her father has sent it to her to help her to sleep:

'I say, you know,' [Nick] said abruptly, 'you shouldn't take opium.'

[. . .]

'Miss Roscoe [. . .] I beg you, don't drink that stuff. Your father must be mad to offer it to you. Let me take the beastliness away.' [. . .]

'[I]t is madness to take opium in this reckless fashion. For Heaven's sake be reasonable. Don't take it.'

He came back to the table, but at his approach she laid her hand upon the glass. She was quivering with angry excitement.

'I will not endure your interference any longer,' she declared, goaded to headlong, nervous fury by his persistence. 'My father's wishes are enough for me. He desires me to take it, and so I will.'

She took up the glass in a sudden frenzy of defiance. He had frightened her—yes, he had frightened her—but he should see how little he had gained by that. She took a taste of the liquid, then paused, again assailed by a curious hesitancy. Had her father really meant her to take it all?

Nick had stopped short at her first movement, but as she began to lower the glass in response to that disquieting doubt, he swooped suddenly forward like a man possessed.

---

[36] Dell, *The Way*, p. 13, p. 14.

[37] Dell, *The Way*, p. 6.

[38] Dell, *The Way*, p. 7.

[39] Dell, *The Way*, pp. 3–4.

[40] Dell, *The Way*, p. 20, p. 19.

For a fleeting instant she thought he was going to wrest it from her, but in the next she understood—understood the man's deep treachery, and with what devilish ingenuity he had worked upon her. Holding her with an arm that felt like iron, he forced the glass back between her teeth, and tilted the contents down her throat. She strove to resist him, strove wildly, frantically, not to swallow the draught. But he held her pitilessly. He compelled her, gripping her right hand with the glass, and pinning the other to her side.

When it was over, when he had worked his will and the hateful draught was swallowed, he set her free and turned himself sharply from her.

She sprang up trembling and hysterical. She could have slain him in that instant had she possessed the means to her hand. But her strength was more nearly exhausted than she knew. Her limbs doubled up under her weight, and as she tottered, seeking for support, she realized that she was vanquished utterly at last.

[. . .]

What followed dwelt ever after in her memory as a hideous dream, vivid yet not wholly tangible. He laid her down upon the couch and bent over her, his hands upon her, holding her still; for every muscle, every nerve twitched spasmodically, convulsively, in the instinctive effort of the powerless body to be free.[41]

As we later learn, Muriel's father, having been shot, is in fact already dying at this point. Nick's objections to the opium are part of his ploy to goad her into drinking it all, so that he can carry out his plan to rescue her by disguising himself as a 'tribesman' and carrying her across the mountains upon his back – as though dead – in a similar disguise.[42] After several days in the mountains, the couple are rescued.[43] Nick proposes and – despite the fact that his violent impulses, his seemingly rapacious desire, and what is insistently described as his 'savage' nature repulse and frighten her – Muriel accepts.[44] Upon overhearing gossip insinuating that Nick is only marrying her out of a sense of obligation, Muriel breaks off the engagement. She travels back to England, followed later by Nick, who has lost an arm in battle. After months of confusion – including Muriel's engagement to another man, the break-up of that engagement, her return to India, Nick's cross-dressing as an 'old native beggar', and his prevention (in that disguise) of the assassination of a British administrator by Indian 'rebels' – Muriel and Nick are finally united in a happy marriage.[45]

[41] Dell, *The Way*, pp. 21–3.
[42] Dell, *The Way*, p. 19.
[43] Dell, *The Way*, pp. 35–6.
[44] Dell, *The Way*, p. 91.
[45] Dell, *The Way*, p. 293.

The novel closes as, mounting the top of Everest at sunrise, Muriel announces her pregnancy.

For Dell's critics, *The Way of an Eagle* represented the 'detrimental diet' of 'hungry girl clerks and housemaids'.[46] And yet, in this opening scene, we are presented with the image of a woman who is already dependent on opium being forcibly and violently drugged by the man who is nonetheless trying to save her and whom, the reader knows, she will come to love and marry by the close of the novel. The scene throws the critical language of hunger, addiction and compulsion into disarray. There is something in *The Way of an Eagle* that both echoes the traditional critique of romance reading and creeps into the obsessive imagining of Ethel M. Dell as a form of bad diet or addiction. This is a novel about women's desires, which is then derided in terms which seem to have leaked out of the novel and crept into its critique: the critical debate symptomatically repeats, and, crucially, simplifies, the subject of the text. This is similar to the 'reading effect' that Shoshana Felman described in the critical debates surrounding *The Turn of the Screw*: 'The scene of critical debate', writes Felman, 'is [. . .] a repetition of the scene dramatized in the text.'[47] In Felman's celebrated essay, she describes how the sophisticated, so-called 'Freudian' readers of *The Turn of the Screw* respond to textual ambiguity as though it were a question demanding a literal answer, a literal answer which, by its very nature, violates the ambiguity of the text.[48] Dell's critics respond to what can be read as an ambiguity in *The Way of an Eagle* by turning a question about women's agency into an account of the text as itself straightforwardly engendering a passive form of degenerate engorged femininity in its readers. This is a novel about compulsion, but that is not to say (as the critics suggest) that the reader of *The Way of an Eagle* is necessarily reproduced in the image of the opium addict. Although metaphors of addiction and hunger have been, and are still, used to censure the typically female readers of bestsellers, in *The Way of an Eagle* the opening description of forcible drugging creates a kind of rupture that is difficult to reconcile with the argument that romantic fiction works only as a kind of drug that pacifies and ideologically shapes hopelessly addicted readers.

In *The Way of an Eagle*, the opening encounter between hero and heroine is bound up in a deep-rooted set of early-twentieth-century cultural anxieties about women's agency, hunger and desires. In this scene, the heroine's dependency on opium may conjure the familiar trope of the addicted romance reader, but the scene also contains striking parallels with the contemporary accounts and visual depictions of the forcible feeding of hunger-striking suffragettes,

[46] Leavis, *Fiction*, pp. 53–4; Fry, *The Artist*, p. 11.
[47] Felman, 'Turning the Screw', p. 101.
[48] Felman, 'Turning the Screw', pp. 104–7.

thereby complicating the recognisable stereotypes of women's passivity. In *The Prisoner: An Experience of Forcible Feeding: A Sketch*, published in 1911, Helen Gordon Liddle described the 'scene' of forcible feeding as a 'battle' in which anonymous male doctors force 'the prisoner' into submission:

> The prisoner refuses to unclose her teeth – the last defence against the food she, out of principle, refuses to take [. . .] He puts his great fingers along her teeth – feels a gap at the back, rams the tool blindly and with evident intention to hurt her, and cause the helpless woman to wince – along the shrinking flesh – how long will it take before superior strength triumphs? – tears start in the prisoner's eyes – uncontrollable tears – tears she would give anything to control.
>
> [. . .]
>
> The pain is maddening – she strains at her hands – her feet are in a vice – her head is held – she tries to speak – her jaw is forced to its widest. They pour the food down [. . .]
>
> The limit is reached, and for the first time the prisoner gives way – great sobs of pain and breathlessness come faster and faster – she cannot bear it – she tries to call out 'Stop!' with that tortured wide-open mouth – and with one wrench she frees her hands and seizes the gag.
>
> [. . .]
>
> A short quick thrust and her mouth is gagged again – the prisoner tries to control herself – her sobs increase – her breathlessness also – there is nothing but the pain and the relentless forcing of food down her throat – her choking despair, and the bitter draught of tonic and digestive medicine which is also poured down her throat.[49]

'At last', Liddle writes, 'it is over, and she is left sick and shaken with the whole scene.'[50] In 'Forcibly Fed: The Story of My Four Weeks in Holloway Gaol' (1913), Sylvia Pankhurst described her experience in a similar manner:

> Then the doctors came stealing in behind. Some one seized me by the head and thrust a sheet under my chin. I felt a man's hands trying to force my mouth open. I set my teeth and tightened my lips over them with all my strength. My breath was coming so quickly that I felt as if I should suffocate. I felt his fingers trying to press my lips apart,—getting inside,—and I felt them and a steel gag running around my gums and feeling for gaps in my teeth.

[49] Helen Gordon Liddle, *The Prisoner: An Experience of Forcible Feeding: A Sketch* (Letchworth: Garden City Press Ltd, 1911), pp. 49–51.

[50] Liddle, *The Prisoner*, p. 51.

I felt I should go mad; I felt like a poor wild thing caught in a steel trap. I was tugging at my head to get it free. [. . .] My breath was coming faster and with a sort of low scream that was getting louder. [. . .]

Then I felt a steel instrument pressing against my gums, cutting into the flesh, forcing its way in. Then it gradually prised my jaws apart as they turned a screw. It felt like having my teeth drawn; but I resisted—I resisted. I held my poor bleeding gums down on the steel with all my strength. [. . .] I was struggling wildly, trying to tighten the muscles and to keep my throat closed up. They got the tube down, I suppose, though I was unconscious of anything but a mad revolt of struggling, for at last I heard them say, 'That's all'; and I vomited as the tube came up.

They left me on the bed exhausted, gasping for breath and sobbing convulsively.[51]

For both these suffragettes, and for Muriel, the scene of forcible feeding, or forcible drugging, follows a strikingly similar pattern of resistance, struggle, defeat, outrage and, finally, exhaustion.

In *The Way of an Eagle*, Dell describes Muriel's 'rigidity of defiance' forced to give way to Nick's greater physical power.[52] For the suffragettes, similarly, the scene of forcible feeding takes the form of a dramatic power struggle between the brute force of the male doctors and the passive but determined resistance of the prisoner who is forced to give way to the anonymous doctors' 'superior strength'.[53] As it dawns on Muriel 'with what devilish ingenuity he had worked upon her', Dell describes her protagonist as the passive object of the man's actions, using the passive voice to describe how, 'when he had worked his will [. . .] the hateful draught was swallowed'.[54] Dell emphasises the visceral physicality of the scene, describing a struggle between 'his hands' – which anticipate the anonymous men's 'hands' and 'fingers' in the suffragette accounts – and 'her' body (the names, 'Nick' and 'Muriel', disappear).[55] Many of the reports of forcible feeding describe the sensation of being 'held' in a 'vice': while Liddle describes the prisoner's feet in a 'vice', Pankhurst recalls feeling 'like a poor wild thing caught in a steel trap'.[56] In a strange account of an avowedly 'playacted' experience of voluntary forcible feeding, which she underwent as an act of solidarity with her 'English sisters' and wrote up in

[51] Sylvia Pankhurst, 'Forcibly Fed: The Story of My Four Weeks in Holloway Gaol', *McClure's Magazine*, August 1913, 87–93 (p. 90).
[52] Dell, *The Way*, p. 20.
[53] Liddle, *The Prisoner*, p. 50.
[54] Dell, *The Way*, p. 22.
[55] Dell, *The Way*, pp. 22–3.
[56] Liddle, *The Prisoner*, p. 50; Pankhurst, 'Forcibly Fed', p. 90.

self-consciously sensational style for the *New York World Magazine* in 1914, the modernist writer Djuna Barnes echoed the dominant rhetorical features of these suffragette accounts, describing 'the hands' at her head 'tightening into a vise [*sic*]', while 'like answering vises [*sic*] the hands at my hips and those at my feet grew rigid and secure'.[57] Muriel, similarly, is described, before the drugging, feeling 'as though an iron trap had closed upon her and held her at his mercy'; when Nick drugs her, she is held in place by 'an arm that felt like iron', later 'like a vice'.[58] One of the most visceral elements of the suffragette accounts lies in the detailed description of the doctors' assaults on the prisoners' mouths: *The Prisoner* describes the suffragette refusing to 'unclose her teeth', but the doctor 'puts his great fingers along her teeth – feels a gap' and 'rams the tool blindly [. . .] along the shrinking flesh'.[59] Pankhurst describes how she 'felt his fingers trying to press my lips apart,—getting inside,—[. . .] feeling for gaps in my teeth'.[60] In Constance Lytton's account of the forcible feeding that she underwent while disguised as a working-class woman called Jane Warton, she recounts her 'resistance' while the doctor 'plied my teeth with the steel implement', and 'dug his instrument down on to the sham tooth'.[61] In *The Way of an Eagle*, Nick is described as having 'forced the glass back between her teeth, and tilted the contents down her throat'.[62]

Like Pankhurst, who describes herself 'struggling wildly, trying to tighten the muscles and to keep my throat closed up', Muriel, in Dell's words, 'strove to resist him, strove wildly, frantically, not to swallow the draught'.[63] Pankhurst, describing a 'mad revolt of struggling', fears that she will 'go mad', while Liddle similarly describes the experience as 'maddening', and Barnes describes herself – even though she underwent the experience on a voluntary basis – as 'burning with revolt at this brutal usurpation of my own functions', contemplating 'how they who actually suffered the ordeal in its acutest horror must have flamed at the violation of the sanctuaries of their spirits'.[64] Both Pankhurst and Liddle describe their resistance breaking down into uncontrollable breathlessness and convulsive sobbing. Dell, echoing, or perhaps anticipating, these suffragette accounts, describes Muriel as 'quivering', 'frenz[ied]', 'trembling and hysterical'.[65] But

---

[57] Djuna Barnes, 'How It Feels to Be Forcibly Fed' (1914), in *Djuna Barnes's New York*, ed. by Alyce Barry (London: Virago, 1990), pp. 174–9 (p. 178, p. 177).

[58] *The Way*, p. 21, p. 22, p. 25.

[59] Liddle, *The Prisoner*, p. 49.

[60] Pankhurst, 'Forcibly Fed', p. 90.

[61] Constance Lytton, *Prisons and Prisoners: Some Personal Experiences* (London: William Heinemann, 1914), p. 269.

[62] Dell, *The Way*, p. 22.

[63] Pankhurst, 'Forcibly Fed', p. 90; Dell, *The Way*, p. 22.

[64] Pankhurst, 'Forcibly Fed', p. 90; Liddle, *The Prisoner*, p. 50; Barnes, 'How it Feels', p. 178.

[65] Dell, *The Way*, p. 22.

Nick 'held her pitilessly': 'He compelled her, gripping her right hand with the glass, and pinning the other to her side.'[66] Like Pankhurst, who describes herself, when they finish 'at last', as 'exhausted', Muriel too finds herself 'exhausted', 'vanquished utterly at last'.[67] In Barnes's newspaper article, she describes how

> Unbidden visions of remote horrors danced madly through my mind. There arose the hideous thought of being gripped in the tentacles of some monster devil fish in the depths of a tropic sea, as the liquid slowly sensed its way along innumerable endless passages that seemed to traverse my nose, my ears, the inner interstices of my throbbing head.[68]

Like Barnes, Muriel experiences a similar kind of splitting of the body and mind, entering a hallucinogenic state (induced partly, of course, by the opium), only to be pursued 'ever after' by a 'hideous dream, vivid yet not wholly tangible'.[69] Barnes, who describes having 'lapsed into a physical mechanism without power to oppose or resent the outrage to my will', dwells finally on a 'spirit betrayed by the body's weakness'.[70] Dell too describes the 'body' reduced to instinct, as – like Pankhurst, who recalls 'sobbing convulsively' – Muriel's 'every muscle, every nerve twitched spasmodically, convulsively, in the instinctive effort of the powerless body to be free'.[71]

When Muriel wakes up she feels panic and fear, recognising that, as the narrative puts it explicitly: 'He had drugged her *forcibly*.'[72] Seeking to escape, she feels his 'hand fastened claw-like upon her dress'.[73] Nick insists that she eat, and what follows repeats the opening scene, once again revealing a striking affinity with the suffragettes' accounts of forcible feeding: 'She stooped and strove wildly, frantically, to shake off the detaining hand. But it held her like a vice, with awful skeleton fingers that she could not, dared not, touch.'[74] Muriel makes a final effort to 'wrest herself free', before breaking down, helpless.[75] As Nick continues to insist that she eat, Muriel finds herself trembling: 'Could he make her eat also against her will, she wondered?'[76] Finally, 'against

---

[66] Dell, *The Way*, p. 22.
[67] Pankhurst, 'Forcibly Fed', p. 90; Dell, *The Way*, p. 22.
[68] Barnes, 'How It Feels', p. 177.
[69] Dell, *The Way*, p. 23.
[70] Barnes, 'How It Feels', p. 178.
[71] Dell, *The Way*, p. 23.
[72] Dell, *The Way*, p. 25, my emphasis.
[73] Dell, *The Way*, p. 25.
[74] Dell, *The Way*, p. 25.
[75] Dell, *The Way*, p. 25.
[76] Dell, *The Way*, p. 26.

her will, almost without conscious movement, she obeyed him. The untempting morsel passed from his hand to hers, and under the compulsion of his insistence she began to eat.'[77] Dell describes her heroine feeling 'as if every mouthful would choke her', but 'urged by the dread certainty that he would somehow have his way'.[78]

During the years in which Dell worked on *The Way of an Eagle*, and in the years immediately following its publication in January 1912, the campaign for the women's vote resounded loudly in the public consciousness. The first suffragette hunger strikes had begun in 1909, and public accounts of forcible feeding appeared in September of the same year, provoking considerable debate in the House of Commons, the press, and in the writing and visual propaganda produced by the Women's Social and Political Union. Dell's biographer suggests that she was writing and rewriting her first novel from 1907 onwards, possibly earlier.[79] The first page of a bound handwritten manuscript in the British Library is dated '27 Sept. 1909' – there are some crossings out and additions in this manuscript, but the text bears a close proximity to the published novel, suggesting that the version Dell was working on in September 1909 (when reports of the forcible feeding of hunger strikers first emerged) was close to the finished text.[80] Both written accounts and visual images of forcible feeding were ubiquitous in the years surrounding the publication of *The Way of an Eagle*. 'Forcible feeding is perhaps the primary image in the public imagination regarding the "meaning" of the suffrage movement,' writes Jane Marcus. 'Consequently it is this experience as presented in suffrage poster art, as recollected in autobiography and as interpreted by historians, which one may see as symbolic of the movement as a whole.'[81] Although it seems unlikely (although not impossible) that Dell consciously drew on the accounts of suffragette forcible feeding, I do want to suggest, not only that the hunger strikes and forcible feeding may have been evoked in the minds of the novel's many readers, but also that at some level, this novel, with its graphic and sensational depiction of violently enforced drugging, is historically entangled with the many, often conflicting, conscious and unconscious meanings attached to contemporary representations of forcible feeding.

---

[77] Dell, *The Way*, p. 26.

[78] Dell, *The Way*, p. 27.

[79] Dell, *Nettie and Sissie*, p. 30.

[80] Autograph MS of *The Way of an Eagle*, 1909–1912, Add MS 45743, British Library Manuscript Collections.

[81] Jane Marcus, 'Introduction', in *Suffrage and the Pankhursts*, ed. by Jane Marcus (London: Routledge & Kegan Paul, 1987), pp. 1–17 (p. 2).

'MASOCHISTIC BRUNETTES'

Writing about the images and accounts of the suffragette forcible feedings, Linda Schlossberg notes that

> The violent, spectacular, and apparently titillating nature of what Keir Hardie called the 'scene' of forcible feeding was often exploited in the British press. Detailed, unsparing illustrations of forcible feedings were frequently depicted in both prosuffrage and conservative periodicals [. . .] The graphic, idealized images of young women being forcibly restrained and orally penetrated suggests that illustrations of the forcible feedings, despite their apparent political intentions, could function as a source of visual pleasure as well as visual horror.[82]

As Jane Marcus asserts, several depictions and accounts of forcible feeding may be 'clearly read as rape scenes, but this did not stop anti-suffrage commentators from reading oral assault as female masochism'.[83] Citing Lisa Tickner's observation that there is 'a sado-masochistic element' in some of the Women's Social and Political Union posters, Schlossberg observes that, 'as representational acts, [forcible feedings] were open to a range of interpretative interventions': 'The meanings or political messages generated by the hunger strikes were never subject to the suffragettes' control; nor were the prison wardens [. . .] able to control the various meanings attributed to the forcible feedings.'[84]

The idea of female masochism – so often attributed to the suffragettes – was also, of course, at the heart of cultural debates about romance reading in the early twentieth century. While images and accounts of forcible feeding were frequently interpreted as depictions of female masochism, romantic novelists like Ethel M. Dell were also criticised for appearing to celebrate, and to solicit, the masochistic desires of women and women readers. Reflecting on the vogue for Dell's novels in an essay written at a later date, Elizabeth Bowen commented that 'Ethel M Dell's pale, masochistic brunettes would today seem ripe for psycho-analysis'.[85] Alongside E. M. Hull's *The Sheik* (1919), *The Way of an Eagle* has been read as one of the earliest examples of a genre that – according

---

[82] Linda Schlossberg, 'Consuming Images: Women, Hunger, and the Vote', in *Scenes of the Apple: Food and the Female Body in Nineteenth- and Twentieth-Century Women's Writing*, ed. by Tamar Heller and Patricia Moran (New York: State University of New York Press, 2003), pp. 87–108 (pp. 89–90).

[83] Marcus, 'Introduction', p. 16. See also Maud Ellmann, *The Hunger Artists: Starving, Writing and Imprisonment* (London: Virago, 1993), p. 33.

[84] Lisa Tickner, *The Spectacle of Women: Imagery of the Suffrage Campaign 1907–14* (London: Chatto & Windus, 1988), p. 38, cited by Schlossberg, 'Consuming Images', p. 90.

[85] Elizabeth Bowen, 'Outrageous Ladies' [n.d.], in *People, Places, Things*, pp. 379–83 (p. 382).

to some critics – not only identifies female sexuality as a form of masochism, but also shapes and reproduces such desires in its readers.[86] In *The Sheik*, E. M. Hull tells the story of Diana Mayo, an English heiress who, while travelling in the Algerian desert, is kidnapped and repeatedly raped by the villainous yet alluring Sheik Ahmed Ben Hassan (played in the 1921 film by Rudolph Valentino), with whom she later falls in love. In *The Way of an Eagle*, although not as graphic as Hull's bestseller, the opening scene of forcible drugging is similarly subsumed within an erotically charged narrative in which Muriel must learn to reinterpret Nick's violence as romantic love.

From the scene of forcible drugging onwards, Dell emphasises Muriel's horror at Nick's apparently violent nature. During their escape into the Indian wilderness, Muriel, washing in a stream, is caught in 'the paralysis of a great horror'.[87] 'Transfixed by terror', she finds herself face-to-face with a 'beast-like', 'tall, blackbearded tribesman', 'His eyes, gleaming, devilish', like those of 'a devouring monster':

> In her agony she tried to shriek aloud, but her voice was gone, her throat seemed locked. She was powerless.
>
> Close to her, for a single instant he paused; then, as in a lightning flash, she saw the narrow, sinewy hand and snakelike arm dart forward to seize her, felt every muscle in her body stiffen to rigidity in anticipation of its touch, and shrank—shrank in every nerve though she made no outward sign of shrinking.[88]

Nick, 'with a panther-like spring, sure, noiseless, deadly', swoops in to Muriel's rescue, and the two men fight 'like demons in a silence that throbbed with the tumult of unrestrained savagery'.[89] In terms of the plot Nick appears in this scene as Muriel's saviour, but when she looks at 'Nick's face bent above the black-bearded face of his enemy' she is reminded of a picture of 'the devil in the wilderness'.[90] When Nick proposes to Muriel, the 'horror' of both the night of the drugging and the sight of Nick killing the 'tribesman' is 'reawakened': 'it seemed to her in those moments of reawakened horror as if by some magnetic

[86] See David Trotter, 'A Horse Is Being Beaten: Modernism and Popular Fiction', in *Rereading the New: A Backward Glance at Modernism*, ed. by Kevin J. H. Dettmar (Michigan: University of Michigan Press, 1992), pp. 191–220 (pp. 206–7); Laura Frost, *The Problem with Pleasure: Modernism and Its Discontents* (New York: Columbia University Press, 2013), pp. 89–129.

[87] Dell, *The Way*, p. 35.

[88] Dell, *The Way*, p. 35.

[89] Dell, *The Way*, p. 35, p. 36.

[90] Dell, *The Way*, p. 36.

force he still held her fast. She strove against it with all her frenzied strength, but it eluded her, baffled her—conquered her.'[91] Muriel's lurking fear of the 'violence and bloodshed that she knew to be hidden away somewhere behind that smiling, yellow mask' is reinforced by the narrative, which shifts between third-person narrative and a form of free indirect discourse that shares not only Muriel's fears, but also Nick's struggle to master himself.[92] Contemplating the 'great consummation of all his desires', Nick is forced to 'curb' himself, to 'master' his 'eagerness' and to 'control' his 'passion' – to tighten the slackening 'bonds of his self-restraint'.[93] Describing Nick receiving a note from Muriel, Dell writes:

> With a swift, passionate movement he carried the paper to his lips. And he remembered suddenly how he had once held her hand there and breathed upon the little cold fingers to give them life. He had commanded himself then. Was he any the less his own master now? And was he fool enough to destroy all in a moment that trust of hers which he had built up so laboriously? He felt as if a fiend had ensnared him, and with a fierce effort he broke free.[94]

When Muriel announces that she must break off the engagement, she sees Nick's 'hands clench [. . .] and an overwhelming sense of danger swept over her'.[95] She sees the 'face she had once seen bent over a man in his death-agony, convulsed with passion, savage, merciless—the face of a devil'.[96] 'If you try to run away from me now', Nick tells her, 'I won't answer for myself.'[97]

The narrative underscores Nick's struggle to master himself, but it also shifts, slipping uncertainly in and out of Nick's and Muriel's perspectives. When Dell describes Nick struggling to master 'the demon in him', it is not entirely clear whether we are offered this from Muriel's viewpoint, from Nick's, or from an omniscient third-person perspective: 'Had she withstood him, had she sought to escape, the demon in him would have burst the last restraining bond, and have shattered in one moment of unshackled violence all the chivalrous patience which during the last few weeks he had spent his whole strength to achieve.'[98] The subject of this sentence seems to shift, so that while at first

[91] Dell, *The Way*, p. 63.
[92] Dell, *The Way*, p. 65.
[93] Dell, *The Way*, p. 80, p. 87.
[94] Dell, *The Way*, p. 88.
[95] Dell, *The Way*, p. 91.
[96] Dell, *The Way*, p. 91.
[97] Dell, *The Way*, p. 91.
[98] Dell, *The Way*, p. 91.

this might be read simply as Muriel's naïve terror of Nick, the sentence curves round as though entering Nick's own meditation on his struggle to control himself. The narrative then returns to Muriel's perspective:

> In every nerve, she felt him drawing near, and in an agony of helpless-ness she awaited him, all the surging horror of that night when he had drugged her rushing back upon her with tenfold force. Again she saw him as she had seen him then, monstrous, silent, terrible, a man of super-human strength, whose mastery appalled her.[99]

Nick's struggle to restrain himself returns Muriel once more to the night of the drugging, rendering her passive before his appalling 'mastery'.

Muriel is repeatedly 'appalled' by Nick's 'mastery', but, although Dell gives us a vivid insight into Muriel's horror, she also hints at the way that Muriel's 'fear' and 'sick[ness]' at this 'uncanny force' will be transformed, by the end of the novel, into a portrait of desire and 'Love'.[100] Writing about mass-produced romance fiction, Tania Modleski has argued that, although romance typically invites the reader to identify with the heroine, the use of third-person narra-tive, coupled with the reader's presumed familiarity with the genre, allows the reader to take up a position of superior knowledge to the heroine and to feel safe in the certainty that, even in the face of violence, everything will work out in the end. As Modleski puts it:

> It is easy to assume, and most popular culture critics have assumed, a large degree of identification between reader and protagonist, but the matter is not so simple. Since the reader knows the formula, she is supe-rior in wisdom to the heroine and thus detached from her. The reader, then, achieves a very close emotional identification with the heroine partly because she is intellectually *distanced* from her and does not have to suffer the heroine's confusion.[101]

In *The Way of an Eagle*, it's certainly true that, in some ways, Dell's use of the third-person narrative, and her allusions to the conventions of romantic fiction, operate to preserve this kind of distance between reader and protagonist. The opening scene between Nick and Muriel's father, for example, operates as a distancing frame, soliciting us as readers to trust the brigadier's own judgement (despite Muriel's own expressed dislike for her father's decision) that Nick will,

---

[99] Dell, *The Way*, p. 92.

[100] Dell, *The Way*, p. 111.

[101] Tania Modleski, *Loving with a Vengeance: Mass-Produced Fantasies for Women* (London: Methuen, 1984), p. 41, p. 55.

as he insists, 'go to the uppermost limit' to protect Muriel.[102] In this scene, Nick displays what Dell describes as the 'first primaeval instinct of human chivalry', and when he steps out into the Indian night disguised as a tribesman with the drugged Muriel slung over his shoulders, Dell positions him as a figure of imperialist masculine virility, describing him in racist terms as 'marching with the sublime audacity of the dominant race'.[103] Throughout the novel, the use of the third-person narrative means that Dell shuttles between vivid descriptions of Muriel's 'surging horror' at Nick's 'mastery', steely accounts of Nick's own struggle to master his 'passion', and other characterisations of Nick as the typical hero of colonial romance.[104] For the reader, this means that although we may sympathise with Muriel's sense of horror at Nick's apparent violence, we are also encouraged to read ahead of Muriel and to reinterpret the feverish descriptions of her 'surging horror' as early indications of Muriel's buried desire for Nick. In a crucial scene in which Nick demands that Muriel acknowledge her own desire, she watches Nick 'electrified by passion' and feels the 'old paralyzing fear [. . .] knocking at her heart'.[105]

In the epiphanic moment when Muriel finally realises her love for Nick, Dell describes this as a form of enslavement:

> She knew now! She knew now! He had forced her to realize it. He had captured her, had kindled within her [. . .] the undying flame. Against her will, in spite of her utmost resistance, he had done this thing. Above and beyond and through her fiercest hatred, he had conquered her quivering heart [. . .] None other could ever dominate her as this man dominated [. . .]
>
> And this was Love—this hunger that could never be satisfied, this craving which would not be stifled or ignored [. . .] the thing she had striven to slay at its birth, but which had lived on in spite of her, growing, spreading, enveloping, till she was lost, till she was suffocated, in its immensity. There could never be any escape for her again. She was fettered hand and foot.[106]

'Truly [love] conquered', writes Dell, 'but it left its prisoners to perish of starvation in the wilderness.'[107] This is a narrative in which Muriel is finally 'captured' by a man who 'Against her will [. . .] had conquered her quivering heart'.[108]

---

[102] Dell, *The Way*, p. 5.
[103] Dell, *The Way*, p. 4, p. 23.
[104] Dell, *The Way*, p. 92, p. 87.
[105] Dell, *The Way*, p. 214.
[106] Dell, *The Way*, p. 253.
[107] Dell, *The Way*, p. 253.
[108] Dell, *The Way*, p. 253.

'Love' – being 'dominated' by a man – is described by Dell as a 'hunger that could never be satisfied', a 'craving which could not be stifled or ignored'.[109] The opening scene of violent forcible drugging is transformed into an apparently masochistic 'hunger' for domination.

It would be easy, on the basis of these quotations, to read Muriel as one of Dell's 'masochistic brunettes' par excellence – to insist that Dell eroticises a degraded form of female subjection, and to argue that her novel solicits a similar form of masochistic desire from its readers.[110] For Dell's critics, this is precisely what her novels did to her readers, who were, in one of Q. D. Leavis's many memorable phrases, 'invited to share the debauch'.[111] For these critics, romance fiction works by soliciting a form of first-person identification, in which the reader identifies closely with the heroine of the novel, allowing her own desires to be shaped and moulded by the romantic narrative. In these critical accounts, as in Q. D. Leavis's horrified analysis of early-twentieth-century bestsellers, the assumption is not only that the reader identifies wholeheartedly with the heroine of romantic fiction, but also that such a form of identification leaves her utterly passive to ideological moulding from the rigidly patriarchal scripts of romantic fiction. And yet, as Cora Kaplan has argued, the forms of identification and fantasy at work in romance reading are surely more complex than is suggested by these critical accounts.

In her analysis of Colleen McCullough's romantic novel *The Thorn Birds* (1977), Kaplan shows how the novel's third-person narrative and 'unstable inscriptions of sexual difference' facilitate potentially transgressive forms of identification that confound the ostensible invitation to the female reader to identify with an image of female passivity.[112] In *The Thorn Birds*, writes Kaplan,

> The text gives us a 'natural' identification with [the female protagonist] Meggie [. . .] but it offers a seductive alternative identification with Ralph [the hero], as a more complex and expressive subjectivity. The [. . .] disruption of the terms of sexual difference is both titillating and vertiginous, making obvious what perhaps is always true in romance reading for women, that the reader identifies with both terms in the seduction scenario, but most of all with the process of seduction.[113]

In this novel, although the reader is invited to identify with the female protagonist, the 'feminine' characterisation of Ralph (who appears as 'mother, father

---

[109] Dell, *The Way*, p. 253.

[110] Bowen, 'Outrageous Ladies', p. 382.

[111] Leavis, *Fiction*, p. 236.

[112] Cora Kaplan, '*The Thorn Birds*: Fiction, Fantasy, Femininity', in *Sea Changes: Essays on Culture and Feminism* (London: Verso, 1986), pp. 117–46 (p. 141).

[113] Kaplan, '*The Thorn Birds*', p. 142.

and lover in relation to Meggie') also means that 'the reader oscillates from the woman's position to the man's position—represented as poles of subjectivity rather than fixed, determinate identities'.[114] The 'unstable inscriptions of sexual difference' in this novel mean that, although the reader may be solicited to identify with the female protagonist, the novel also invites forms of identification and fantasy that disrupt the fixed gendered positions associated with typical romance.[115]

In *The Way of an Eagle*, the use of the third-person narrative voice, coupled with Nick's vertiginously shifting identifications as a virile imperialist, a colonial subject, a feminine and maternal figure, and a 'cripple', mean that it is also possible to read this text as soliciting similarly transgressive forms of identification on the part of the reader.[116] Although Nick is characterised from the start as a heroic figure who is 'ready to go through hell' for Muriel, his appearance as a figure of virile imperialist masculine power is also immediately complicated by Dell's presentation of him as a physically unattractive figure, whose sunburnt skin ('burnt to a deep yellow-brown'), 'wrinkled' features ('they might have belonged to a very old man') and 'insignificant' figure make him appear in stark contrast to his fellow officer, a 'magnificent man with the physique of a Hercules'.[117] Despite his role as a figure of potent and violent imperial masculinity, Nick is also characterised throughout the novel as a 'savage', and a 'native'.[118] When Nick informs Muriel of his plan to escape the fort by disguising himself as a 'tribesman', he comments that he is 'as yellow as a Chinaman already', and on another occasion he describes his face as like that of an 'Egyptian mummy'.[119] When Nick rescues Muriel from the 'devilish' tribesman in the mountains, he is strangely doubled with this racist figure of colonial sexual threat, whose otherness is, as Martin Hipsky has noted, 'transferred' on to Nick.[120] In the closing scenes of the novel Nick appears in the disguise of an Indian beggar, sitting at the gates of the British Residency, where an unwitting Muriel throws coins to him: Muriel finds the Indian-beggar-Nick 'repulsive, but in a fashion fascinating', and is reminded 'of a wizened old monkey who had wandered from his kind'.[121] Alongside these identifications as a 'savage' colonial subject, Nick is also described, in a number of passages, in distinctly feminine terms. When Muriel wakes up after the drugging she feels

---

[114] Kaplan, 'The Thorn Birds', p. 135, p. 139.
[115] Kaplan, 'The Thorn Birds', p. 141.
[116] Dell, The Way, p. 250.
[117] Dell, The Way, p. 5, p. 2, p. 3, p. 5.
[118] Dell, The Way, p. 112.
[119] Dell, The Way, p. 19, p. 145.
[120] Martin Hipsky, *Modernism and the Women's Popular Romance in Britain, 1885–1925* (Ohio: Ohio University Press, 2011), p. 174, p. 181.
[121] Dell, The Way, p. 292.

'gentle hands' ministering to her and hears a 'motherly voice'.[122] Nick bathes her face 'with a care equal to any woman's'.[123] When he proposes, Nick displays an 'almost womanly gentleness', and when Muriel watches him caring for his sick niece she witnesses 'a tenderness maternal'.[124] After the loss of his arm, Nick describes himself as 'a single-handed pigmy', and when as a result of his wounding he is unable to go out and rescue a boat stranded at sea, he identifies as both a woman and a 'cripple'.[125]

As we have seen, in *The Way of an Eagle*, the third-person narrative slides in and out of both Muriel's and Nick's perspectives, inviting the reader, in places, to identify as much with Nick as with Muriel. By soliciting, or at least offering the possibility of, the reader's identification with Nick Ratcliffe – a figure with complex and multiply overdetermined identifications as a virile masculine imperialist, a colonial subject, a woman and a 'cripple' – *The Way of an Eagle* certainly does not counter its outwardly conservative and racist colonial and sexual politics. But it does draw attention to the more mobile and shifting forms of identification and fantasy that surely underpin most readers' investments in romantic fiction. For the woman reader, the invitation to identify with Nick Ratcliffe offers a transgressive alternative to the invitation to identify with the passive figure of Muriel. Writing about Hollywood cinema, Laura Mulvey argues that the invitation to a form of 'trans-sex identification' encourages women spectators to 'rediscover' an originally bisexual disposition that is, in a heteronormative and patriarchal culture, subject to severe forms of repression.[126] This kind of identification may not, in itself, be politically progressive, but it does put the reader in touch with unconscious identifications that the more explicit heteronormative politics of the bestselling romance seeks to repress, disrupting the apparently fixed gendered positions of romantic fiction.

'QUEEN' OF THE BESTSELLERS

Reviewing Dell's 1922 novel *Charles Rex*, Rebecca West crowned Dell as 'queen' of the 'best-sellers'.[127] Although damning of Dell and her readers, West's tone of helplessly fascinated curiosity also belies her ostensible condemnation: 'I am surprised to find that I can blush,' she begins.[128] Summarising *Charles Rex*, West writes with relish, drawing out the strangely unacknowledged

---

[122] Dell, *The Way*, p. 23, p. 24.

[123] Dell, *The Way*, p. 30.

[124] Dell, *The Way*, p. 65, p. 198.

[125] Dell, *The Way*, p. 171, p. 250.

[126] Laura Mulvey, 'Afterthoughts on "Visual Pleasure and Narrative Cinema"', in *Visual and Other Pleasures* (Basingstoke: Macmillan, 1989), pp. 29–38 (p. 33).

[127] Rebecca West, 'The Tosh Horse', in *The Strange Necessity: Essays and Reviews* (London: Jonathan Cape, 1931), pp. 319–25 (p. 323).

[128] West, 'The Tosh Horse', p. 319.

sexual ambiguities in a plot that features a cross-dressing working-class girl disguised as a boy who desires to be beaten by her future husband, the aristocratic Lord Saltash. Antoinette, a circus-rider (her mother is later revealed to be a celebrated modern dancer in the style of Isadora Duncan, who dies while performing the 'dance of Death' in Paris), is known throughout the novel by her boy-name Toby, and much of the plot is taken up with a straight-faced attempt to answer the question of whether or not she is a virgin.[129] 'But I blush, and I wonder,' West writes:

> This is the story of a middle-aged voluptuary who, when he is cruising about the Mediterranean, comes on an Italian hotel proprietor beating a page-boy, and interrupts the sport. That night he finds the boy concealed as a stowaway on the yacht, and immediately realizes—though he keeps silence—that here is a girl in disguise. For five chapters the story titillates us (us includes, one amazedly estimates, the mass of the population of Surbiton, Bournemouth, and Cheltenham) with a description of the peculiar intercourse that takes place between them in these circumstances. There is a specially pleasing incident when they are playing cards and the girl-boy cheats, and Lord Saltash beats her with a riding-switch. We afterwards learn that she had cheated on purpose that she might have this delicious revelation of the gentleman's quality.[130]

West concludes her review by pointing to the strangeness of the fact that, while 'Mr D. H. Lawrence's sincere and not for one second disgusting *The Rainbow*' has been 'banned', Ethel M. Dell writes on for a ravenous public.[131] Amongst the sights that 'must fill the heart of any serious English writer with wistfulness' is that of 'the old ladies reading their Ethel Dells'.[132] 'Truly', West concludes, 'we are a strange nation.'[133]

Despite her disdain, West acknowledges the 'thrilling' nature of the novel, the excited breathlessness of her own prose mimicking the element of excess, something 'strange' and uncontainable, at the heart of Dell's writing.[134] In 'Outrageous Ladies', Elizabeth Bowen situated Dell's 'masochistic brunettes' alongside 'a long run of expensive sinners, [. . .] a host of *gamines* [. . .] and a hell-cat dynasty, founder Scarlet [*sic*] O'Hara'.[135] Bowen commented on the ease

---

[129] Ethel M. Dell, *Charles Rex* (London: Hurst and Blackett, 1969), p. 210, p. 339.
[130] West, 'The Tosh Horse', pp. 323–4.
[131] West, 'The Tosh Horse', p. 324.
[132] West, 'The Tosh Horse', p. 325.
[133] West, 'The Tosh Horse', p. 325.
[134] West, 'The Tosh Horse', p. 323, p. 325.
[135] Bowen, 'Outrageous Ladies', p. 382.

with which we consign the 'absurdity of the day-before-yesterday's best-seller' to 'dust', and reflected on the temptation to patronise the 'public's taste' for the 'once glamorous' heroine's 'blushe[s]', 'flutter[s]' and 'sigh[s]'.[136] 'Fashions in ladies change,' Bowen acknowledged, and 'grotesqueries are laid bare', but, she asked pointedly: 'Readers were naïve, were they—in the past?'[137] 'It was the triumph of those dream-queens that they *were* outrageous,' she remarks, underscoring, like West, something 'outrageous' and significant in this kind of writing.[138]

In Peter Brooks's account of the melodramatic imagination, he argues that the melodramatic excess of popular culture points to what he calls a 'moral occult'.[139] For Brooks, melodramatic excess gestures to the desire for a moral order that no longer obtains in a disenchanted modernity. In this account,

> Melodrama starts from and expresses the anxiety brought by a frightening new world in which the traditional patterns of moral order no longer provide the necessary social glue. It plays out the force of that anxiety with the apparent triumph of villainy, and it dissipates it with the eventual victory of virtue.[140]

But in its excessiveness, the melodramatic is haunted by the 'vertiginous feeling of standing over the abyss created when the necessary center of things has been evacuated and dispersed'.[141] In the case of *The Way of an Eagle*, melodramatic excess reveals the moral vacuity of a patriarchal order that, by 1912 and in the face of historical pressure from the suffrage movement, found itself struggling (despite its redoubled violence) to claim any moral authority. In the transition from violent force-feeding to a form of desire imagined as a 'hunger that could never be satisfied', there is a kind of excess that the novel fails to contain – an identification and diagnosis of the violence at the heart of both feminine and masculine ideals, which cannot easily be masked over by the novel's ostensibly happy ending (Muriel announcing her pregnancy to her husband as they mount the top of Everest). The violent scene of forcible drugging produces something uncontainable, something that exceeds the conventional critique of Dell's novels as simply complicit in the forms of patriarchal violence that they seem to expose as much as celebrate.

---

[136] Bowen, 'Outrageous Ladies', p. 382.

[137] Bowen, 'Outrageous Ladies', p. 382.

[138] Bowen, 'Outrageous Ladies', p. 382.

[139] Peter Brooks, *The Melodramatic Imagination: Balzac, Henry James, Melodrama, and the Mode of Excess* (1976), 2nd edn (New Haven and London: Yale University Press, 1995), p. 5.

[140] Brooks, *The Melodramatic Imagination*, p. 20.

[141] Brooks, *The Melodramatic Imagination*, p. 21.

Not only, however, does the violence of the novel exceed the bounds of the apparently happy ending, the forms of desire explored within the novel also seem more complex than simple expressions of a degraded form of masochistic femininity. When Nick accuses Muriel of failing to be 'honest' with herself, she determines 'to know the truth': 'Now or never would she read the enigma.'[142] Nick rebukes Muriel for her failure to read her own desire, insisting that now she has grown from a 'child' into a 'woman' she 'know[s] what Love is': 'You don't call it by its name, but none the less you know it.'[143] However, his sexist accusation of a typically female form of self-deception and trickery ('You will be false to yourself'; 'It's a way women have', he claims), and his insistence upon the legibility of desire, struggles to mask the novel's portrayal of a form of psychic complexity in which desire is not always legible, and female sexuality is not always transparent to itself or others.[144] Although Muriel insists that Nick has 'dominated' her, this desire nonetheless takes the form of a 'hunger that could never be satisfied'.[145] Muriel struggles to name 'it', 'this thing', a 'hunger' and 'craving' which possesses her and cannot be satiated, and which spirals out from her attempt to describe it, until she herself becomes 'lost' in 'its immensity': 'the thing she had striven to slay at its birth, but which had lived on in spite of her, growing, spreading, enveloping, till she was lost, till she was suffocated, in its immensity.'[146]

In Dell's penultimate novel, *The Juice of the Pomegranate*, published in 1938, the heroine, Diana, sitting in her older sister's drawing room, spots a book hidden behind a cushion:

> Now we really shall see what the brainy Blanche reads in her leisure moments! Something she's none too proud of obviously! Great Scott! It's an Ethel M. Dell! [. . .] Blanche [. . .] You're a snob, and I'm going to punish you for it. I shall put this book where all your high-brow friends will mark and learn—even if they refuse to read. It'll be a terrible exposure for you, but it'll damn well serve you right.[147]

Returning, later, to the drawing room, Diana notices that the book is missing, and asks the servant, Enid, what has become of it:

> 'My lady never leaves a Dell book lying about for visitors to see, madam, so I took it away.'

[142] Dell, *The Way*, p. 212.
[143] Dell, *The Way*, p. 213.
[144] Dell, *The Way*, p. 213, p. 214.
[145] Dell, *The Way*, p. 253.
[146] Dell, *The Way*, p. 253.
[147] Ethel M. Dell, *The Juice of the Pomegranate* (London: Cassell & Co., 1941), p. 53.

'I see. Bad style, is she?' There was a mischievous gleam in Diana's glance.
'I'm sure I don't know, madam.' Enid's tone was repressive.
'Ever read them yourself?' asked Diana.
'Yes, madam,' said Enid.
'And like them?'
'Yes madam,' said Enid again.

Diana lighted her cigarette. 'I congratulate you, Enid,' she said. 'We may like bad things, but it isn't all of us who have the courage to say so. You read it while you're sitting up this evening and enjoy it!'[148]

Dell may have written this scene with a 'mischievous gleam' in her own eye, but there is also something quite serious at stake in this staged scene of reading.

In *The Juice of the Pomegranate*, following this scene, Diana goes out dancing. She is plied with alcohol, seduced, and, as we later find out, drugged and raped by the villain, who is then revealed to be her step-brother, and who convinces her to marry him after discovering that she is pregnant. They are married and he takes her to France, where he bullies and abuses her while conducting clandestine business as the 'paid agent of a foreign Secret Service'.[149] When the hero turns up to rescue her, Diana's husband tries to run him over in a car, at which Diana grabs the wheel, leading to an accident in which her husband is killed. Diana suffers a miscarriage and is life-threateningly injured but, after many months, recovers to marry her hero. In the scene following the rape, Diana quarrels with her sister for insisting on the virtues of married life, complaining: 'You married people all know the very varied ingredients that go to make up the matrimonial mixture, and yet you always try to serve it up as if it were sheer treacle and nothing else.'[150] Blanche (the clandestine reader of Ethel M. Dell novels, which she hides from her 'high-brow friends') argues that the 'true way of happiness' should be 'first the dream, then—fulfilment; and after that, the awakening'.[151] In response, Diana sarcastically asks Blanche if she plucked this narrative 'out of an Ethel M. Dell novel', describing Dell as 'that most contemptible of all novelists'.[152] 'It's a good thing I didn't read it', Diana claims, 'or my literary taste might have been vitiated for ever.'[153] *The Juice of the Pomegranate*, however, does not follow the pattern ascribed by Diana to an 'Ethel M. Dell novel', suggesting perhaps that Dell felt the interest of her books lay less in the stress on the 'sheer treacle' of dreams and wish-fulfilment than

[148] Dell, *The Juice*, pp. 56–7.
[149] Dell, *The Juice*, p. 260.
[150] Dell, *The Juice*, p. 95.
[151] Dell, *The Juice*, p. 96.
[152] Dell, *The Juice*, p. 96.
[153] Dell, *The Juice*, p. 96.

on the 'awakening' – the 'awakening' to the 'varied ingredients that go to make up the matrimonial mixture', and even an 'awakening' to the forms of sexual, physical and emotional violence that, in Diana's case, form the prelude to and the substance of her first marriage.[154]

Dell's first novel may not stage the scene of reading quite so obviously as in *The Juice of the Pomegranate*, but the opening scene of *The Way of an Eagle* does present a violent scene of forced consumption that both echoes and complicates the traditional critique of the romance genre as a 'treacle' or 'mind opiate' for the devouring masses.[155] I'm not suggesting that Dell's first novel self-consciously ironises the critical account of the gluttonous, addicted romance reader, or that she explicitly or consciously gestures to contemporaneous accounts of suffragette force-feeding. But, by demonstrating the ways in which this novel can be, and might have been, read alongside the debates surrounding the similarly overdetermined image of the suffragette forcible feeding, I want to foreground the limitations in the idea that this novel simply reproduces the female reader as a passive masochist, gorging on images of her own subjection. For Orwell and Leavis, *The Way of an Eagle* was representative of a form of romance that produces a type of addictive, compulsive and – crucially – passive reading. In early-twentieth-century criticism, Dell and her readers appear as the tabooed opposite of literary modernism, forced to stand in for the dangers of popular fiction as a form of ideological manipulation. And yet, while Dell's novels certainly do espouse conservative and patriarchal ideas about gender, sexuality and race, their popularity also points to the overlooked complexities of women readers' fantasy lives, disrupting the dominant image of the romance reader as a passive and addicted glutton.[156]

For critics like Q. D. Leavis, the danger of romance reading was that it risked replacing reality with fantasy, leaving readers like Gerty MacDowell unable to distinguish between the 'clichés' of 'cheap fiction' and the realities of 'actual life'.[157] For Leavis, popular novelists had 'discovered the novel as a means of satisfying their suppressed desires and so [. . .] the starved desires of the vast bulk of the public'.[158] The 'reasons' for this were 'best explained by a psychoanalyst', not a literary critic.[159] Like a number of modernist critics

---

[154] Strachey, 'Some Unconscious Factors', p. 326.
[155] Dell, *The Juice*, p. 95; Leavis, *Fiction*, p. 56.
[156] On the act of reading romance fiction as itself a kind of protest against the patriarchal reality in which readers live, see Janice Radway, *Reading the Romance: Women, Patriarchy, and Popular Culture*, 2nd edn (London: Verso, 1987).
[157] Leavis, *Fiction*, p. 245.
[158] Leavis, *Fiction*, p. 168.
[159] Leavis, *Fiction*, p. 168.

(including, as we've seen, Roger Fry and Clive Bell), Leavis is almost as scornful of psychoanalysis as she is of popular culture. Like both Mansfield and Woolf, who were dismissive of the dominance of psychoanalysis in popular novels, Leavis reserves a particularly acute distaste for the proliferation of what she calls the 'jargon of popular psychology' in bestsellers such as *The Sheik* (which she describes as a 'typist's day-dream'), commenting that 'the novels of Gilbert Frankau are so thickly studded with mention of inhibitions and the subconscious that it is hardly possible to find a page without one or both'.[160] For Leavis, however, her distaste for psychoanalysis is more than a case of disdain for a form of wild psychoanalysis that appeared as the subject-matter of popular novels: she is also scornful of psychoanalysis because of the ease with which it seems to describe the very mechanisms of popular culture. For Leavis, the bestseller replaces the proper activities of reading, thinking and feeling with debased forms of substitute living that she describes in terms borrowed from the language of psychoanalysis: bestsellers, according to Leavis, replace reading with 'wish-fulfilment', 'day-dreaming', 'fantasy-spinning' and 'fantasying'.[161] Popular novels, Leavis claims, are 'unhealthy' – they indulge the 'morbid cravings' of readers who are invited to indulge in 'emotional orgies'.[162] 'In the bestseller', Leavis writes, 'the author has poured his own day-dreams, hot and hot, into dramatic form [. . .] the author is himself—or more usually herself—identified with the leading character, and the reader is invited to share the debauch.'[163] '[A]s the century grows older', Leavis laments, 'the bestseller becomes less a case for the literary critic than for the psychologist—in place of Aphra Behn we have Ouida with the voluptuous day-dream instead of the dispassionate narration of a complicated plot.'[164]

For Leavis, psychoanalysis and popular culture were both complicit in producing (or, in the case of psychoanalysis, theorising) readers who are always entirely passive, reduced to and enslaved by their irrational unconscious desires, which are in turn captured in thrall to the pernicious ideologies perpetuated by popular culture.[165] In Leavis's portrait of the reader, she recognises that psychoanalysis might help to analyse the fantasies that drive our investments in popular culture, but she tends to regard and to dismiss psychoanalysis as a functionalist account of how we internalise social norms. When Leavis published *Fiction and the Reading Public* in 1932, psychoanalysts were, at the

---

[160] Leavis, *Fiction*, p. 259, p. 138, p. 260.

[161] Leavis, *Fiction*, p. 51, p. 54, p. 60.

[162] Leavis, *Fiction*, p. 89.

[163] Leavis, *Fiction*, p. 236.

[164] Leavis, *Fiction*, p. 164.

[165] On the close proximity of psychoanalysis and mass consumer culture in the early twentieth century, see Rachel Bowlby, *Shopping with Freud* (London and New York: Routledge, 1993).

same time, caught up in a related debate about what Freud famously described, in 1931, as the long and 'very circuitous path' to 'normal' femininity.[166] For the psychoanalysts, as for Leavis, the question was, in part, about the nature of the mechanisms through which ideological ideas about femininity are transformed into women's lived experiences. As Jacqueline Rose has argued, the psychoanalysts involved in this debate were attempting to explain the 'exact mechanisms whereby ideological processes are transformed, via individual subjects, into human actions and beliefs'.[167] 'Like Marxism', Rose writes,

> psychoanalysis sees the mechanisms which produce those transformations as determinant, but also as leaving something in excess. If psychoanalysis can give an account of how women experience the path to femininity, it also insists, through the concept of the unconscious, that femininity is neither simply achieved nor is it ever complete. The political case for psychoanalysis rests on these two insights together— otherwise it would be indistinguishable from a functionalist account of the internalisation of norms.[168]

In Leavis's portrait of the romance reader, and in her invocations of psychoanalysis, she tends to produce what Rose (referring to the culturalist side of the psychoanalytic debate about femininity) describes as an 'image of utter passivity' – an image of the woman reader that recognises the 'restrictiveness of culture', while forgetting or 'abandon[ing] the unconscious altogether'.[169] And yet, as feminist psychoanalytic critics have pointed out, psychoanalysis both recognises what Rose describes as 'the fully social constitution of identity and norms' while also insisting on 'that point of tension between ego and unconscious where [those norms] are endlessly remodelled and endlessly break'.[170]

By turning to psychoanalysis, we can find an account of women's fantasy lives that draws attention not only to the mobility of fantasy, but also to the gap between the rigid ideological scenarios that are so frequently inscribed within romantic fiction, and the diverse ways that individual women engage with those fantasies. As Rose has written elsewhere:

> For Freud, fantasy refers to a psychic domain, no less important—indeed no less real—than the world we live and move in; but it is distinguished from that world by the fertility, the potentially endless transformative

---

[166] Sigmund Freud, 'Female Sexuality' (1931), *Standard Edition*, XXI, pp. 221–44 (p. 230).
[167] Jacqueline Rose, *Sexuality in the Field of Vision*, 2nd edn (London: Verso, 2005), p. 7.
[168] Rose, *Sexuality*, p. 7.
[169] Rose, *Sexuality*, pp. 7–8.
[170] Rose, *Sexuality*, p. 7.

capacities of the mind. We use fantasy, conscious and unconscious, to explore things that have not happened and never will, to see in our mind's eye worlds out of reach. In fantasy, we are capable of thoughts, often terrifying and exhilarating, which we never dreamt we had [. . .] If asked to express them consciously, we would never dare.[171]

As we have seen in this chapter, Dell's writing is one of the many places in early-twentieth-century popular culture where women's sexual fantasies are bound up with a troublingly patriarchal and racist colonial narrative. But, as I've tried to show, Dell's writing also complicates the assumption that her readers simply feasted on images of their own (and others') subjection. Dell's writing, with its wild melodramatic excess, and its fascination with the enigmatic nature of desire, also draws attention to those aspects of the unconscious that resist the coercive forces of the dominant patriarchal order. Although Dell's writing is complicit with the sexist and racist colonial politics of the early twentieth century, her novels also complicate, and resist, the dominant critical characterisation of her readers as simple gluttons, gorging on images of their own subjection.

'CHEW[ING] UP' ETHEL M. DELL

Roger Fry and Clive Bell may have been dismissive of psychoanalytic attempts to theorise the unconscious dimensions of reading, but in March 1930 their friend James Strachey gave a paper to the British Psycho-Analytical Society that satirises his Bloomsbury colleagues' attempts to preserve a neat division between 'pure' aesthetic experience and the gluttonous fantasies of the Ethel M. Dell reader. In April 1930, Ernest Jones wrote to Sigmund Freud, praising Strachey's 'very excellent and original paper' on the 'Psycho-Analysis of Reading'.[172] A few weeks earlier, members of the British Psycho-Analytical Society had gathered to discuss the unconscious life of reading. First to present was Strachey, Freud's chief translator for the Hogarth Press and a prominent figure in the cross-pollination of 'Bloomsbury' modernism and psychoanalysis. The audience included, amongst others, Ernest Jones, Melanie Klein, Susan Isaacs, Alix Strachey, D. W. Winnicott, and Virginia Woolf's brother and sister-in-law, the psychoanalysts Adrian and Karin Stephen.[173] Strachey's paper, later published as 'Some Unconscious Factors in

---

[171] Jacqueline Rose, 'Sylvia Plath—Again', in *On Not Being Able to Sleep: Psychoanalysis and the Modern World* (London: Vintage, 2004), pp. 49–71 (p. 55).

[172] Sigmund Freud and Ernest Jones, *The Complete Correspondence of Sigmund Freud and Ernest Jones 1908–1939*, ed. by R. Andrew Paskauskas (Cambridge, MA: Belknap Press of Harvard University Press, 1993), pp. 669–70.

[173] Following Strachey's paper, Barbara Low (a schoolteacher, psychoanalyst and friend of D. H. Lawrence) presented a paper in which she too traced inhibitions and difficulties in reading to memories and fantasies rooted in early childhood. *The Minute Book of the*

Reading', traced adult inhibitions in reading back to the oral fantasies of early childhood, both drawing on and complicating his Bloomsbury friends' disdain for the supposedly infantile gratifications of popular culture.

Beginning his paper with the idea of literacy as a characteristic that distinguishes 'the more advanced forms of civilization from the primitive', Strachey remarked on the practice of measuring the 'relative degree of civilization in different countries from the percentage of illiterates among their inhabitants'.[174] But he also emphasised the peculiarly modern nature of the mass-literacy ideal: 'Indeed,' he commented, injecting a satirically self-reflective note, 'until the last fifty years, even in the most civilized communities these accomplishments have been restricted to an extremely limited number of individuals.'[175] This brief but historically precise allusion to the expansion of literacy between 1880 and 1930 would have been understood by Strachey's audience as a reference to the boom in literacy following the 1870 Education Act. Numerous members of the British Psycho-Analytical Society were intimately connected to what a 1929 editorial in the *Nation and Athenaeum* described as the 'radical transformation of English education' in this period.[176] Gesturing to this context of radical upheaval in both adult and children's education, Strachey proposed to trace the psychic importance of reading in the 'economics of the mind of modern man'.[177] Setting his essay up as a pointedly modern intervention into debates concerning mass literacy and high cultural ideals of 'civilization', Strachey burrowed down into the unconscious infantile roots of the modern reading experience.

Summoning the common metaphors that we use to describe reading, Strachey notes our tendency to

> speak of a 'voracious reader' or of 'an omnivorous reader'; of 'an unwholesome book' or of 'a stodgy book' or of a book being 'rather strong meat'; or, again, we talk of 'browsing in the library', of finding a book 'indigestible', or of 'devouring' its pages.[178]

Scientific Proceedings of the British Psycho-Analytical Society from November Sixth 1929, 19 March 1930, Society and Institute Records, British Psychoanalytical Society S/B/01/A/01; Anna Freud, 'British Psycho-Analytical Society: First Quarter, 1930', *Bulletin of the International Psycho-Analytical Association*, 11 (1930), 352–3.

[174] Strachey, 'Some Unconscious Factors', p. 322.
[175] Strachey, 'Some Unconscious Factors', p. 322.
[176] 'The School Leaving Age', *Nation and Athenaeum*, 45.17 (27 July 1929), 558–9 (p. 558). See Helen Tyson, '"Little Mussolini" and the "Parasite Poets": Psychoanalytic Pedagogy, Modernism, and the Illegible Child', in *Wild Analysis: From the Couch to Cultural and Political Life*, ed. by Shaul Bar-Haim, Elizabeth Sarah Coles and Helen Tyson (London: Routledge, 2021), pp. 85–104.
[177] Strachey, 'Some Unconscious Factors', p. 322.
[178] Strachey, 'Some Unconscious Factors', p. 324.

While 'boys and girls preparing for a good afternoon's read will so often pro-vide themselves not only with a book, but with a bag of sweets to consume along with it', the adult male 'retire[s] into the solitude of his study [. . .] with a whisky and soda, a pipe, and a good novel'.[179] There is, Strachey writes, a 'pecu-liar appearance of intense and continuous absorption in a person immersed in a book', which reminds the observer of 'an infant enjoying its meal'.[180] This type of absorbed infantile consumption is, Strachey argues, characteristic of our relationships to popular culture:

> The audience at a picture palace show just the same signs of absorption as the schoolboy with his detective story; the smoker in his easy chair is just as likely to turn on the wireless as to read a novel; and if we talk of 'devouring' a book, we talk equally of 'drinking in' music and of 'lapping up' knowledge. [. . .] The blissful absorption, the smooth, uninterrupted enjoyment, that characterize the mental states of the novel-reader, the cinema-goer, the wireless-listener and the rest, suggest, of course, that their nourishment is liquid and that they are sucking it in.[181]

'But', Strachey continues, 'all reading, alas, is not of this nature': 'There are the other books—the ones that we have to get our teeth into and chew up before we can digest them.'[182]

Distinguishing between forms of popular culture that we can 'suck down' contentedly like baby milk (novels, the cinema and the wireless) and those 'other books' (read: high modernism) that are harder to digest, Strachey traces these oral metaphors back to their roots in unconscious infantile oral fantasies. He proposes a division between two attitudes corresponding to two infantile oral phases: a pre-ambivalent phase where everything goes 'smoothly and eas-ily, and an ambivalent one where difficulties arise at every step'.[183] Echoing his modernist contemporaries' disdain for the apparently infantile and feminine gratifications of popular novels, Strachey comments that 'In the case [. . .] of a typist reading a best-seller or of a schoolboy reading a thriller, no doubt the subject-matter with its variously disguised gratifications of the reader's wishes plays an essential part'.[184] But there is, Strachey insists, a 'further element of satisfaction' in the act of reading itself, which is 'essentially oral'.[185] Strachey's

---

[179] Strachey, 'Some Unconscious Factors', p. 325.
[180] Strachey, 'Some Unconscious Factors', p. 325.
[181] Strachey, 'Some Unconscious Factors', p. 325.
[182] Strachey, 'Some Unconscious Factors', pp. 325–6.
[183] Strachey, 'Some Unconscious Factors', p. 326.
[184] Strachey, 'Some Unconscious Factors', pp. 324–5.
[185] Strachey, 'Some Unconscious Factors', p. 325.

interest in this essay is not so much in the gratifications afforded to readers by the subject-matter of books, but in the fantasies attached to the act of reading itself, and in the psychic pleasure to be gained from different cultural forms, whether difficult high modernist literature or bestsellers and thrillers. Strachey eschews the clichéd psychoanalytic account of literary texts as projections of the reader's thwarted desires, offering instead what Jacques Derrida (himself referring to Strachey's essay) called a 'psychoanalytic graphology' – a psychoanalytic study of the literary 'signifier' rather than the signified.[186] For Strachey, the smooth forms of popular culture satisfy pre-ambivalent (loving, feeding, consuming) infantile oral fantasies, while reading difficult books tends to push us back into the ambivalent (destructive, cannibalistic, paranoid) infantile oral fantasies.[187]

In what reads like a case study of E. M. Forster's Leonard Bast, Strachey introduces a patient who was eager to display his cultural capital: he 'pretended to be deeply interested in literature and to be extremely well read, and constantly interlarded his conversation with quotations'.[188] Despite the patient's literary aspirations, however, 'he found it almost impossible to read'.[189] Strachey recounts the 'terrible difficulties' with which this reader had to contend:

> He would read with a pencil in his hand, and after going through each page with the utmost care and attention, and after convincing himself that he had understood it, he would put a tick at the bottom. He would then go through it again 'to confirm it' and put a cross stroke through the tail of the tick. [. . .] Sometimes each paragraph had to have its tick, and sometimes each sentence. If things were going badly or if he was reading something specially important, each separate word was treated in the same way.[190]

'But', Strachey insisted, 'this is only an exaggerated example of a very common phenomenon':

---

[186] Jacques Derrida, 'Freud and the Scene of Writing', in *Writing and Difference*, trans. by Alan Bass (Abingdon: Routledge, 2001), pp. 246–91 (pp. 290–1, Derrida's emphasis); Jacques Derrida, *Of Grammatology*, trans. by Gayatri Chakravorty Spivak (Baltimore: Johns Hopkins University Press, 1976), p. 88, pp. 333–4, n. 37.

[187] See also Edward Glover, 'The Significance of the Mouth in Psycho-Analysis', *The British Journal of Medical Psychology*, 4.2 (1924), 134–55; Edward Glover, 'Notes on Oral Character Formation', *International Journal of Psycho-Analysis*, 6 (1925), 131–54; Edward Glover, 'On the Aetiology of Drug-Addiction', *International Journal of Psycho-Analysis*, 13 (1932), 298–328.

[188] Strachey, 'Some Unconscious Factors', p. 323.

[189] Strachey, 'Some Unconscious Factors', p. 323.

[190] Strachey, 'Some Unconscious Factors', p. 323.

Even approximately normal people are sometimes overcome by a feeling that they have 'missed' something in a paragraph they have just been reading, and feel obliged to go through it again.[191]

Tracing our adult relationship to words back to early childhood lessons in reading, Strachey suggests that when, as adults, we struggle with a difficult text, we are returned to a vexed scene of infantile struggle in which we laboured to mouth the words on the page out loud.[192] This early struggle to articulate – with its necessary 'movements of the lips, tongue, throat, jaw-muscles and teeth' – also has 'deep psychological connections with the oral stage of libidinal development and particularly with its second phase'.[193] In reading, Strachey argues, we are 'taking someone else's thoughts inside', or 'eating another person's words'.[194] But this connection to the second, ambivalent, oral phase means that when we read difficult literary texts, there is the 'tendency to the release of a number of sadistic and destructive impulses':

> Each word is then felt as an enemy that is being bitten up, and, further, for that very reason, as an enemy that may in its turn become threatening and dangerous to the reader. It seems to be an uneasy doubt as to whether this enemy has really been disposed of, or whether he is not lurking somewhere, overlooked between the lines perhaps, or missed by some other mistake, that causes the obsessional reader to turn back, to read and re-read, to read each word aloud, to fix each word with a tick, and yet never to be reassured. But it must not be forgotten that the relation is all the time a two-sided one, and that he is simultaneously loving the words, rolling them round in his mouth and eventually making them a part of himself.[195]

This description of the vexed, fraught, ambivalent, and yet nonetheless intimate encounter with those 'other books' offers a vivid characterisation of many a reader's encounter with a difficult modernist novel.

At first glance, Strachey appears to echo a widespread tendency in modernist literary culture to distinguish between the mature and civilising virtues of modernism and the infantilising and feminine forces of popular culture. And yet, I want to suggest that Strachey is in fact satirising this binary approach to readers and rendering it unstable. Mary Jacobus has written of Strachey's

---

[191] Strachey, 'Some Unconscious Factors', p. 323.
[192] Strachey, 'Some Unconscious Factors', p. 326.
[193] Strachey, 'Some Unconscious Factors', p. 326.
[194] Strachey, 'Some Unconscious Factors', p. 326.
[195] Strachey, 'Some Unconscious Factors', p. 327.

essay as a 'send-up' of the 'gullible psychoanalytic reader', suggesting that 'the interest' of Strachey's essay 'lies less in what it has to say about the unconscious factors in reading [. . .] than in locating the scene of reading in the historically specific private and public spaces of his time, the spaces of modernity where the modern citizen comes into being'.[196] It is also, I want to argue, a 'send-up' of, and a riposte to, some of Strachey's highbrow modernist friends and contemporaries – those who, as we have seen, were not just sceptical about psychoanalysis but also all too eager to set themselves apart from the 'hungry girl clerks and housemaids' of the modern reading public.

Strachey's essay reaches its satirical crescendo when, in a scene that echoes Leopold Bloom reading *Titbits* in the outhouse in James Joyce's *Ulysses*, he introduces a patient who spent a great deal of time reading in public lavatories: 'Much of his knowledge of current events was derived from reading the small squares of newspaper that are placed in some lavatories, though not with a view to being read.'[197] His greatest satisfaction, which nonetheless caused him considerable guilt and distress, was to 'eat something (the specific food was a custard tart) at the very moment of defaecation'.[198] Interpreting this as a 'symbolic act of coprophagy' – in other words, a symbolic act of eating faeces – Strachey goes on to suggest that 'a coprophagic tendency lies at the root of *all* reading':

> Perhaps the clearest evidence of these unconscious processes is to be seen in the orgies of newspaper reading which have accompanied the spread of literacy to the lower classes of the community. Inconceivably vast masses of ink-stained paper are ejected every day into the streets; there they are seized and devoured with passionate avidity, and a few moments later destroyed with contempt or put to the basest possible uses; no one can find enough abuse for the rags of this gutter Press, but no one feels he has breakfasted unless one of them is lying beside his coffee and his toast.[199]

It would be easy to read this as yet another elitist attack on the 'lower class' consumption of the 'rags of this gutter Press'. But Strachey is careful to emphasise that '*no one* feels he has breakfasted unless one of [these rags] is lying beside his coffee and his toast'.[200] Suggesting that 'a coprophagic tendency lies at the root of *all* reading', Strachey undoes his implicit distinction between high and low

---

[196] Jacobus, *Psychoanalysis*, p. 33.
[197] Strachey, 'Some Unconscious Factors', p. 328; see also Jacobus, *Psychoanalysis*, p. 36.
[198] Strachey, 'Some Unconscious Factors', p. 328.
[199] Strachey, 'Some Unconscious Factors', p. 328, p. 329.
[200] Strachey, 'Some Unconscious Factors', p. 329, my emphasis.

culture, insisting that the scene of reading is, regardless of the reader or of the material consumed, always, at its roots, a site of our most primitive and infantile fantasies and desires. It is not only the consumer of popular culture that is infantilised in Strachey's essay: while the modern consumer sucks down detective novels and romances like an infant enjoying its meal, the reader of those 'other books' is returned to a troubled scene of childhood difficulty. Modernism here – not solely popular culture – becomes, quite literally, infantilising.

Throughout his essay Strachey draws on modernist anxieties surrounding the scene of popular consumption, but he also repeatedly troubles the binary division between mature, disinterested modernist culture and the infantile satisfactions of popular culture. 'It may', Strachey comments, 'be impossible to suck down the works of Mr Bertrand Russell, or to chew up those of Miss Ethel M. Dell', but, he adds, 'it is surprising what successful efforts may be made in both these directions'.[201] As we have seen throughout this chapter, 'chew[ing] up' Ethel M. Dell was not as simple, nor as easy, as her critics suggested.

[201] Strachey, 'Some Unconscious Factors', p. 326.

3

READING *THE WAVES*, READING YOU: VIRGINIA WOOLF AND THE CULTURE OF REDEMPTION

As darkness descends in *To the Lighthouse* (1927), Mr Carmichael lies awake reading Virgil: 'One by one the lamps were all extinguished, except that Mr Carmichael, who liked to lie awake a little reading Virgil, kept his candle burning rather longer than the rest.'[1] Woolf doesn't specify whether Mr Carmichael reads Virgil's epic, pastoral or elegiac poetry, but the image, appearing at the beginning of 'Time Passes', certainly hints at the possible psychological uses of reading in dark times. Mr Carmichael may find solace, or comfort, or heightened understanding in the words of the Roman poet, but in 'Time Passes' – a passage of writing that records both the personal tragedies of the Ramsay family and the wider losses of the First World War – Woolf presents her own readers with what David James has described as 'discrepant solace'.[2] This is, James argues, a form of writing that both 'stages and inspects language's necessarily impossible attempt' to 'redress' the absences that it traces.[3] For James, *To the Lighthouse* offers 'neither the outright refutation of solace [. . .] nor a plea to transcend history's harm through [what Tyrus Miller characterises as] the "admirable design of words"'.[4] This is a kind of writing in which

[1] Woolf, *To the Lighthouse*, p. 103.
[2] James, *Discrepant Solace*, pp. 45–8.
[3] James, *Discrepant Solace*, p. 46.
[4] James, *Discrepant Solace*, p. 47. Summarising two influential critical responses to modernism, James cites Neil Lazarus's assertion that modernism engenders 'disconsolation' in its readers, and Tyrus Miller's similar observation that late modernism 'sought to deflate' the 'symbolic resources' of Joycean encyclopedism and Woolfian lyricism. See Tyrus Miller,

language enacts its own fraught effort to navigate 'the sands of oblivion', as Woolf puts it towards the end of 'Time Passes', and in doing so navigate itself, its resources of resuscitation, knowing what it has 'fetched up from oblivion' cannot ultimately be 'rescued from the pool of Time'.[5]

Woolf's quest for a kind of writing that could resist the consolations of beauty is, in James's words, 'dramatized' in *To the Lighthouse*, 'by a style that seems to argue with its very own capacity to confront the inconsolable'.[6] Later in 'Time Passes', the anonymous figures that pace the beach express a longing for consolation, but this desire is both punctured and heightened by Andrew Ramsay's death in the trenches – announced in a famously abrupt pair of square brackets. 'At that season', Woolf writes,

> those who had gone down to pace the beach and ask of the sea and sky what message they reported or what vision they affirmed had to consider among the usual tokens of divine bounty—the sunset on the sea, the pallor of dawn, the moon rising, fishing boats against the moon, and children pelting each other with handfuls of grass, something out of harmony with this jocundity, this serenity.[7]

Although the figures pacing the beach search for 'the most sublime reflections' and 'the most comfortable conclusions', the 'intrusion' of an 'ashen-coloured ship' and 'a purplish stain upon the bland surface of the sea' – the 'intrusion' of war and of death – 'stayed their pacing':

> Impatient, despairing yet loth to go (for beauty offers her lures, her consolations), to pace the beach was impossible; contemplation was unendurable; the mirror was broken.[8]

And yet, even as this passage marks Woolf's suspicion of the 'lures' and 'consolations' of beauty, it is followed swiftly by another set of square brackets encasing another scene of reading:

> [Mr Carmichael brought out a volume of poems that spring, which had an unexpected success. The war, people said, had revived their interest in poetry.][9]

Late Modernism: Politics, Fiction, and the Arts between the World Wars (Berkeley: University of California Press, 1999), p. 19, p. 20; Neil Lazarus, *The Postcolonial Unconscious* (Cambridge: Cambridge University Press, 2011), p. 32.

5 James, *Discrepant Solace*, p. 47.
6 James, *Discrepant Solace*, p. 47.
7 Woolf, *To the Lighthouse*, p. 109.
8 Woolf, *To the Lighthouse*, p. 109, p. 110.
9 Woolf, *To the Lighthouse*, p. 110.

Although Woolf does not specify the nature of the public's 'interest in poetry', nonetheless, this allusion to the scene of reading once again suggests the possible consolations afforded by poetry in the aftermath of war. In *To the Lighthouse* Woolf places the question of literary consolation in the foreground of this radically experimental passage of writing, simultaneously underscoring the consoling rhythms of her own writing, while also interrogating both the possibilities and the politics of literary consolation in the aftermath of the First World War. In this novel, Woolf not only dramatises a quest for 'discrepant solace', but also, in her portraits of reading, dramatises a set of questions about the role of reading literature in dark times.

In *The Waves* (1931), Woolf continued to explore the role of reading in the lives of her characters, creating a novel that stages and scrutinises the psychic, social and political investments that readers place in books. An 'abstract mystical eyeless book', *The Waves* is Woolf's most self-consciously abstract, poetic, difficult book.[10] 'I feel more & more sure that I will never write a novel again,' Woolf observed, having finished *Orlando* – 'Little bits of rhyme come in'; 'Something abstract poetic next time'.[11] Complaining of 'this appalling narrative business of the realist: getting on from lunch to dinner: it is false, unreal, merely conventional', Woolf explicitly opposed her method to that of the 'realist' and the 'conventional' novelist, asking, 'Why admit anything to literature that is not poetry—by which I mean saturated?'[12] Woolf described *The Waves* as 'prose yet poetry; a novel & a play'.[13] In her 1927 essay 'Poetry, Fiction and the Future', Woolf began by observing that 'Nobody indeed can read much modern literature without being aware that some dissatisfaction, some difficulty is lying in our way': 'writers are [. . .] forcing the form they use to contain a meaning that is strange to it.'[14] There is an echo here not only of Eliot's observation that 'poets in our civilization [. . .] must be *difficult*', but also of his claim that part of this difficulty resides in the poet's need to be 'more comprehensive, more allusive, more indirect, in order to force, to dislocate if necessary, language into his meaning'.[15] Woolf imagined the birth of a new form 'among the so-called novels [. . .] which we shall scarcely know how to christen': like *The Waves*, this new form would be 'written in prose, but in prose which has many of the characteristics of poetry'; it would 'be dramatic, and yet not a play'.[16]

---

[10] Woolf, *Diary*, III, p. 128.

[11] Woolf, *Diary*, III, p. 77, p. 185. See also Woolf, *Diary*, III, p. 28, pp. 209–10.

[12] Woolf, *Diary*, III, pp. 209–10.

[13] Woolf, *Diary*, III, p. 128.

[14] Woolf, *Essays*, IV, p. 429.

[15] T. S. Eliot, 'The Metaphysical Poets' (1921), in *Selected Prose of T. S. Eliot*, ed. by Frank Kermode (London: Faber and Faber, 1975), pp. 59–67 (p. 65).

[16] Woolf, *Essays*, IV, p. 435.

In writing *The Waves*, Woolf was, as these quotations testify, profoundly aware of the 'difficulty' that this, 'the most complex, & difficult of all my books', presented to her readers.[17] Leonard Woolf thought 'the first 100 pages extremely difficult' and was, Woolf noted in her diary, 'doubtful how far any common reader will follow'.[18] On completing the book, she felt that it was 'fundamentally unreadable'.[19] 'I think then that my difficulty is that I am writing to a rhythm & not to a plot,' Woolf wrote, worrying that 'though the rhythmical is more natural to me than narrative, it is completely opposed to the tradition of fiction & I am casting about all the time for some rope to throw to the reader'.[20] Writing to a rhythm rather than presenting a linear narrative, Woolf worried that her reader might drown.

And yet, although Woolf may have worried about the difficulties that her writing presented to its readers, in this chapter I want to argue that the figure of the reader is at the heart of *The Waves*. As I noted in the introduction to this book, in a plan dated 13 June 1930, Woolf sketched out the episodes of the book from 'The garden', through 'school', 'College', 'London', 'Maturity', 'Death' and 'Love', to a final section devoted to 'Books. & sensation'.[21] Although there is no final episode dedicated to 'Books. & sensation', scenes of reading appear throughout both the drafts and the final text of *The Waves*. All of Virginia Woolf's novels depict scenes of reading: from Rachel Vinrace reading Ibsen in *The Voyage Out* (1915), to Mr and Mrs Ramsay reading Walter Scott and Shakespeare in *To the Lighthouse* (1927), Sara reading *Antigone* in *The Years* (1937), or Mrs Swithin reading her 'Outline of History' in *Between the Acts* (1941).[22] But it is in *The Waves* that Woolf offers her fullest portrait of the imaginative, psychological and political investments that we, as readers, place in books. 'Books. & sensation' is up there, in the plan, with 'Death' and 'Love'.

---

[17] Woolf, *Diary*, III, p. 298.

[18] Woolf, *Diary*, IV, p. 36.

[19] On publication, as the Cambridge University Press editors note, Woolf expressed 'surprise at the reaction the novel received in the "mass-circulation" newspapers': 'How odd this is,' she wrote, 'so far most of the low-brow reviewers (whose sense I respect) find the Waves perfectly simple.' Although, as the editors note, 'almost all the early reviewers' commented on the 'difficulty' of *The Waves*, Woolf found that 'this unintelligible book is being better "received" than any of them'; 'And it sells—how unexpected, how odd that people can read that difficult grinding stuff!' Woolf, *Letters*, IV, p. 357; Woolf, *Letters*, IV, p. 389, cited by Ian Blyth, Michael Herbert and Susan Sellers, 'Introduction', in *The Waves*, pp. xxxix–c (p. lxx); Woolf, *Diary*, IV, p. 47.

[20] Woolf, *Letters*, IV, p. 204.

[21] Woolf, *The Waves: The Two Holograph Drafts*, p. 400.

[22] Virginia Woolf, *The Voyage Out*, ed. by Lorna Sage (Oxford: Oxford University Press, 2009), pp. 137–9; Woolf, *To the Lighthouse*, pp. 95–9; Woolf, *The Years*, pp. 117–22; Virginia Woolf, *Between the Acts*, ed. by Mark Hussey (Cambridge: Cambridge University Press, 2011), pp. 6–7.

Throughout *The Waves*, the six voices or 'characters' (Woolf found it 'odd' that *The Times* praised her 'characters' when she 'meant to have none') repeatedly turn to books and to poetry, articulating their desires for various forms of what Leo Bersani has characterised – and dismissed – as cultural 'redemption'.[23] In the scenes of reading depicted in *The Waves*, Bernard, Rhoda, Louis and Neville all turn to art and to poetry as a source of consolation in the wake of Percival's death. In *The Waves*, the longing for 'redemption' appears not only in the scenes of mourning for Percival, but also, as we shall see in this chapter, in Neville's fantasy of poetry as a scholarly refuge from the horrors of mass modernity, and in Louis's vision of poetry as a source of communal belonging and a form of transcendence. In these scenes, however, far from participating in the 'culture of redemption', Woolf challenges the dominant fantasies in early-twentieth-century culture about the role of literature in psychic, social and political life. In *The Waves*, Woolf dramatises the scene of reading, modelling the real psychological uses of literature in troubled times, while also scrutinising the potential historical evasions and political abuses of a redemptive understanding of art. In *The Waves*, the scenes of reading depict the projected reader of Woolf's own literary modernism, evoking both Woolf's desires and her anxieties about the role of her own writing in her readers' psychic, social and political lives. By soliciting us, as readers, to identify with the readers depicted in the text, Woolf asks us to consider how far our own encounter with Woolf's modernist prose enacts an alternative to the fantasies of redemption explored within the novel. In *The Waves*, Woolf stages a series of scenes of reading that complicate the characters' expressed longings for a redemptive encounter with art. And yet, although *The Waves* may appear to offer an alternative to the fantasies of redemption that circulated in early-twentieth-century culture, it also enacts an ultimately ambivalent struggle with the different forms of reading that it both diagnoses and seeks to reimagine.

THE WAVES AND THE POETICS OF REDEMPTION

In the trio of essays that he wrote in the midst of the First World War, Freud forged a theory of mourning that insisted upon the individual's capacity to overcome their grief for what has been lost, and to replace the lost object – whether a loved person, or 'some abstraction [. . .] such as one's country, liberty, an ideal, and so on' – with a new one.[24] Contrasting the 'normal' work of mourning with the pathological state of melancholia, Freud argued that in melancholia the individual clings to the lost object, transforming a libidinal tie

---

[23] Woolf, *Diary*, IV, p. 47; Bersani, *The Culture of Redemption*.

[24] Freud, 'Thoughts for the Times on War and Death'; Sigmund Freud, 'On Transience' (1916 [1915]), *Standard Edition*, XIV, pp. 303–7; Sigmund Freud, 'Mourning and Melancholia' (1917 [1915]), *Standard Edition*, XIV, pp. 237–60 (p. 243).

into an '*identification* of the ego with the abandoned object'.[25] In mourning, in contrast, the mourner progresses through a painful process in which he or she gradually consents to the 'command of reality'.[26] Although the mourner may experience a form of internal revolt, nonetheless, 'bit by bit, at great expense of time and cathectic energy', the libidinal ties to what has been lost are severed, and 'when the work of mourning is completed the ego becomes free and uninhibited again'.[27] For Freud, mourning takes the form of a psychic work with a beginning, a middle and, most crucially, an end. In melancholia, by contrast, the 'shadow of the object f[a]ll[s] upon the ego', producing a painful and prolonged, perhaps even interminable relationship to what has been lost.[28]

For Freud, in these wartime essays, the work of mourning was also bound up with a theory about art's capacity to rebuild a shattered civilisation. Like T. S. Eliot's *The Waste Land*, Freud's writings on mourning bear a powerful resemblance to a modernist aesthetics in which (to quote Eliot) artists sought to shore up 'ruins' with the 'fragments' of European culture.[29] 'When once the mourning is over,' Freud wrote in his essay 'On Transience', 'it will be found that our high opinion of the riches of civilization has lost nothing from our discovery of their fragility. We shall build up again all that war has destroyed, and perhaps on firmer ground and more lastingly than before.'[30] The theory of mourning that Freud elaborates in these essays bears all the signs of its genesis in a moment when, as Freud acknowledges, the war had 'shattered our pride in the achievements of our civilization'.[31] As Jacqueline Rose has argued, the theory of mourning can be read as a 'drive for political, or cultural, as much as psychic self-protection' born out of a 'moment of cultural dismay'.[32] Freud's insistence on what Judith Butler describes as the 'interchangeability of objects' feels jarring and at odds with Freud's own writing about the nature of the unconscious.[33] The claims that Freud makes about the capacity for cultural renewal also feel complicit with Leo Bersani's idea of a 'culture of redemption' in which, as Bersani argues, modernist writers and psychoanalysts turned to art to make up for the 'catastrophe of history'.[34]

---

[25] Freud, 'Mourning and Melancholia', p. 243, p. 249, Freud's emphasis.

[26] Freud, 'Mourning and Melancholia', p. 245.

[27] Freud, 'Mourning and Melancholia', p. 245.

[28] Freud, 'Mourning and Melancholia', p. 249.

[29] T. S. Eliot, *The Waste Land* (1922), in *The Complete Poems and Plays of T. S. Eliot* (London: Faber and Faber, 2004), pp. 59–80 (V. 431).

[30] Freud, 'On Transience', p. 307.

[31] Freud, 'On Transience', p. 307.

[32] Jacqueline Rose, 'Virginia Woolf and the Death of Modernism', in *On Not Being Able to Sleep*, pp. 72–88 (p. 73).

[33] Judith Butler, *Precarious Life: The Powers of Mourning and Violence* (London: Verso, 2006), p. 21; Bersani, *The Culture of Redemption*, p. 22.

[34] Bersani, *The Culture of Redemption*, p. 22.

In *The Culture of Redemption*, Bersani criticises a redemptive account of cultural experience, in which, he argues, art and literature are conceived – for both artists and readers or spectators – as a 'redemptive replication of damaged or worthless experience'.[35] In this 'culture of redemption', 'great masterworks' are, Bersani claims, supposed to 'save us—save us from our lives, which in some way are failed lives in need of repair and redemption'.[36] For the proponents of the culture of redemption, 'art is', Bersani argues, 'reduced to a kind of superior patching function', while 'the catastrophes of individual experience and of social history matter much less (thereby making active reform and resistance less imperative) if they are somehow "understood" and compensated for in art'.[37]

In Bersani's account, modernist writers and psychoanalysts were the guilty advocates of a form of cultural experience that held out the promise of transfiguring and healing the horrors of both individual and historical experience. For Bersani, one of the chief culprits was Melanie Klein, whose theory of reparation he reads alongside *À la recherche du temps perdu* as exemplary of a modernist faith in the power of art to redeem both writers and readers from the traumas of the past. For Bersani, the drive for political, cultural and psychic self-protection that appears in Freud's wartime essays on mourning was transformed, in Klein's work, into a theory of reparation that also underpins the most egregious evasions at work in the modernist culture of redemption. In Klein's account of psychic life, mourning appears not solely – as in Freud's account – as an experience of grief for the dead, or for lost abstractions ('such as one's country, liberty, an ideal, and so on'), but as a foundational experience in infantile psychic life – an experience on which all later relationships and experiences, including cultural experiences, are founded.[38] In infancy, Klein argued, experiences of nourishment and pleasure at the mother's breast inspire fantasies of the 'good' breast, while experiences of frustration and hunger inspire aggressive fantasies of the 'bad' breast, in which the baby 'wishes to bite up and to tear up his mother and her breasts, and to destroy her also in other ways'.[39] In what Klein came to call the 'paranoid-schizoid position', the baby projects all of his rage on to a dangerous and persecutory 'bad' breast, indulging in violent fantasies of tearing up the mother's body, reducing her to pieces.[40] By contrast, in what

---

[35] Bersani, *The Culture of Redemption*, p. 20.

[36] Bersani and Dutoit, *Arts of Impoverishment*, p. 3.

[37] Bersani and Dutoit, *Arts of Impoverishment*, pp. 3–4.

[38] Freud, 'Mourning and Melancholia', p. 243.

[39] Melanie Klein, 'Love, Guilt and Reparation' (1937), in *Love, Guilt and Reparation and Other Works 1921–1945* (London: Vintage, 1998), pp. 306–43 (p. 308).

[40] Klein, 'Love, Guilt and Reparation', p. 308. See also Joan Riviere, 'On the Genesis of Psychical Conflict in Earliest Infancy', *International Journal of Psycho-Analysis*, 17 (1936), 395–422 (p. 404). For Klein's introduction of the term 'paranoid-schizoid position', see

Klein called the 'depressive position', these fantasised attacks on the mother's body give way to overwhelming feelings of sorrow and guilt: the infant undergoes an experience of mourning accompanied by the desire to 'save the loved object, to repair and restore it'.[41] For Klein, reparation appears as a creative endeavour to restore the damaged object:

> It is a 'perfect' object which is in pieces; thus the effort to undo the state of disintegration to which it has been reduced presupposes the necessity to make it beautiful and 'perfect'. The idea of perfection is, moreover, so compelling because it disproves the idea of disintegration. In some patients who had turned away from their mother in dislike or hate [. . .] I have found that there existed in their minds nevertheless a beautiful picture of the mother, but one which was felt to be a *picture* of her only, not her real self. The real object was felt to be unattractive—really an injured, incurable and therefore dreaded person. The beautiful picture had been dissociated from the real object but had never been given up, and played a great part in the specific ways of their sublimations.[42]

These attempts to 'save the loved object, to repair and restore it [. . .] are determining factors for all sublimations'.[43]

In Bersani's interpretation, Klein presents a linear narrative of infantile development: the infant begins with the paranoid-schizoid position, in which he is dominated by sadistic and paranoid aggressive fantasies, and then progresses to the depressive position, in which, succumbing to depression and guilt about his fantasised attacks on his mother, he feels 'an over-riding urge to preserve, repair or revive the loved objects [. . .] to make reparation'.[44] In Klein's account, as Bersani reads it, this guilty *'desire to restore'* is the driving force behind both artistic creation and the pleasures and consolations we gain from reading.[45] And yet, in Klein's writings from the 1930s and 1940s, even as the theory of reparation takes on a greater historical urgency, the reparative fantasies that Klein describes are also shot through with, and rendered fragile by,

---

Melanie Klein, 'Notes on Some Schizoid Mechanisms' (1946), in *Envy and Gratitude and Other Works 1946–1963* (London: Vintage, 1997), pp. 1–24.

[41] Melanie Klein, 'A Contribution to the Psychogenesis of Manic-Depressive States' (1935), in *Love, Guilt and Reparation*, pp. 262–89 (p. 270). See also Melanie Klein, 'Mourning and Its Relation to Manic-Depressive States' (1940), in *Love, Guilt and Reparation*, pp. 344–69.

[42] Klein, 'A Contribution to the Psychogenesis of Manic-Depressive States', p. 270.

[43] Klein, 'A Contribution to the Psychogenesis of Manic-Depressive States', p. 270.

[44] Melanie Klein, 'On the Theory of Anxiety and Guilt' (1948), in *Envy and Gratitude*, pp. 25–42 (pp. 35–6).

[45] Klein, 'A Contribution to the Psychogenesis of Manic-Depressive States', p. 270.

the sadistic fantasies that they seek to contain. The fantasy of reparation is, as Julia Kristeva, Jacqueline Rose and Lyndsey Stonebridge have all observed, bound up in a cyclical logic in which reparation is repeatedly threatened by the violence that it seeks to repair. For Bersani, Klein prescribes a linear passage from sadism through to reparation, in which reparation masks over and compensates for the violence of the past. And yet, Klein warned her readers against interpreting her descriptions of psychic processes as a 'chronological account'; she theorised 'positions', not 'stages' or 'phases of development', and insisted that they 'may well happen simultaneously'.[46] 'Klein's concept of the "position"' is not, as Kristeva writes, 'a "stage" as the term was understood by the psychoanalysts who preceded her'.[47] Rather, Klein's theory of psychic 'positions' emphasises 'a shifting psychic vantage point and [challenges] the strict chronology claimed by the proponents of psychoanalytic stages'.[48]

In her 1940 essay on 'Mourning and Its Relation to Manic Depressive States', Klein described how the ego might be 'driven by depressive anxieties (anxiety lest the loved objects as well as itself should be destroyed) to build up omnipotent and violent phantasies, partly for the purpose of controlling and mastering the "bad", dangerous objects, partly in order to save and restore the loved ones'.[49] Writing about the reparative fantasy of the 'good' object characterised by 'extreme perfection', Klein observed that

> The desire to control the object, the sadistic gratification of overcoming and humiliating it, of getting the better of it, the *triumph* over it, may enter so strongly into the act of reparation (carried out by thoughts, activities or sublimations) that the 'benign' circle started by this act becomes broken. The objects which were to be restored change again into persecutors, and in turn paranoid fears are revived.[50]

Repeatedly, Klein and her followers return to the figure of a 'vicious circle'.[51] 'Klein's logic', writes Kristeva, 'does not function as a "causal sequence" from

---

[46] Klein, 'On the Theory of Anxiety and Guilt', p. 31.

[47] Julia Kristeva, *Melanie Klein*, trans. by Ross Guberman (New York: Columbia University Press, 2001), p. 66.

[48] Kristeva, *Melanie Klein*, pp. 66–7.

[49] Klein, 'Mourning and Its Relation to Manic-Depressive States', p. 349, p. 349, n. 2.

[50] Klein, 'Mourning and Its Relation to Manic-Depressive States', p. 351.

[51] Riviere, 'On the Genesis of Psychical Conflict', p. 405. See also Klein, 'On the Theory of Anxiety and Guilt', p. 31; Melanie Klein, *The Psycho-Analysis of Children*, trans. by Alix Strachey, rev. by H. A. Thorner (London: Vintage, 1997), p. 150; Klein, 'Notes on Some Schizoid Mechanisms', p. 15; Melanie Klein, 'The Origins of Transference' (1952), in *Envy and Gratitude*, pp. 48–56 (p. 53); Melanie Klein, 'Envy and Gratitude' (1957), in *Envy and Gratitude*, pp. 176–235 (p. 231); Melanie Klein, 'Some Reflections on "The Oresteia"' (1963), in *Envy and Gratitude*, pp. 275–99 (pp. 294–5).

point A to point B, but as a *circular effort.*[52] As Stonebridge argues in response to Bersani's criticisms, 'For Klein, the individual does not so much develop from "A" to "B" (from the destructive element, for instance, to its transcendence through psychic reparation) but is constantly defined and redefined by the vicissitudes of anxiety.'[53] Although Klein's writings do, like the writing of many of her modernist contemporaries, sketch the framework for a theory of the therapeutic and reparative powers of art, the theory also fails to sustain itself in these terms: reparation, in Klein's writing, is always fragile and precarious.

The fragility of reparation is, as Stonebridge makes clear, bound up in the history of the 1920s, 1930s and 1940s. Noting the echoes with the 1919 Treaty of Versailles and its aftermath, Stonebridge shows how the Kleinian theory of reparation carried with it the history of European attempts at post-war reparation, evoking not just the idea of 'compensation for war damage owed by the aggressor', but also, for 'vocal' members of the European intelligentsia such as John Maynard Keynes, appearing as 'something exorbitant, excessive and punitive, in short, an invitation to more aggression'.[54] The Kleinian theory of reparation bears testament to its origins in a moment that desperately desired redemption from the psychic, social and political violence of recent and ongoing history, but was also shaped by, shot through with, and frequently undone by that violence.

In *The Waves*, following the death of Percival, the characters all turn, amidst their grief, to art and to literature. In their monologues, Woolf's characters articulate conflicted longings for cultural encounters that might resolve the psychic and political ambiguities of mourning for their dead friend, the colonial administrator Percival. At first glance, this might seem to confirm Leo Bersani's worst suspicions concerning modernism's complicity with an evasive 'culture of redemption' in which art appeases the ravages of grief. Where Freud's essays on mourning invoke the need to replace both the literal dead and the lost 'ideals' of nation, liberty and civilisation with a renewed and strangely amnesiac faith in the buttressing potential of the 'riches of civilization', the work of mourning in *The Waves* might be read similarly as an attempt to eulogise empire (another shattered 'abstraction' or 'ideal') in the figure of Percival.[55] And yet, although *The Waves* intertwines the work of mourning with the processes of reading and looking at art, it also places the relationship between mourning and cultural experience under critical scrutiny.

In his work on 'discrepant solace', David James has challenged Bersani's polemical account of the culture of redemption, arguing that the imagined

---

[52] Kristeva, *Melanie Klein*, p. 199, Kristeva's emphasis.
[53] Stonebridge, *The Destructive Element*, p. 39. See also Rose, *Why War?*, p. 163.
[54] Stonebridge, *The Destructive Element*, p. 32.
[55] Freud, 'Mourning and Melancholia', p. 243; Freud, 'On Transience', p. 307.

witness of aesthetic redemption appears as 'something of a monolithic fiction, a fiction that depends upon the portrait of a reader who allegedly conflates the promise of material repair with the recuperative force of representational ingenuity'.[56] 'Whatever we feel about consolation's politics,' James adds,

> there is something uncomfortably condescending about assuming that readers are incapable of recognizing the imaginative refuge of art for what it is, without romanticizing it as a cure, and without assuming that their embrace of an enchanting text will durably appease either the material costs of social dispossession or the mental costs of psychic deterioration.[57]

Like James, I think that Bersani is too sweeping in his condemnation of the apparent lures of modernist aesthetics – there's a danger, as James notes, of critics sneering at readers who seek solace, which is not, in itself or by necessity, politically evasive. In *The Waves*, however, the search for consolation *is* politicised, because of what, in Woolf's framing of the novel, Percival stands for: patriarchal imperial power, and the fascistic allure of the leader.[58] At school, Louis describes Percival as 'some mediaeval commander', the schoolboys 'trooping after him [. . .] to be shot like sheep'; 'he is a hero', 'a God', in whose presence the group of friends 'assume the sober and confident air of soldiers in the presence of their captain'.[59] Bernard imagines Percival in India: 'By applying the standards of the West, by using the violent language that is natural to him', the 'Oriental problem is solved'; when Percival dies, Bernard expostulates to people in the street, 'You have lost a leader whom you would have followed'; 'you would have had to respect him'.[60] As Gabrielle McIntire comments:

> While Woolf never actually *names* fascism in the novel, the ways in which she represents the group's ambivalent awe for a quasi-mystical confraternity, the characters' alternating fascination and abhorrence for order and authority, the group's hero-worship of Percival, and [. . .] the quasi-monologic arrest of Bernard's closing soliloquy, all point to a sustained meditation on the nearness of fascist rhetoric and sentiment to the politics and rhetoric of everyday English life.[61]

---

[56] James, *Discrepant Solace*, p. 15.

[57] James, *Discrepant Solace*, p. 15.

[58] See also Jane Marcus, 'Britannia Rules *The Waves*', in *Hearts of Darkness: White Women Write Race* (New Brunswick: Rutgers University Press, 2003), pp. 59–85; Kathy J. Phillips, *Virginia Woolf against Empire* (Knoxville: University of Tennessee Press, 1994).

[59] Woolf, *The Waves*, p. 28, p. 107, p. 96.

[60] Woolf, *The Waves*, p. 107, p. 121, p. 122.

[61] Gabrielle McIntire, 'Heteroglossia, Monologism, and Fascism: Bernard Reads *The Waves*', *Narrative*, 13.1 (2005), 29–45 (p. 30).

In the scenes following Percival's death, the characters' attempts to use art and literature as part of a troubled work of mourning are inextricably bound up with the fantasies of masculine authority, imperial power and proto-fascist unity that, as critics have long noted, accrue to the figure of Percival in this novel. And yet, in *The Waves*, Woolf challenges the politics of mourning for Percival while also exploring the real psychic urgency of consolation for individual readers, producing an account of reading that is both attuned to the powerful role of art in individual processes of mourning, while nonetheless remaining suspicious of producing an elegy for a figurehead of imperialist and proto-fascistic patriarchal power.

In *The Waves*, the figure of Percival – who stands at the absent centre of the friendships that the novel describes – is animated both by Woolf's bleakly ominous critique of patriarchal and imperialist power, and at the same time by a deeply felt and sincere attempt to write about grief. On finishing the final pages of *The Waves*, Woolf wrote: 'I have been sitting these 15 minutes in a state of glory, & calm, & some tears, thinking of Thoby & if I could write Julian Thoby Stephen 1881–1906 on the first page. I suppose not.'[62] Vanessa Bell wrote to Woolf:

> I have been for the last 3 days completely submerged in The Waves—and am left rather gasping, out of breath, choking, half-drowned, as you might expect. I must read it again when I may hope to float more quietly, but meanwhile I'm so overcome by the beauty [. . .] it's impossible not to tell you or give you some hint of what's been happening to me. [. . .] Of course there's the personal side, the feelings you describe on what I must take to be Thoby's death [. . .] Even then I know it's only because of your art that I am so moved. I think you have made one's human feelings into something less personal—if you wouldn't think me foolish I should say that you *have* found the 'lullaby capable of singing him to rest.'[63]

While the first-person monologues mean that, as readers, we are solicited to identify closely with intensely felt and vividly rendered grief, the absence of Percival's own voice means that, as readers, we are also solicited to detect Woolf's satirical treatment of his ignominious death – 'thrown, riding in a race' in India – and to criticise the characters' unthinking celebration of Percival as a charismatic colonial leader.[64] None of the characters, least of all Bernard,

---

[62] Woolf, *Diary*, IV, p. 10.

[63] Vanessa Bell, *Selected Letters of Vanessa Bell*, ed. by Regina Marler (London: Bloomsbury, 1993), p. 361, original emphasis. On Woolf's mourning for her brother and *The Waves*, see Gillian Beer, *Virginia Woolf: The Common Ground* (Edinburgh: Edinburgh University Press, 1996), pp. 85–6.

[64] Woolf, *The Waves*, p. 195.

ever explicitly voices any discontent with the politics of eulogising a figure who appears to Woolf's readers as a troublingly violent and vacuous colonial administrator. And yet, where the characters do express their discontent with the poetics of consolation, Woolf opens up a critical space for reflection on the complex relationship between consolatory poetics and politics. 'I am *not* going to lie down and weep a life of care,' Bernard rebukes himself, even as he echoes Shelley's 'Stanzas Written in Dejection'.[65] In his final monologue, Bernard expresses a desire for consolation while jostling with a fear that the attempt to channel sorrow into the forms of poetry might fail to do justice to the pain of grief, or to the person lost. Amidst his and Jinny's articulations of anguished regret at the 'trifl[ing] but torturing' memories of their dead friend ('I did not go with him to Hampton Court. That claw scratched; that fang tore; I did not go'), Bernard entertains an ambivalent, both longed for and dreaded, vision of the future: 'I saw the first leaf fall on his grave. I saw us push beyond this moment, and leave it behind us for ever.'[66] It's at precisely this moment that poetry 'inevitably' – in the form of a line from Ben Jonson – rises up:

> And then sitting side by side on the sofa we remembered inevitably what had been said by others; 'the lily of the day is fairer far in May'; we compared Percival to a lily—Percival whom I wanted to lose his hair, to shock the authorities, to grow old with me; he was already covered over with lilies.
>
> So the sincerity of the moment passed; so it became symbolical; and that I could not stand. Let us commit any blasphemy of laughter and criticism rather than exude this lily-sweet glue; and cover him with phrases, I cried.[67]

In these hesitations about the risks of poetic consolation, Woolf opens up a critical space which allows the readers of the novel, if not the characters themselves, to question the politics of eulogising imperial leaders in the shape of Percival. Not only, however, does Woolf challenge the politics of consolation, but, as we shall see in the scenes that follow, Woolf also begins to map out alternative forms of cultural encounter that, while allowing the reader the psychic space for mourning, also refuse to subscribe to the fantasies of aesthetic redemption that circulated within early-twentieth-century culture.

---

[65] Woolf, *The Waves*, p. 121, my emphasis.

[66] Woolf, *The Waves*, p. 212.

[67] Woolf, *The Waves*, pp. 212–13. The allusion is to Ben Jonson's 'To the immortall memorie, and friendship of that noble paire, Sir Lvcivs Cary, and Sir H. Morison'. Michael Herbert, Susan Sellers and Ian Blyth, 'Explanatory Notes', in Woolf, *The Waves*, pp. 239–395 (p. 387, n. 212: 25).

Describing a modernist 'practice of countermourning', Sanja Bahun has argued that 'modernist literature can be understood as an alternative mourning rite [. . .] distinguished by the unusual tendency to give form to the very impossibility to mourn'.[68] For Bahun,

> What is distinct in the modernists' attempts to replace reified forms of mourning with experimental expressions of grief is a routine questioning of the 'healing' aspect of traditional mourning practices. For this reason, the alternative mourning that their texts offer is at once therapeutic and interminable [. . .]; modernist literature performs an impossible mourning, driven by the force of its unattainable 'cure'. [. . .] Being 'awkward' and 'tormenting' monuments, [countermonuments] acquire their heightened social function precisely through the perpetuation of the loss they memorize.[69]

In the scenes of reading depicted in *The Waves*, Woolf portrays her characters working through similar 'alternative mourning rite[s]'. In these scenes, Woolf challenges both the healing aspect of traditional mourning practices and the culture of heroic memorialisation, while nonetheless articulating her characters' longings for different forms of consolation. The characters engage with poetry and with art, in a way that challenges Freud's portrait of the work of mourning as a process with a fixed end-point, and his associated faith in the possibility that the 'riches of civilization' might, despite their destruction, be built up again 'on firmer ground and more lastingly than before'.[70] In Woolf's novel, mourning has more in common with the interminable temporality of Freudian melancholia, and with the circular rhythms that characterise Klein's writing about mourning and reparation. 'In mourning', wrote Klein in 1940, 'as well as in infantile development, inner security comes about not by a straightforward movement but in waves.'[71]

In *The Waves*, Woolf dramatises her characters' desires for reparation, but she also holds these desires up for scrutiny, revealing the complex entanglement of the quest for psychic reparation with overdetermined, and conflicting, fantasies of masculine imperial authority, democratic community and proto-fascist unity. In *The Waves*, Woolf's portraits of reading are, like Klein's account of reparation, marked by forms of psychic and historical violence that thwart

---

[68] Sanja Bahun, *Modernism and Melancholia: Writing as Countermourning* (Oxford: Oxford University Press, 2014), p. 8.
[69] Bahun, *Modernism and Melancholia*, p. 18.
[70] Freud, 'On Transience', p. 307. See also Rose, 'Virginia Woolf and the Death of Modernism', p. 73.
[71] Klein, 'Mourning and Its Relation to Manic-Depressive States', p. 361.

the individual reader's path to reparation. Like Klein, for whom reparation is haunted by the violence that it seeks to contain, in Woolf's scenes of reading the desire for different forms of aesthetic wholeness – whether expressed as a longing for scholarly refuge, for communal feeling, or as a longing for a cultural encounter that might assuage the ravages of grief – is repeatedly threatened by the destructive drives of an era of looming fascism.

'THIS IS MY FUNERAL SERVICE': BERNARD IN THE NATIONAL GALLERY

Although Bernard rejects the 'lily-sweet glue' of words, in the immediate aftermath of Percival's death he does turn to painting. Wishing to delay the inevitable return from his state of shocked grief to the 'usual order' of the city, Bernard goes to the National Gallery:

> I will go up these steps into the gallery and submit myself to the influence of minds like mine outside the sequence. [. . .] Here are pictures. Here are cold madonnas among their pillars. Let them lay to rest the incessant activity of the mind's eye, the bandaged head, the men with ropes, so that I may find something universal underneath. Here are gardens; and Venus among her flowers; here are saints and blue madonnas. Mercifully these pictures make no reference; they do not nudge; they do not point. Thus they expand my consciousness of him and bring him back to me differently. I remember his beauty.[72]

'This is my funeral service,' claims Bernard. 'We have no ceremonies, only private dirges and no conclusions, only violent sensations, each separate. Nothing that has been said meets our case. We sit in the Italian room at the National Gallery picking up fragments.'[73] Bernard echoes *The Waste Land*: 'These fragments I have shored against my ruins.'[74] And yet, while Eliot's poem falters on the psychic and political ambiguities of shoring up 'ruins' with 'fragments', Bernard's own attempt to use art to buttress himself against the ravages of grief is similarly fraught with contradiction and ambiguity.[75]

Looking at the paintings in the National Gallery, Bernard describes how 'Lines and colours almost persuade me that I too can be heroic', and laments that, unlike his hero Percival, he cannot 'clench' his 'fist'.[76] In his final monologue, Bernard returns to this scene and recalls a feeling of 'freedom' and

---

[72] Woolf, *The Waves*, pp. 122–3.
[73] Woolf, *The Waves*, pp. 123–4.
[74] Eliot, *The Waste Land*, pp. 59–80 (V. 431).
[75] See Peter Howarth, 'Eliot in the Underworld: The Politics of Fragmentary Form', *Textual Practice*, 20.3 (2006), 441–62 (p. 444, p. 458).
[76] Woolf, *The Waves*, p. 123.

'immunity', which he describes as a 'conquest' that 'stirred in me such exaltation that I sometimes go there, even now, to bring back exaltation and Percival'.[77] In this passage, Bernard describes the vivid but disordered sensations produced in him by the paintings:

> The pressure is intermittent and muffled. I distinguish too little and vaguely. The bell is pressed and I do not ring or give out irrelevant clamours all jangled. I am titillated inordinately by some splendour; the ruffled crimson against the green lining; the march of pillars; the orange light behind the black, pricked ears of the olive trees. Arrows of sensation strike from my spine, but without order.[78]

Bernard's vivid account of his own sensory and emotional response to the paintings, coupled with his repeated emphasis on 'lines and colours' (presented by Woolf in quotation marks), suggests a comparison with the work of the post-impressionist art critics Roger Fry and Clive Bell.[79] In his account of 'significant form' Bell claimed that the 'representative element' in traditional artworks (the 'Venus among her flowers', 'saints and blue madonnas') was 'irrelevant', arguing instead that the formal qualities of art alone, 'lines and colours combined in a particular way, certain forms and relations of forms, stir our aesthetic emotions'.[80] For Bell, 'The relations and combinations of lines and colours, these aesthetically moving forms', produced a uniquely pure and elevated disinterested 'aesthetic emotion'.[81] For Bell, this 'aesthetic emotion' was utterly distinct from our everyday passions, containing the capacity to 'transport[s] us from the world of man's activity to a world of aesthetic exaltation': 'For a moment we are shut off from human interests; our anticipations and memories are arrested; we are lifted above the stream of life.'[82]

For Roger Fry, similarly, as for many modernist poets and writers, the formal features of an artwork could confer on the viewer a special form of 'unity' which was, Fry argued, achieved through the 'balancing of the attractions of the eye about the central line of the picture'.[83] Writing to Fry about the central image in *To the Lighthouse*, Woolf commented that 'One has to have a central

---

[77] Woolf, *The Waves*, p. 123, p. 212.

[78] Woolf, *The Waves*, p. 124.

[79] Woolf, *The Waves*, 124.

[80] Clive Bell, *Art* (London: Chatto & Windus, 1914), p. 25, p. 8.

[81] Bell, *Art*, p. 8.

[82] Bell, *Art*, p. 9.

[83] Roger Fry, 'An Essay in Aesthetics' (1909), in *Vision and Design* (Harmondsworth: Penguin, 1937), p. 35, cited by Kate McLoughlin, 'Woolf's Crotchets: Textual Cryogenics in *To The Lighthouse*', *Textual Practice*, 28.6 (2014), 949–67 (p. 952).

line down the middle of the book to hold the design together'.[84] Responding
to the conclusion of *To the Lighthouse*, in which Lily Briscoe finishes her
painting by drawing 'a line there, in the centre', critics have often appealed to
Fry's formalist criticism to understand Woolf's own statements about 'unity'
in the 'design' of that novel.[85] And yet, despite the tendency to read it as an
'elegy' that, through its unique formal structure, 'laid' the deaths of Woolf's
parents 'to rest', *To the Lighthouse* also challenges both the post-impressionist
ideal of formal 'unity' and the idea of elegy as resolution, implicitly question-
ing the politics, and even the psychic possibility, of such a laying to rest.[86] As
Kate McLoughlin argues, Woolf 'explicitly owned the idea of *broken* unity'
– she described 'Time Passes' as 'entailing a "consequent break of unity in
my design"'.[87] Reading the square brackets in 'Time Passes' as 'unsealed' and
disruptive 'textual crypts', McLoughlin argues that these 'textual crypts' reveal
an 'incomplete interment on the psychic level and, on the technical level, devi-
ation from the post-impressionist desiderata [. . .] of "structural design and
harmony"'.[88]

In a similar way, although Bernard appears to search for an aesthetic
encounter that will buttress him against the ruins of grief, he also hesitates over
the temptation to find a consoling 'unity' in paintings.[89] Sitting in the Italian
room at the National Gallery, Bernard feels that 'something is added to my
interpretation':

---

[84] Woolf, *Letters*, III, p. 385.

[85] Woolf, *To the Lighthouse*, p. 170. On Woolf's engagement with post-impressionist aesthetics, see Jane Goldman, *The Feminist Aesthetics of Virginia Woolf: Modernism, Post
Impressionism, and the Politics of the Visual* (Cambridge: Cambridge University Press,
1998); Goldman, '*To the Lighthouse*'s Use of Form'; Benjamin Harvey, 'Woolf, Fry and
the Psycho-Aesthetics of Solidity', in *Virginia Woolf's Bloomsbury, Volume 1: Aesthetic
Theory and Literary Practice*, ed. by Gina Potts and Lisa Shahriari (Basingstoke: Palgrave
Macmillan, 2010), pp. 104–20.

[86] Reflecting on *To the Lighthouse*, Woolf wrote: 'I used to think of him & mother daily;
but writing The Lighthouse laid them in my mind. And now he comes back sometimes,
but differently. (I believe this to be true—that I was obsessed by them both, unhealthily;
& writing of them was a necessary act.)' In her 'Sketch of the Past', describing again how
'the presence of my mother obsessed me', Woolf wrote: 'I suppose that I did for myself
what psycho-analysts do for their patients. I expressed some very long felt and deeply
felt emotion. And in expressing it I explained it and then laid it to rest.' Woolf, *Diary*, III,
p. 208; Virginia Woolf, 'Sketch of the Past' (1939–40), in *Moments of Being*, ed. by Jeanne
Schulkind, rev. by Hermione Lee (London: Pimlico, 2002), pp. 78–160 (p. 92, p. 93); both
cited by McLoughlin, 'Woolf's Crotchets', p. 952.

[87] Woolf, *Diary*, III, p. 36; cited by McLoughlin, 'Woolf's Crotchets', p. 957, p. 961, my
emphasis.

[88] McLoughlin, 'Woolf's Crotchets', p. 963.

[89] Bell, *Art*, p. 9; Fry, 'An Essay in Aesthetics', p. 35.

Something lies deeply buried. For one moment I thought to grasp it. But bury it, bury it; let it breed, hidden in the depths of my mind some day to fructify. After a long lifetime, loosely, in a moment of revelation, I may lay hands on it, but now the idea breaks in my hand. Ideas break a thousand times for once that they globe themselves entire. They break; they fall over me. 'Line and colours they survive, therefore . . .'[90]

Bernard's reference to a 'moment of revelation' may echo the 'redemption' that Bell explicitly located in aesthetic experience, but Bernard, in contrast to Bell, refuses to seize on the revelatory moment.[91] Sitting in the National Gallery, Bernard insists that 'something' is 'added' to his 'interpretation', that 'Something lies deeply buried', but decides to 'bury it', to 'let it breed, hidden in the depths of my mind some day to fructify'; for 'now', he observes, 'the idea breaks in my hand'.[92]

In this scene, although Bernard echoes the reparative drive of modernist aesthetics, the anticipated 'moment of revelation' is delayed. In place of the triumphant 'moment' so often associated with modernist aesthetics, Bernard describes an encounter with the artwork that is dispersed across time, deferred to an uncertain future. As with Freud's concept of *Nachträglichkeit*, Bernard describes an experience in which the psychic significance of his encounter in the National Gallery is, in Rita Felski's words, 'diffused across a temporal continuum'.[93] As we saw in Chapter 1, in Felski's summary of *Nachträglichkeit*,

> the term names a traumatic event that is registered at a later date when the individual belatedly grasps its import [. . .] Thanks to this time-lag between the occurrence of an event and its resonance, meaning is delayed, washed forward into the future rather than anchored in one defining moment. And even as fragments of past experience persist into the present, their meaning mutates under the pressure of new insight. Retrospection recreates the past even as it retrieves it, in a mutual contamination and commingling of different times.[94]

For Felski, Freud's account of 'afterwardsness' 'speaks directly to the enigmas of textual transmission' – to the fact that 'works bear the imprint of their historical moment, while also accounting for their potential to resonate across time'.[95]

---

[90] Woolf, *The Waves*, p. 124.
[91] Woolf, *The Waves*, p. 124; Bell, *Art*, p. 276.
[92] Woolf, *The Waves*, p. 124.
[93] Felski, *The Uses of Literature*, p. 119.
[94] Felski, *The Uses of Literature*, p. 119.
[95] Felski, *The Uses of Literature*, pp. 119–20.

In Bernard's visit to the National Gallery, he certainly experiences the power of Titian's paintings, but he also describes another enigmatic feature of cultural experience. For Bernard, his encounter with paintings is entangled with his own attempt to work through the trauma of Percival's death, but, although much of Bernard's language suggests a desire for reparation, the anticipated moment of 'revelation' is fractured and deferred. Bernard acknowledges a desire for some future 'revelation', but, for now, he allows the sensations that he experiences to wash over him and fragment, like waves breaking on the shore.

Rhoda and the Echoes of Shelley

When Rhoda learns of Percival's death, she asks: 'Where shall I go then? To some museum [. . .]? There shall I recover beauty, and impose order upon my raked, my dishevelled soul?'[96] Rejecting the quest for 'beauty' and 'order', Rhoda is scornful of Louis, who, she imagines, 'will smooth out the death of Percival to his satisfaction'.[97] Tempted by the consolations of beauty in a stocking shop – 'I could believe that beauty is once more set flowing'; 'Pain is suspended' – Rhoda acknowledges, but also rejects, the urge 'to shelter under the wing of beauty from truth which I desire'.[98] 'I should stand in a queue and smell sweat,' Rhoda announces, 'and scent as horrible as sweat; and be hung with other people like a joint of meat among other joints of meat.'[99] In a scene that is writ large with Rhoda's snobbery about the urban masses, she visits a music hall (in the drafts, this is Wigmore Hall), and listens to 'music among somnolent people who have come here after lunch on a hot afternoon'.[100] Although the scene is laden with Rhoda's disgust for the 'heavy bodies [. . .] gorged with food, torpid in the heat', when the voice of the singer in the operetta erupts, Rhoda feels as though 'An axe has split a tree to the core'.[101] In this passage, Rhoda describes the feelings conveyed by the music in terms that once again echo the formalist writings of Fry and Bell:

> Now that lightning has gashed the tree and the flowering branch has fallen and Percival, by his death, has made me this gift, let me see the thing. There is a square; there is an oblong. The players take the square and place it upon the oblong. They place it very accurately; they make a perfect dwelling-place. Very little is left outside. The structure is now visible; what is inchoate is here stated; we are not so various or so mean; we

96 Woolf, *The Waves*, p. 127.
97 Woolf, *The Waves*, p. 127.
98 Woolf, *The Waves*, p. 126.
99 Woolf, *The Waves*, p. 127.
100 Woolf, *The Waves*, pp. 127–8.
101 Woolf, *The Waves*, p. 128.

have made oblongs and stood them upon squares. This is our triumph; this is our consolation.[102]

For Rhoda, the abstract forms of music serve both as an outlet and as a form of psychic container for her grief, providing 'triumph' and 'consolation':

> The sweetness of this content overflowing runs down the walls of my mind, and liberates understanding. Wander no more, I say; this is the end. The oblong has been set upon the square; the spiral is on top.[103]

But the feeling of relief is short-lived. When the players return, 'mopping their faces', Rhoda resolves to leave the music hall and to 'make a pilgrimage'.[104]

Taking a penny bunch of violets, Rhoda goes to Greenwich and makes an 'offering' to Percival, casting her violets into the Thames where the ships sail (significantly, given Percival's colonial death) 'to India': 'Into the wave that dashes upon the shore, into the wave that flings its white foam to the utter-most corners of the earth, I throw my violets, my offering to Percival.'[105] In the drafts, Rhoda describes this as 'my funeral service', 'my ceremony, my dirge'.[106] Despite Rhoda's scorn for a redemptive poetics, her childhood experience of reading Shelley returns, in this scene and in others, to echo in Rhoda's mind as she performs her mourning ritual. In the scene that I discussed in Chapter 1, Rhoda reads Shelley's poem 'The Question' in the school library. Reading Shelley as a child, Rhoda feels a '*check* in the flow of my being', a 'deep stream presses on some obstacle; it *jerks*; it tugs; some knot in the centre resists'.[107] As an adult mourning the death of her friend, Rhoda feels that resistance give way, announcing that 'Now I will at last free the *checked*, the *jerked-back* desire to be spent, to be consumed'.[108] The garland of flowers from Shelley's poem is transformed, in this passage, into the bunch of violets that Rhoda presents as her 'offering' to Percival. Later in life, reflecting on Percival's death, Rhoda recalls how she 'threw my bunch into the spreading wave', and observes: 'I seldom think of Percival now.'[109] And yet, although she may not consciously think about Percival, the lines from 'The Question' resurface again as Rhoda imagines launching herself 'over the precipice' into the waves with 'Flowers

[102] Woolf, *The Waves*, pp. 128–9.
[103] Woolf, *The Waves*, p. 129.
[104] Woolf, *The Waves*, p. 129.
[105] Woolf, *The Waves*, p. 130.
[106] Woolf, *The Waves: The Two Holograph Drafts*, p. 258, p. 259.
[107] Woolf, *The Waves*, p. 43, my emphasis.
[108] Woolf, *The Waves*, p. 130, my emphasis.
[109] Woolf, *The Waves*, p. 164.

only, the cowbind and the moonlight-coloured May': 'Gathering them loosely in a sheaf I made of them a garland and gave them—Oh, to whom?'[110] In the drafts, the earlier scene of reading is explicitly recalled here as a memory: 'I remembered leaning on my elbow [. . .] at school [. . .] & saying I would pick flowers & give them—O to whom?'[111] In the final text, however, the repetitions of the childhood scene of reading are woven seamlessly into the text, suggesting something closer to the work of Proustian involuntary memory than conscious recall. The lines from Shelley accompany Rhoda throughout her life, returning across time, edging in and out of consciousness, and acquiring deferred significance as part of her negotiation with the very idea of turning to art for consolation in the face of death.

Rhoda explicitly rejects the lures of consolation in the aftermath of Percival's death, but Woolf's representation of her encounters with Shelley enacts an alternative to the evasive tendencies of the culture of redemption. Both Bernard's and Rhoda's encounters with art and with poetry are subject to the temporal logic of afterwardsness, in which cultural experience alters and takes on a changed and shifting significance over time. For both of these characters, their attempts at mourning are bound up with their encounters with art and with poetry, but these cultural encounters are non-linear, unfinished, ongoing, refusing the refuge of aesthetic redemption.

NEVILLE AND THE FANTASY OF SCHOLARLY REFUGE

In *The Waves*, Woolf's quarrel with the culture of redemption appears not only in the scenes of mourning for Percival, but also in her characterisation of the male poet and scholar's fantasy of literature as a refuge from the horrors of modernity. In the portraits of Neville as a schoolboy and university student, Woolf offers a vivid picture of the psychic life of an aspiring male scholar, revealing how the idea of literature as a refuge intersected with powerful fantasies about literature as a buttress of masculine upper-class authority. As a schoolboy, Neville reads 'Catullus in a third-class railway carriage', while imagining his destiny as a university 'don':[112]

> Now I pretend again to read. I raise my book, till it almost covers my eyes. But I cannot read in the presence of horse-dealers and plumbers. I have no power of ingratiating myself. I do not admire that man; he does not admire me. Let me at least be honest. Let me denounce this piffling, trifling, self-satisfied world; these horse-hair seats; these coloured photographs of piers and parades. I could shriek aloud at the smug self-satisfaction, at

[110] Woolf, *The Waves*, p. 165.
[111] Woolf, *The Waves: The Two Holograph Drafts*, p. 318.
[112] Woolf, *The Waves*, p. 54, p. 55.

the mediocrity of this world, which breeds horse-dealers with coral ornaments hanging from their watch-chains. There is that in me which will consume them entirely. My laughter shall make them twist in their seats; shall drive them howling before me. No; they are immortal. They triumph. They will make it impossible for me always to read Catullus in a third-class railway carriage. They will drive me in October to take refuge in one of the universities, where I shall become a don; and go with schoolmasters to Greece and lecture on the ruins of the Parthenon. It would be better to breed horses and live in one of those red villas than to run in and out of the skulls of Sophocles and Euripides like a maggot, with a high-minded wife, one of those University women.[113]

In this portrait of Neville, Woolf reveals the violent class prejudice that underpins his fantasy of scholarly life. Opposing his own act of reading Catullus to the cultural trappings of working-class life, Neville seeks to transcend the 'mediocrity' of the third-class railway carriage through his commitment to Latin poetry. Acknowledging that he is driven both by a fear and by an envy of the working-class men he claims to 'denounce', Neville participates in a characteristically modernist romanticising of the 'immortal' working-class man even as he reiterates Woolf's own often-expressed snobbery about 'those red villas'.[114] Blaming the 'horse-dealers and plumbers' for making it 'impossible for me always to read Catullus in a third-class railway carriage' and for 'driv[ing]' him 'to take refuge in one of the universities', Neville nonetheless expresses a profound ambivalence about his destined role as a university scholar, who, he imagines, weaves his way in and out of the texts of Sophocles and Euripides like a maggot through their skulls, or – as Woolf put it in a draft – a 'master of the dead'.[115]

At university, Neville advocates an impersonal and disinterested scholarly approach to literary texts, articulating a typical scholarly distrust of identification and personal emotion. Picking up Bernard's copy of Byron's poems, Neville is scornful of Bernard's tendency to identify with the heroes of Romantic poetry:

You have been reading Byron. You have been marking the passages that seem to approve of your own character. I find marks against all those sentences which seem to express a sardonic yet passionate nature [. . .] You thought, as you drew your pencil there, 'I too throw off my cloak like that, I too snap my fingers in the face of destiny.'[116]

---

[113] Woolf, *The Waves*, pp. 54–5.

[114] On Woolf's attitude to suburban 'red villas', see Clara Jones, 'Virginia Woolf and "The Villa Jones" (1931)', *Virginia Woolf Studies Annual*, 22 (2016), 75–95.

[115] Woolf, *The Waves: The Two Holograph Drafts*, p. 492.

[116] Woolf, *The Waves*, pp. 67–8.

Neville, in contrast, claims 'I am one person—myself. I do not impersonate Catullus, whom I adore.'[117] Following his rebuke of Bernard for identifying with Byron, Neville continues:

> I am the most slavish of students, with here a dictionary, there a note-book in which I enter curious uses of the past participle. But one cannot go on for ever cutting these ancient inscriptions clearer with a knife. Shall I always draw the red serge curtain close and see my book, laid like a block of marble, pale under the lamp? That would be a glorious life, to addict oneself to perfection; to follow the curve of the sentence wherever it might lead, into deserts, under drifts of sand, regardless of lures, or seductions; to be poor always and unkempt; to be ridiculous in Piccadilly.
>   [. . .] I hate your greasy handkerchiefs—you will stain your copy of *Don Juan*.[118]

Not only does Neville's attempt at 'slavish' scholarship suggest his subscription to a 'critical attitude' that, as Woolf argued elsewhere, 'pinches the mind', his refusal to identify with the objects of his study also echoes the dominant schol-arly 'prohibition' on personal emotions that characterised (in different ways) the neo-Kantian formalism of the art critics Roger Fry and Clive Bell, the liter-ary criticism of T. S. Eliot, and the more institutionalised forms of close reading developed by I. A. Richards and the Scrutineers.[119] For these formalist critics, as we saw in Chapters 1 and 2 of this book, the taboo on the reader's emotional life formed part of an attempt to banish the feminised affective dimensions of literary experience in favour of a form of mature and masculine scholarly mastery. For Neville too, in these scenes, the posture of critical disinterest is tethered to a form of reading that elevates the reader into a position of schol-arly mastery.

And yet, although Neville may imitate the scholar's refusal to 'impersonate' Catullus, the language with which Neville describes scholarly life is saturated with an erotic drive. Although he presents an image of classical literary study as a process of patient sculpting ('cutting these ancient inscriptions clearer with a knife'), Neville also relishes the intense pleasures of solitary scholarly study, imagining the 'glorious life' of the scholar, who, he fantasises, is granted the

---

[117] Woolf, *The Waves*, p. 68.

[118] Woolf, *The Waves*, p. 68.

[119] '"Anon" and "The Reader": Virginia Woolf's Last Essays', ed. by Brenda Silver, *Twentieth Century Literature*, 25.3/4 (Autumn–Winter 1979), 356–441 (pp. 433–4). On Woolf's hostility to the institutionalisation of English studies in universities, see Cuddy-Keane, *Virginia Woolf*, pp. 68–75.

licence to 'addict' himself 'to perfection' and to follow the 'curve of the sentence' as a displaced substitute for the 'lures' and 'seductions' of more fleshly curves. Later in the novel, Neville describes his own investment in books as driven by a desire to 'oppose the waste and deformity of the world, its crowds eddying round and round disgorged and trampling'.[120] In this passage, Neville describes the act of reading as part of a quest to counter the 'horror and deformity' of mass modernity with the 'perfection' of classical poetry, but he also explicitly renounces his earlier posture of scholarly disinterest:

> One must slip paper-knives, even, exactly through the pages of novels, and tie up packets of letters neatly with green silk, and brush up the cinders with a hearth broom. Everything must be done to rebuke the horror of deformity. Let us read writers of Roman severity and virtue; let us seek perfection through the sand. Yes, but I love to slip the virtue and severity of the noble Romans under the grey light of your eyes, and dancing grasses and summer breezes and the laughter and shouts of boys at play—of naked cabin-boys squirting each other with hose-pipes on the decks of ships. Hence I am not a disinterested seeker, like Louis, after perfection through the sand. Colours always stain the page; clouds pass over it. And the poem, I think, is only your voice speaking. Alcibiades, Ajax, Hector and Percival are also you. They loved riding, they risked their lives wantonly, they were not great readers either.[121]

'[S]lip[ping] the virtue and severity of the noble Romans under the grey light' of his lover's eyes, Neville also 'slip[s]' the 'severity' of the critical taboo on personal emotions, identifying the voice of the poem with the voice of his lover and acknowledging that he is not the 'disinterested seeker' idealised by the critics. Allowing the 'colours' of personal experience to 'stain the page', Neville also identifies his lover with 'Alcibiades, Ajax, Hector and Percival', and reveals the entanglement of his reading practices with what he acknowledges, later in the passage, as his quest for something to 'console' him 'for the lack of many things', including 'the depravity of the world, and the flight of youth and Percival's death'.[122] In one of the drafts of this passage, the blurring between the real and the fictional that takes place when Neville identifies his lover with the heroes of ancient epics and with his dead friend Percival is rendered more explicitly: Alcibiades, Hector and Percival are imagined to have 'shared your taste for golf, & risked their lives wantonly flying the Channel in a fog; &

---

[120] Woolf, *The Waves*, pp. 143–4.
[121] Woolf, *The Waves*, p. 144.
[122] Woolf, *The Waves*, p. 144.

were in the trenches in France'.[123] This image of Percival alongside the classical heroes highlights his position as a semi-mythical figure, but the anachronistic and bathetic image of the heroes from ancient Greece playing golf, flying aeroplanes and fighting in the trenches of the First World War also underscores Woolf's suspicion of the role classical texts were put to as mediators of a military masculinity. In all of these scenes, Neville's claim to scholarly disinterest is revealed as a masquerade: his acts of reading are coloured both by personal desires and longings (the voice of his lover, the memory of his dead friend, 'the shouts of boys at play') and by a fragile but nonetheless (and perhaps, on the basis of its fragility, all the more) tenacious fantasy of literature as a retreat. For Neville, in these portraits, the ideal of scholarly disinterest appears as a kind of screen, covering up a powerful and intersecting set of fantasies about literature as a source of upper-class masculine authority, and as a form of psychic refuge from the 'horror and deformity' of modernity.

LOUIS AND THE 'BINDING POWER' OF POETRY

In her influential essay on *The Waves* and imperialism, Jane Marcus argued that the male characters' repeated allusions to poetry reveal the ways that imperialist, and later fascist, masculinity buttressed itself through the writing and reading of poetry. For Marcus, *The Waves* is not only 'about the ideology of white British colonialism', but also 'the Romantic literature that sustains it'.[124] In Marcus's argument, *The Waves* exposes the 'complicity' of the poet – and, implicitly, the reader – 'in the creation of a collective national subject through an elegy for imperialism':

> The Western valorization of individual selfhood is marked by Woolf in her exhaustion of the form of the soliloquy, and the notion of individual literary genius is disposed of by an overdetermined intertextuality with Romantic poetry, which [. . .] demonstrates how powerful certain phrases and images are in the invocation of patriotism and nationalist claims for English 'genius'.[125]

In *The Waves*, the scenes of reading at the boys' public school and at the university not only reveal the extent to which these patriarchal institutions enlisted literature as a buttress of upper-class masculine authority, they also echo and anticipate Woolf's more explicit institutional critiques of the intimate connections between patriarchal group politics, imperialism and latent fascism. In a 1926 review of the letters of Sir Walter Raleigh, 'one of the best Professors

---

[123] Woolf, *The Waves: The Two Holograph Drafts*, p. 604.
[124] Marcus, 'Britannia Rules', p. 65.
[125] Marcus, 'Britannia Rules', p. 63, p. 66.

of Literature of our time', Woolf was scathing in her analysis of the entanglement between university English, empire and militarism, damning Raleigh's
tendency to use the lecture theatre to preach a love of 'the British Empire', not
literature.[126] For Woolf, as she put it in another essay, the university lecture
theatre was a platform that gave rise to 'the most debased of human passions—
vanity, ostentation, self-assertion, and the desire to convert'.[127] Citing Raleigh's
misogynistic claim that 'critical admiration' is 'an emotion for spinsters', Woolf
highlighted his insistence on 'some close connection between writing and fighting': 'When the guns fired in August 1914,' Woolf wrote bitingly, 'no one
saluted them more rapturously than the Professor of English at Oxford.'[128] In
A Room of One's Own, Woolf referred again to Raleigh's letters, imagining
'an age to come of pure, of self-assertive virility, such as the letters of professors [. . .] seem to forebode, and the rulers of Italy have already brought into
being'.[129] For Woolf, there was a direct link between the 'self-assertive virility' of Raleigh's imperialist lectures on English literature and the 'unmitigated
masculinity' of Italian fascism.[130] By the time that she came to publish *Three
Guineas*, in 1938, Woolf would argue that the forms of masculine authority
enshrined in the 'vain and vicious system' of university lecturing were part of a
patriarchal system that not only shaped British imperialism, but also contained
the latent 'germ' of home-grown fascism.[131]

In *The Waves*, in the portraits of Louis reading, Woolf explores the overlapping connections between his fantasy of literature as a buttress of masculine
authority, his longing for a form of psychic retreat, and his desire for forms of
communal belonging. In Louis's soliloquies on reading, the desire for refuge is
entangled with a powerful fantasy of literature not only as a source of imperialist patriarchal authority, but also as a repository of communal belonging – a
form of communal belonging that is, however, troublingly overshadowed by
the oceanic fantasies that would, as Jessica Berman has shown, increasingly
come to govern an age of looming fascism in Britain and Europe.[132]

Louis has long been recognised as one of Woolf's most acute examinations
of the psychological mechanisms of imperialism: as David Bradshaw has written, 'all the characters in *The Waves* are either card-carrying, acquiescent or
novice colonialists', but 'it is above all Louis' who appears as the most vocal

---

[126] Virginia Woolf, 'A Professor of Life' (1926), in *Essays*, IV, pp. 342–8 (p. 344).

[127] Virginia Woolf, 'Why?' (1934), in *Essays*, VI, pp. 30–6 (p. 33).

[128] Woolf, *Essays*, IV, p. 345, p. 346.

[129] Virginia Woolf, *A Room of One's Own* (1929), in *A Room of One's Own and Three Guineas*, p. 77.

[130] Woolf, *A Room of One's Own*, p. 77.

[131] Woolf, *Three Guineas*, p. 121, pp. 226–7, n. 30.

[132] Berman, *Modernist Fiction*, p. 140.

imperialist.[133] Although Louis identifies as an outsider, his feelings of marginali-
sation as an Australian subject lead him to take up a position running a colonial enterprise in London. Throughout the novel, Louis's feelings of exclusion
propel his repeatedly reiterated quest to find feelings of belonging and authority through the act of reading. Perpetually troubled by his colonial roots, Louis
is envious of the other boys' ascent to the universities, while he is destined to
'make money', to 'consort with cockneys and clerks, and tap the pavements of
the city'.[134] At public school, Louis 'rejoice[s]' in the 'orderly progress' of the
chapel services, taking pleasure in submitting himself to the words of authority
as his headmaster reads from the Bible: 'my heart expands in his bulk, in his
authority.'[135] Recalling a painful experience of childhood exclusion, Louis feels
it swallowed up and patched over in subservience to the headmaster's words:

> Now all is laid by his authority, his crucifix, and I feel come down over
> me the sense of the earth under me, and my roots going down and down
> till they wrap themselves round some hardness at the centre. I recover
> my continuity, as he reads. I become a figure in the procession, a spoke
> in the huge wheel that turning, at last erects me, here and now.[136]

Reading, or, in this case, being read to, embeds Louis's fragile sense of identity,
but what might at first appear as a benign scene of reparation takes on ominous
tones as Louis finds himself absorbed into the 'procession' as a mere 'spoke' in
the 'huge wheel' of patriarchal tradition.

In his soliloquies, Louis repeatedly describes an endeavour to turn fragmented experience into something that will 'endure': 'From discord, from
hatred,' he observes, 'my shattered mind is pieced together by some sudden perception.'[137] But these moments of reparation are repeatedly crushed, and Louis
finds himself subject to bitter fragmentation. Watching the schoolboys 'forming
into fours and marching in troops', saluting their 'general', Louis is enraptured:
'How majestic is their order, how beautiful their obedience! If I could follow, if
I could be with them, I would sacrifice all I know.'[138] Louis acknowledges the
violence of the schoolboy 'troops' (they 'leave butterflies trembling with their
wings pinched off; they throw dirty pocket-handkerchiefs clotted with blood
screwed up into corners. They make little boys sob in dark passages'), but

---

[133] David Bradshaw, 'Beneath *The Waves*: Diffusionism and Cultural Pessimism', *Essays in Criticism*, 63.3 (2013), 317–43 (p. 332, p. 334). See also Phillips, *Virginia Woolf Against Empire*, p. 153.
[134] Woolf, *The Waves*, pp. 50–1.
[135] Woolf, *The Waves*, pp. 25–6.
[136] Woolf, *The Waves*, p. 26.
[137] Woolf, *The Waves*, p. 29.
[138] Woolf, *The Waves*, p. 35.

still he persists in his admiration, finding himself on the outside, violently torn with envy, excluded, yet longing to join the herd.[139] Excluded from the kind of patriarchal group formation that, in *Three Guineas*, Woolf would diagnose as a source of latent fascism, Louis turns instead to literature – literature becomes a repository for his displaced desire to form part of the militant 'troop' of schoolboys:

> As I stand here with my hand on the grained oak panel of Mr. Wick-ham's door I think myself the friend of Richelieu, or the Duke of St. Simon holding out a snuff-box to the King himself [. . .] My witticisms 'run like wildfire through the court.' Duchesses tear emeralds from their ear-rings out of admiration—but these rockets rise best in darkness, in my cubicle at night. I am now a boy only with a colonial accent holding my knuckles against Mr. Wickham's grained oak door.[140]

The fantasy of belonging to the French aristocracy is rendered fragile by Louis's awareness of his 'colonial accent'; 'But when the darkness comes', he adds, 'I put off this unenviable body—my large nose, my thin lips, my colonial accent—and inhabit space. I am then Virgil's companion and Plato's.'[141]

At the final school assembly, the headmaster hands out 'bound volumes' of 'Horace, Tennyson, the complete works of Keats and Matthew Arnold'.[142] Louis comments on the divisions that life will impose on the boys; 'But', he insists, 'we have formed certain ties':

> Above all, we have inherited traditions. [. . .] On these walls are inscribed the names of men of war, of statesmen, of some unhappy poets (mine shall be among them). Blessings be on all traditions, on all safeguards and circumscriptions! I am most grateful to you men in black gowns, and you dead, for your leading, for your guardianship.[143]

Louis's repeated emphasis on 'tradition' evokes T. S. Eliot's insistence on 'tradition' as that 'which compels a man to write not merely with his own generation in his bones, but with a feeling that the whole of the literature of Europe from Homer [. . .] has a simultaneous existence and composes a simultaneous order'.[144] Louis articulates his desire to form a part of this 'tradition', and his

---

[139] Woolf, *The Waves*, pp. 35–6.
[140] Woolf, *The Waves*, p. 40.
[141] Woolf, *The Waves*, p. 40.
[142] Woolf, *The Waves*, p. 44.
[143] Woolf, *The Waves*, pp. 44–5.
[144] T. S. Eliot, 'Tradition and the Individual Talent' (1919), in *Selected Prose of T. S. Eliot*, pp. 37–44 (p. 38).

references to the 'dead' and to dead poets also echo Eliot's famous assertion that 'No poet [. . .] has his complete meaning alone. His significance, his appreciation is the appreciation of his relation to the dead poets and artists.'[145] But Louis's awestruck subservience not only to the 'unhappy' poets, but also to 'men of war', 'statesmen', 'men in gowns' and the 'dead', alongside his gratitude for their 'leading', also suggests the complicity of this vision with an oppressively patriarchal and militaristic political tradition.

In an early draft, Woolf described Louis, at school, with a 'plain little book', a 'grammar of the Latin language'.[146] 'Thereby', Woolf writes,

> he associated with Horace & Lucretius He was introduced associated to an august soul. [. . .] leaving his body, in its jacket & collar on the bench he ascended into [. . .] a cavernous region, very clear & black, like the polished ice over a mountain tarn [. . .] His body & jacket dissolved. His mind knew no confines. He was disembodied, expanded,) commensurate with the whole air.[147]

The school bell interrupts Louis's reverie and he is snapped back to the school dining room. But Woolf continues: 'Loneliness had these alcoves, these islands, hollowed out' where 'some of the children withdrew', 'the soul crept away' and found 'communion' with 'Rome or Greece'.[148]

It is tempting to read this seductive account of 'communion' with the writers of the past as a celebration not only of the pleasures of reading, but also of a type of reading that is participatory, communal and – potentially – democratic. In an early journal entry, Virginia Stephen, aged twenty-one, articulated her own pleasure in reading in similar terms:

> I read some history [. . .] I think I see for a moment how our minds are all threaded together—how any live mind today is of the very same stuff as Plato's & Euripides. [. . .] It is this common mind that binds the whole world together; & all the world is mind. Then I read a poem say—& the same thing is repeated. I feel as though I had grasped the central meaning of the world, & all these poets & historians & philosophers were only following out paths branching from that centre in which I stand.[149]

[145] Eliot, 'Tradition and the Individual Talent', p. 38.
[146] Woolf, *The Waves: The Two Holograph Drafts*, 'Draft 1', p. 24.
[147] Woolf, *The Waves: The Two Holograph Drafts*, 'Draft 1', p. 24.
[148] Woolf, *The Waves: The Two Holograph Drafts*, 'Draft 1', p. 24.
[149] Virginia Woolf, *A Passionate Apprentice: The Early Journals 1897–1909*, ed. by Mitchell A. Leaska (London: Hogarth Press, 1990), pp. 178–9. On this journal entry, see Brenda Silver, 'Cultural Critique', in *The Gender of Modernism: A Critical Anthology*, ed. by Bonnie Kime Scott (Indianapolis: Indiana University Press, 1990), pp. 646–58 (p. 648).

In the draft of *The Waves*, the description of Louis's 'communion' with the writers of the past both echoes Virginia Stephen's image of the 'common mind' and anticipates her later, political, insistence on the democratic 'common ground' of literature. And yet, in *The Waves*, Louis's vision of literature as a possible source of communal feeling is also bound up in troubling ways with fantasies of communal submission to authority that are far from democratic.

Sitting in a London eating-house while trying to read his book, Louis remains, as an adult, painfully aware of his position as an outsider:

> A meaty, vapourish smell of beef and mutton, sausages and mash, hangs down like a damp net in the middle of the eating-house. I prop my book against a bottle of Worcester sauce and try to look like the rest.
>
> Yet I cannot. (They go on passing, they go on passing in disorderly procession.) I cannot read my book, or order my beef, with conviction. I repeat, 'I am an average Englishman; I am an average clerk', yet I look at the little men at the next table to be sure that I do what they do.[150]

Louis describes the 'rhythm of the eating-house' in terms that echo *The Waste Land*: for Louis, as for Eliot, the demotic voices of 'average men' ('I would take a tenner; for it blocks up the hall') combine with the rhythms of the waitresses to produce an effect 'like a waltz tune, eddying in and out, round and round'.[151] 'The circle', Louis claims, 'is unbroken; the harmony complete', but although he observes the 'central rhythm', Louis himself feels shut out from 'the common mainspring' by people who, upon overhearing his attempts to imitate 'their accent', 'prick their ears, waiting for me to speak again, in order that they may place me—if I come from Canada or Australia'.[152] Feeling 'alien, external', Louis makes a renewed effort to focus on his book:

> I will read in the book that is propped against the bottle of Worcester sauce. It contains some forged rings, some perfect statements, a few words, but poetry. You, all of you, ignore it. What the dead poet said, you have forgotten. And I cannot translate it to you so that its binding power ropes you in, and makes it clear to you that you are aimless; and the rhythm is cheap and worthless; and so remove that degradation which, if you are unaware of your aimlessness, pervades you, making you senile, even while you are young. To translate that poem so that it is easily read is to be my endeavour. I, the companion of Plato, of Virgil, will knock at the grained oak door. I oppose to what is passing this ramrod

---

[150] Woolf, *The Waves*, p. 72.
[151] Woolf, *The Waves*, p. 73.
[152] Woolf, *The Waves*, p. 75.

of beaten steel. I will not submit to this aimless passing of billycock hats and Homburg hats and all the plumed and variegated head-dresses of women. [. . .] And the grinding and the steam that runs in unequal drops down the window pane; and the stopping and the starting with a jerk of motor-omnibuses; and the hesitations at counters; and the words that trail drearily without human meaning; I will reduce you to order.[153]

In Louis's meditation on the 'binding power' of poetry, we find Woolf pressing at a series of questions concerning the possibilities, limitations, violence and exclusions of this fantasy of unity in art. Louis's appeal to the 'dead poet', whose words the denizens of the eating-house have 'forgotten', once again recalls Eliot's insistence on the individual's relation to the 'dead poets' as a means of participating in 'tradition'.[154] But the violent imagery of a form of poetry that aspires to a 'binding power' that 'ropes you in' with its 'forged rings' – a 'ramrod of beaten steel' that will put a halt to the transience of modernity – places a question mark over this fantasy of tradition as a form of communion with the poets. Despite his endeavour to 'translate that poem' so that it is 'easily read', Louis foregrounds the question not only of who is and who is not roped in, or 'bound', by this scene of reading, but also of whether such a binding is itself desirable. We might interpret Louis's wish to translate the poem into something that is 'easily read' as a democratic desire to make his poet accessible to the waitresses and 'average men' – in the drafts, this is rendered as an 'endeavour' to 'translate the Greek so that it is available to clerks in city restaurants'.[155] But this is in order to rope them in, to make it clear to them that they are 'aimless' and degraded, to 'reduce [them] to order'. This is neither a fantasy of making culture accessible to the common reader, nor a radical claim for the democratic 'common ground' of literature. It is a fantasy of using culture to control and bind the unruly masses.

Later, as he signs documents for an unspecified colonial enterprise, Louis invokes his identification with the poets and the philosophers that he read at school: 'I, now a duke, now Plato, companion of Socrates', but his signed name also encompasses 'the tramp of dark men and yellow men migrating east, west, north and south; the eternal procession, women going with attaché cases down the Strand as they went once with pitchers to the Nile'.[156] 'All the furled and close-packed leaves of my many-folded life are', Louis claims, 'now summed in my name.'[157] Taking up an attitude of self-sacrificing commitment to the

---

[153] Woolf, *The Waves*, p. 74.
[154] Eliot, 'Tradition and the Individual Talent', p. 38.
[155] Woolf, *The Waves: The Two Holograph Drafts*, p. 499.
[156] Woolf, *The Waves*, p. 133.
[157] Woolf, *The Waves*, p. 133.

project of imperial expansion, Louis postures: 'My shoulder is to the wheel; I roll the dark before me, spreading commerce where there was chaos, in the far parts of the world. If I press on, from chaos making order, I shall find myself where Chatham stood, and Pitt, Burke and Sir Robert Peel.'[158] Turning back to his experience of 'read[ing] my poet in an eating-house', Louis roots this fantasy of imperial patriarchal authority in the scene of reading:

> I have read my poet in an eating-house, and, stirring my coffee, listened to the clerks making bets at the little tables, watched the women hesitating at the counter. I said that nothing should be irrelevant [. . .] I said their journeys should have an end in view; they should earn their two pound ten a week at the command of an august master; some hand, some robe, should fold us about in the evening. When I have healed these fractures and comprehended these monstrosities [. . .] I shall give back to the street and the eating-shop what they lost when they fell on these hard times and broke on these stony beaches. I shall assemble a few words and forge round us a hammered ring of beaten steel.[159]

Louis's determination to 'give back' what has been 'lost when they fell on these hard times' may at first appear as a democratic expression of community at a time of economic hardship, but this is once again undermined both by Louis's disdain for the working classes and by his fantasy of group submission to 'the command of an august master'. Although Louis's fantasies of aesthetic communion may appear seductive, his wish that 'some hand, some robe, should fold us about in the evening' once again reveals his desire for collective submission to authority. In his reiterated longing for a form of poetry that will 'forge round us a hammered ring of beaten steel', Louis's idea of poetry as a repository of communal feeling appears troublingly bound up in the fantasies of communal surrender to authority that, increasingly in the early 1930s, came to dominate British and European politics.

In these reflections on the 'binding power' of poetry, Louis traverses the knife edge that, as Gabrielle McIntire has demonstrated, appears repeatedly in *The Waves* between, on the one hand, the communal vision of 'mystical interpenetration and "oceanic" oneness', and, on the other hand, the 'oneness of the State that fascism demanded'.[160] Although Louis's fantasies of literature as a source of communal feeling resonate with the novel's more pervasive fascination with states of blissful oceanic oneness, they also bear a troubling resemblance with the fantasies of oneness that dominated the fascist rhetoric of the 1930s.

[158] Woolf, *The Waves*, p. 134.
[159] Woolf, *The Waves*, p. 134.
[160] McIntire, 'Heteroglossia', p. 42.

The Waves is permeated by the forms of 'symbiosis and oceanic feeling' that, as Alice Kaplan has observed, are produced in the 'rhythms' and 'intonations' of 'fascism's "gathering" stages'.[161] And yet, as Jessica Berman argues,

> even as *The Waves* expresses an oceanic feeling, desire for wholeness, and pressure for international community like that which pervades the proto-fascist rhetoric of [Oswald] Mosley's New Party (as well as much twentieth-century neo-conservative and fascist literature), *The Waves* specifically confronts the limitations of this political and literary discourse.[162]

In her portraits of Louis reading, Woolf dramatises and exposes the violence at work in his fantasy of poetry as a site of communal wholeness. By staging scenes in which readers find themselves enchanted with fantasies of communal belonging, Woolf signals the deep attractions of her own writing, while also cautioning her readers to be wary of such fantasies of aesthetic belonging. In these scenes, Woolf not only explores the negative aspects of the dominant fantasies that surrounded the scene of reading in the early 1930s, but also seeks to imagine and to enact modernist alternatives to the fascist appropriation of aesthetic communality. And yet, although *The Waves* seeks to imagine an alternative modernist scene of reading, the novel also explores its own ambivalent and troubled relationship to the dangers of literary identification at a time of rising fascism.

Projected Readers

In a scene that I quoted at the beginning of this book, Neville describes an immersive and intimate experience of reading poetry:

> I go to the book-case. If I choose, I read half a page of anything. I need not speak. But I listen. I am marvellously on the alert. Certainly, one cannot read this poem without effort. The page is often corrupt and mud-stained, and torn and stuck together with faded leaves, with scraps of verbena or geranium. To read this poem one must have myriad eyes, like one of those lamps that turn on slabs of racing water at midnight in the Atlantic, when perhaps only a spray of seaweed pricks the surface, or suddenly the waves gape and up shoulders a monster. One must put aside antipathies and jealousies and not interrupt. One must have patience and infinite care and let the light sound, whether of spiders' delicate feet on a leaf or the chuckle of water in some irrelevant drainpipe, unfold too.

[161] Kaplan, *Reproductions of Banality*, p. 13, cited by Berman, *Modernist Fiction*, p. 139.
[162] Berman, *Modernist Fiction*, p. 140.

Nothing is to be rejected in fear or horror. The poet who has written this page (what I read with people talking) has withdrawn. There are no commas or semicolons. The lines do not run in convenient lengths. Much is sheer nonsense. One must be sceptical, but throw caution to the winds and when the door opens accept absolutely. Also sometimes weep; also cut away ruthlessly with a slice of the blade soot, bark, hard accretions of all sorts. And so (while they talk) let down one's net deeper and deeper and gently draw in and bring to the surface what he said and she said and make poetry.[163]

Neville describes an immersive, intimate, and yet anxious, reading experience. He may read 'half a page of anything', but, as I argued in the introduction, Neville's description of the difficulties of reading 'this poem' reverberates with a distinctly modernist experience of reading. A modernist aesthetics of impersonality leaves the reader unmoored. 'The poet' – like the narrator of this, Woolf's most elusive and impersonal novel – 'has withdrawn'. There are, in this poem, as in many a modernist poem written in free verse, 'no commas or semicolons', and 'The lines do not run in convenient lengths'. 'Much is', as modernism's detractors repeatedly claimed, 'sheer nonsense.'[164]

In this scene, Neville describes an anxious attitude of hyper-alertness, marked in the short, sharp imperatives interspersed amongst long, fluid sentences. The reader 'must' 'have patience', take 'care', 'be sceptical'; he 'must put aside antipathies and jealousies'. As we have seen in this chapter, Neville, initially, prides himself on his impersonal, scholarly approach to literary texts, subscribing to many of the dictates of early-twentieth-century literary criticism. Like I. A. Richards, who outlined the need for readers to be vigilant, wary of 'erratic associations' and the 'interference of emotional reverberations from a past which may have nothing to do with the poem', Neville describes an attempt to 'put aside' personal feelings which, like those disruptive 'emotional reverberations', threaten to 'interrupt'.[165] Describing the scene of reading as a site of struggle, in which analytic cautiousness competes with surging emotional currents, Neville echoes the pioneers of a form of 'close reading' that, as Isobel Armstrong has argued, was founded, at least in part, as an attempt to contain feminine affect with masculine reason.[166] And yet, although Neville may echo the scholar's endeavour to regulate the emotional and psychic disturbances produced by reading poetry,

---

[163] Woolf, *The Waves*, pp. 158–9.

[164] On modernism, difficulty and 'nonsense', see Diepeveen, *The Difficulties of Modernism*, p. 14, p. 47.

[165] Richards, *Practical Criticism*, p. 23; Woolf, *The Waves*, p. 158, p. 159.

[166] Armstrong, *The Radical Aesthetic*, pp. 88–9.

he also performs a departure both from the strictures of close reading and from the dynamics of mastery that Woolf, like Armstrong, viewed as endemic to the institutions of literary studies.

For Neville, the unpunctuated and irregular lines of the poem that he reads produce an experience that is at once arduous, immersive and disorientating, much like the 'dizzy[ing]' experience that Woolf described in her 1924 account of T. S. Eliot's poetry:

> As I sun myself upon the intense and ravishing beauty of one of his lines, and reflect that I must make a dizzy and dangerous leap to the next, and so on from line to line, like an acrobat flying precariously from bar to bar, I cry out, I confess, for the old decorums, and envy the indolence of my ancestors who, instead of spinning madly through mid-air, dreamt quietly in the shade with a book.[167]

While Woolf's metaphor of reading as acrobatics conveys the non-linear mental leaps required by the reader of *The Waste Land*, who must attempt to hold the poem's multiply connecting fragments together simultaneously in her mind, Neville similarly evokes the demand made by modernist poetry on the reader to have 'myriad eyes'.[168] For Neville, the rush of images, ideas and feelings that dart past the reader are hard to grasp. The experience of reading is compared to a lamp turning on 'slabs of racing water', suggesting that the images, affects and meanings of the poem are, for the most part, submerged, popping up perhaps only fleetingly like 'the spray of seaweed' that 'pricks the surface', but at other times surging forth violently, as when 'suddenly the waves gape and up shoulders a monster'.[169] The poem, like Woolf's novel, demands 'patience and infinite care', because features that might in another context appear to be insignificant 'nonsense' – like 'the light sound, whether of spiders' delicate feet on a leaf or the chuckle of water in some irrelevant drainpipe' (both of which sound like images from Eliot's early poetry) – are nonetheless crucial to an experience of poetry as a process of 'unfold[ing]' rather than as a vehicle of a message ripe for the reader to pick.[170] In *A Room of One's Own*, Woolf described the shift between nineteenth- and twentieth-century poetry, noting that while 'one responds easily, familiarly' to the poetry of Alfred Tennyson and Christina Rossetti, the 'living poets express a feeling that is actually being made and torn out of us at the moment'.[171] 'One fears it,' Woolf wrote, 'one watches it

---

[167] Woolf, *Essays*, III, pp. 434–5.
[168] Woolf, *The Waves*, p. 158. On the experience of reading *The Waste Land*, see Howarth, *The Cambridge Introduction*, pp. 68–73; Howarth, 'Eliot in the Underworld'.
[169] Woolf, *The Waves*, p. 158.
[170] Woolf, *The Waves*, p. 159.
[171] Woolf, *A Room of One's Own*, p. 11.

with keenness and compares it jealously and suspiciously with the old feeling one knew. Hence the difficulty of modern poetry.'[172] 'One must be sceptical,' Neville comments in similar terms, 'but throw caution to the winds and when the door opens accept absolutely.'[173] The act of reading demands that the reader 'let down one's net deeper and deeper', sinking the mind like a fishing net into the poem, in order to 'bring' latent meanings 'to the surface', to connect different voices ('what he said and she said') and 'make poetry'.[174]

For Armstrong, the model of 'close reading' developed in the work of I. A. Richards and William Empson was founded on an attempt to banish the affective dimensions of literary experience to the realm of the feminine and irrational. Armstrong notes that 'Fascism's manipulation of mass feeling may have been enough reason for this. But the result was a failure to develop an adequate *analytical* language for affect.'[175] Such a model of 'close reading', Armstrong argues, 'rests on an account of the text as *outside*, something external which has to be grasped—or warded off': 'the text is seen as *other*: it is object to a Kantian subject who stands over and against the world in a position of power.'[176] '[C]lose reading', Armstrong argues, 'has never been close enough.'[177] For Armstrong, the close reading promoted by the early-twentieth-century literary critics relied on a thought/feeling dichotomy that, in turn, props up a 'master/slave model of reading which is the dominant model in our culture'.[178] Seeking an alternative to this 'master/slave' model of textual mastery, Armstrong proposes a theory of the reader as a 'Kleinian subject', who 'is likely to find in the "body" of the text what they fear, hate and desire':[179]

> Perhaps a fear of the vengeance of the text and our own creates a need for 'dry' rationalism which keeps this at bay. But my point is that such rationalism can actually fail to see the textual strategies by which thought works. It expels 'semiotic' material, reinforcing a thought/feeling binary

---

[172] Woolf, *A Room of One's Own*, p. 11.

[173] Woolf, *The Waves*, p. 159.

[174] Woolf, *The Waves*, p. 159. As Peter Howarth comments, 'the experience of actually reading a lot of modernist poetry is more like an immersion.' For Howarth, the disorientating forms of modernist poetry serve not so much to alienate as to absorb the reader into the connective webs of the poem, and to dissolve the boundaries between individual and collective, poem and society. Similarly, for Neville, the poem that he reads is, although difficult, deeply absorbing, echoing the ways in which Woolf's own reader is absorbed into the text of *The Waves*. Howarth, *The Cambridge Introduction*, p. 5, pp. 6–7.

[175] Armstrong, *The Radical Aesthetic*, p. 18, Armstrong's emphasis.

[176] Armstrong, *The Radical Aesthetic*, p. 87, Armstrong's emphasis.

[177] Armstrong, *The Radical Aesthetic*, p. 95.

[178] Armstrong, *The Radical Aesthetic*, p. 102.

[179] Armstrong, *The Radical Aesthetic*, p. 102.

which limits our definitions of the rational. A more expanded notion of what thinking is would enable one to accept that a 'narcissistic' moment of identification may be an essential prerequisite of critical reading. To belong to the structure of another experience, stronger than seduction, more like paranoia, may be an essential *phase* in the reading process, because it escapes the master/slave model of reading which is the dominant model in our culture. We may not, as critics do not, remain with the terrors of closeness, but it may be that only a closeness to a text's terrors keeps one sane. A refusal to consent to closeness may produce a traumatized reading, rather as, in early life, a failure of active relationships inhibits growth in both parent and child. I am not here recommending a 'mother/child' relationship between text and reader—rather using it as an analogy, a paradigm, for the structure of relationship open to all of us.[180]

In order to 'see how the text thinks', Armstrong writes, 'it is important to read in the desire of the other':

> This is not an ethical imperative for a gluey empathy, but a *fact* of reading. As the text calls out its need to 'enter into a relationship with someone', the answering need to understand accepts the displacement understanding requires. This is much more like the rigours of transference than empathy.[181]

For Armstrong, this Kleinian model of literary identification sheds light on the potentially radical nature of a truly 'close' encounter with the literary text, refusing the defensive drive to 'mastery' characteristic of much twentieth-century literary criticism.

As Melba Cuddy-Keane has argued, Armstrong's characterisation of identification as 'part of a process by which a text engages its readers in a relation with what is other than the self' has a strong affinity with the depictions of reading in Woolf's essays, where she celebrates the scene of reading as a site of democratic exchange and community, the 'common ground' of literature.[182] 'Such identification', argues Cuddy-Keane, 'is neither projection nor appropriation; it is a movement toward a relational engagement with the voice, or rather voices, in the text.'[183] It is not, as Cuddy-Keane adds, 'simple empathetic sympathy; it demands a willingness to displace one's own thinking and to participate in "how the text thinks"'.[184] In *The Waves*, similarly, Neville's description of reading is,

[180] Armstrong, *The Radical Aesthetic*, p. 102.
[181] Armstrong, *The Radical Aesthetic*, pp. 101–2, Armstrong's emphasis.
[182] Cuddy-Keane, *Virginia Woolf*, p. 126; Woolf, *Essays*, VI, p. 278.
[183] Cuddy-Keane, *Virginia Woolf*, p. 127.
[184] Cuddy-Keane, *Virginia Woolf*, p. 127.

as in Armstrong's account of reading, much closer to the 'rigours' and transformative effects of 'transference' than either the carefully regulated distance of scholarly reading, or the 'gluey empathy' of more recent claims for the virtues of empathetic literary identification.[185] Neville may be a cautious reader, but he also finds himself, in Armstrong's words, 'caught up with, imbricated in the structure of the text's processes'.[186]

In all of the scenes of reading that I've been describing in this chapter, this is precisely what Woolf's readers are encouraged to recognise: that we, as readers, are, in Armstrong's words, 'caught up with, imbricated in', entangled intimately with the 'structure of the text's processes'.[187] For many of Woolf's readers, Neville's description of reading 'this poem' is resonant: the experience of reading the present-tense first-person monologues of *The Waves*, interspersed with those curious, impersonal, richly poetic interludes, is, like Neville's experience of reading this poem, a disorientating, immersive experience.[188] Writing about Proust, Woolf described the experience of reading *À la recherche du temps perdu* in terms that map closely on to the experience of reading *The Waves*. Not only, Woolf pointed out, are the 'commonest objects' described with an intensity that transforms everyday objects into the stuff of poetry, but the 'commonest actions [. . .] instead of being discharged automatically, rake up in their progress a whole series of thoughts, sensations, ideas' and 'memories, which were apparently sleeping on the walls of the mind'.[189] 'What are we to do with it all?' Woolf asked, 'as these trophies are piled up round us':

> The mind cannot be content with holding sensation after sensation passively to itself; something must be done with them; their abundance must be shaped. [. . .]
>
> Much of the difficulty of reading Proust comes from this content obliquity. In Proust, the accumulation of objects which surround any central point is so vast and they are often so remote, so difficult of approach and of apprehension that this drawing-together process is gradual, tortuous, and the final relation difficult in the extreme.[190]

'Moreover,' as Woolf added to her account of Proust,

> if we ask for help in finding our way, it does not come through any of the usual channels. We are never told, as the English novelists so frequently

---

[185] Armstrong, *The Radical Aesthetic*, pp. 101–2.
[186] Armstrong, *The Radical Aesthetic*, p. 94.
[187] Armstrong, *The Radical Aesthetic*, p. 94.
[188] Woolf, *The Waves*, p. 158.
[189] Virginia Woolf, 'Phases of Fiction' (1929), in *Essays*, V, pp. 40–88 (pp. 66–7).
[190] Woolf, *Essays*, p. 67.

tell us, that one way is right and the other wrong. [. . .] Direction or emphasis, to be told that that is right, to be nudged and bidden to attend to that, would fall like a shadow on this profound luminosity and cut off some section of it from our view.[191]

Like the poem that Neville takes down from the bookcase – a poem that refuses its reader the reassuringly familiar features of lyric poetry – Woolf's novel similarly refuses her reader the conventional novelistic anchors of omniscient authorial guidance and clearly delineated chapters. Although the reader might long for authorial 'direction', in *The Waves*, layers accumulate, phrases are repeated, one person's words merge into and resurface in another's monologue or in one of the anonymous interludes, overloading the reader's short-term memory so that, as a reader, you cannot store things in the then-and-there boxes afforded by linear narrative.[192] As readers of this scene of reading, and as readers of Woolf's novel, we, like Neville, are drawn into, sink into, the almost hallucinatory imagery embedded in Woolf's flowing sentences, the sea 'monster' shouldering up, only to swallow us in the rush of fragmented imagery and gaping waves.[193] The reader of *The Waves* is enjoined to identify with Neville's experience of reading and to reflect on the ways in which it also describes his or her own experience of reading a similarly strange, poetic and deeply immersive text. Similarly, when we read about Rhoda's lifelong entanglement with a poem by Percy Bysshe Shelley, or when we read about Bernard's encounter with paintings in the National Gallery, the reader is being asked to identify with these characters in their intimate encounters with works of art, and to reflect on the ways in which we too are bound up in, absorbed by, the rhythms of Woolf's prose.

And yet, although for both Armstrong and Woolf, this form of intimate relationship with the literary text holds democratic possibilities, it is also, as Armstrong's invocation of Melanie Klein attests, fraught with the 'terrors of closeness'.[194] Despite recent critical attempts to claim Klein as a theorist of 'reparative reading', Klein's own writings about the fantasies that underpin

---

[191] Woolf, *Essays*, p. 67.

[192] As Gillian Beer writes, 'Many of the objections to *The Waves* as an image of reality resolve into questions of tense. The interludes, which describe the progress of the sun through a single day and across the world, are put in past tense. The episodes are chiefly in the present, and not always even the progressive present. "I go to the bookcase" . . . "I come back from the office"; "I detect; I perceive": such statements suggest habitual and repeated acts and avoid placing the event in a single moment of time. The pure present tense also implicitly suggests self-observation and a kind of instantaneous act of memory, the activity of the watching mind.' Beer, *Virginia Woolf*, p. 82.

[193] Woolf, *The Waves*, p. 158.

[194] Armstrong, *The Radical Aesthetic*, p. 102.

our acts of reading paint an altogether more ambivalent scene.[195] For Klein, the individual reader is always carrying about with her a complex inner world that contains traces of both reparative and aggressive infantile fantasies, both of which inform her relationship to books.[196] Responding to Martha Nussbaum's arguments about literature's capacity to 'promote concern for someone different from oneself', Mary Jacobus points out the limits to some of the contemporary attempts to invoke Klein's writing as evidence for the moral or ethical value of literary identification.[197] Although, as Jacobus notes, 'Identification emerges' in Klein's writing 'as the foundation for reparation and, ultimately, for creativity', Klein also defines 'identification in both positive and negative terms, revealing its dark underside as well as its link to understanding'.[198] Although Klein's writings, like Woolf's, do sketch the framework for a theory of the reparative powers of art, this theory also, as I argued at the beginning of this chapter, fails to sustain itself in these terms, revealing the fragility of reparation in a period dominated by historical and psychic violence.

In *The Waves*, Woolf offers a form of literary encounter that, by immersing the reader in the intimate, and frequently overlapping, first-person soliloquies of her six speakers, seeks to bring into being a form of collective experience. The reader of *The Waves* is repeatedly solicited to participate in the experiences of 'communion' and 'common feeling' described by Bernard, Neville, Louis, Rhoda, Susan and Jinny.[199] In these moments, when, as Rhoda puts it, 'the walls of the mind become transparent', we, as readers, are invited to participate in the oceanic aesthetic of *The Waves*.[200] Writing about modernist poetry (in a passage that I quoted in my introduction), Peter Howarth comments that 'By disorienting and bewildering, [modernist poetry] attempts to immerse its reader in a kind of unity unavailable to detached thought, and recreate lost forms of collective being'.[201] 'Yet', as

---

[195] On 'reparative reading', see Sedgwick, 'Paranoid Reading and Reparative Reading'. For more recent 'postcritical' attempts to extend Sedgwick's thinking, see Rita Felski, *The Limits of Critique* (Chicago: University of Chicago Press, 2015).

[196] On the 'inner world', see Joan Riviere, 'The Inner World in Ibsen's *Master Builder*', *International Journal of Psycho-Analysis*, 33 (1952), 173–80; Joan Riviere, 'The Unconscious Phantasy of an Inner World Reflected in Examples from English Literature', *International Journal of Psycho-Analysis*, 33 (1952), 160–72; R. D. Hinshelwood, 'The Elusive Concept of "Internal Objects" (1934–1943): Its Role in the Formation of the Klein Group', *International Journal of Psycho-Analysis*, 78 (1997), 877–97.

[197] Martha Nussbaum, *Upheavals of Thought: The Intelligence of the Emotions* (Cambridge: Cambridge University Press, 2001), p. 352, cited by Mary Jacobus, *The Poetics of Psychoanalysis: In the Wake of Klein* (Oxford: Oxford University Press, 2005), p. 87.

[198] Jacobus, *The Poetics of Psychoanalysis*, p. 67, p. 87.

[199] Woolf, *The Waves*, p. 99, p. 114.

[200] Woolf, *The Waves*, p. 183.

[201] Howarth, *The Cambridge Introduction*, p. 31.

Howarth also observes, 'this very expansiveness is both [modernism's] attraction and its chief political problem.'[202] Although, in *The Waves*, Woolf seeks to reimagine the scene of reading as a site of democratic collective belonging (where the reader is an active participant in the act of 'mak[ing] poetry'), she also, as we have seen, points to the ways in which such a fantasy of collective belonging leaves the scene of reading ripe for fascist appropriation.[203] For Jessica Berman, *The Waves* not only 'confronts the limitations' of fascist discourse, it also forcefully rejects the fascist appropriation of communal aesthetics, 'presenting an oppositional cosmopolitan politics that resists the lure of the corporate state and that is prescient in its understanding of the danger of the fascist aesthetic'.[204] In the scenes of reading that I have been examining in this chapter, however, the distinction between modernist cosmopolitanism and the fascist demand for individual surrender to the group is precarious. Like Melanie Klein, Woolf examines the darker side of these forms of close identification with the literary text. In the political context of the 1930s, although the process of identification might disrupt the critic's ascent to a position of textual mastery and seek to enact the 'common ground' of literature, it also, as we have seen in the character of Louis, bears an uncomfortable resemblance to the fascist demand for self-surrender to the totalitarian state.

In one of the scenes following Percival's death, Louis returns home from his office to his attic room and picks up a book of poetry. As he sits down to read the fifteenth-century anonymous lyric 'O western wind', Woolf transcribes the poem into her text, interspersing each half-line with Louis's free associations:

> I open a little book. I read one poem. One poem is enough.
> O western wind . . .
> O western wind, you are at enmity with my mahogany table and spats, and also, alas, with the vulgarity of my mistress, the little actress, who has never been able to speak English correctly—
> O western wind, when wilt thou blow . . .
> Rhoda, with her intense abstraction, with her unseeing eyes the colour of snail's flesh, does not destroy you, western wind, whether she comes at midnight when the stars blaze or at the most prosaic hour of midday. She stands at the window and looks at the chimney-pots and the broken windows in the houses of poor people—
> O western wind, when wilt thou blow . . .[205]

In this passage, Louis reiterates his fantasy of poetry as a refuge from the transience of modernity: poetry, he claims, will transcend the squalor of urban

[202] Howarth, *The Cambridge Introduction*, p. 31.
[203] Woolf, *The Waves*, p. 159.
[204] Berman, *Modernist Fiction*, p. 140, p. 156.
[205] Woolf, *The Waves*, pp. 160–2.

poverty, withstand the coming and going of lovers, and serve to memorialise the dead. Confirming Rhoda's suspicion that he would attempt to 'smooth out the death of Percival to his satisfaction', Louis imagines Percival in heroic terms, buried with poet's laurels: 'flowering with green leaves and [. . .] laid in the earth with all his branches still sighing in the summer wind'.[206]

In a passage from 'Byron & Mr Briggs' – a fragmentary draft for a book on 'Reading' that she first proposed in a diary entry in 1921 – Woolf turned to the same poem in an attempt to think through 'what sort of processes it stirs up in the mind of a common reader':

> Passionate; direct. [. . .] Western wind, when will thou blow—how wist-fully it begins, with a sort of weary delaying compared with the direct attack of the concluding lines [. . .] Some sailor wrote it, far away look-ing towards England. 'Christ if my love were in my arms and I in my bed again!' [. . .] <I must> returns to the poem itself; not connecting it with rain <,> or sailor <,> or any <[> individual <]> experience in particular. I cannot except by constantly repeating the poem itself <as a whole>, keep in touch with the emotion. I am tempted directly I begin to analyse to get far away from what I feel. After reading it several times I cease to get any emotion. But later I shall think involuntarily of 'the small rain' [. . .] for it describes rain that I have seen but never thought of calling small. [. . .] But if I say the poem through these details are merged in a whole; in the direct shock of emotion which I receive, and cannot explain to myself or communicate to others.[207]

This, Woolf writes, is 'not very satisfactory as an analysis', but, instead of offer-ing an 'analysis' of the poem, Woolf attempts to sketch the reader's mind in the process of 'trying to make a whole', 'trying to sort out <lay bare> and sharpen its perceptions', 'trying to refer its impressions as accurately <closely> as possi-ble to the poem itself'.[208] The reader has to keep 'return[ing] to the poem itself', 'constantly repeating the poem [. . .] as a whole', in order to render faithfully the experience of holding together the individual 'details' that are, in the moment of reading, 'merged in a whole' that is also an enigmatic 'shock of emotion'.[209]

As Louis reads 'O western wind', the repetition of the previous lines with the accretion of each line of the poem ('O western wind . . .'; 'O western wind, when wilt thou blow . . .'; 'O western wind, when wilt thou blow, / That the

---

[206] Woolf, *The Waves*, p. 162, p. 127.
[207] Woolf, 'Appendix II: Byron & Mr Briggs', in *Essays*, III, pp. 473–99 (pp. 486–7).
[208] Woolf, *Essays*, III, p. 487.
[209] Woolf, *Essays*, III, p. 486, p. 487. See also Alice Fox, *Virginia Woolf and the Literature of the English Renaissance* (Oxford: Clarendon Press, 1990), pp. 70–1.

small rain down can rain?') seems to replicate the experience of reading poetry that Woolf describes in 'Byron & Mr Briggs': as each line of the poem builds, the reader is continually referred back to the previous lines of the poem, as part of an effort to hold the individual parts of the poem in relationship to the 'whole'.[210] As a reader, Louis, like Woolf's 'common reader', 'plait[s] into one cable the many threads' of the poem, in an attempt to make a 'whole'.[211] In Louis's case, however, the quest for 'wholeness' is bound up in his troublingly violent quest for poetic transcendence: Louis's process of reading is intertwined with his 'colossal labour' as an imperialist ('driv[ing] a violent, an unruly, a vicious team'), and aligned with his 'destiny' – not only as a reader and a poet, but also as an imperialist – to 'plait into one cable the many threads, the thin, the thick, the broken, the enduring of our long history'.[212] And yet, the juxtaposition of the line-by-line repetitions of the poem, interspersed with Louis's anxieties about the 'incoherences' of his day-to-day life, simultaneously bears witness to the difficulty, indeed the impossibility, of resolving the 'discord' of modernity through a turn to poetry.[213] Louis's repeated returns to the opening line, 'O western wind . . .', juxtaposed with the interruptions of violence, vulgarity and death, also suggest that, despite his desire for a poetry of redemption, the rhythms and repeated refrains of poetic language refuse to bend to the reader's drive towards transcendence.

* * *

Woolf's writing, as I have been arguing throughout this chapter, confronts us with some of the most powerful fantasies at work in modernist culture (and beyond) about the role of literature in psychic, social and political life, but at the same time unsettles those fantasies and places them under scrutiny. The scenes of reading in *The Waves* display the overdetermined role of literary texts in the psychic, social and political lives of their readers. Although Woolf does expose her characters' investments in literary texts that serve as mediators of patriarchal, imperialist and even fascistic fantasies, at the same time she offers a sincere but nonetheless troubled account of the ways in which readers use literary objects as part of a vexed form of mourning. *The Waves* not only exposes the drive towards mastery in early-twentieth-century scenes of reading (Neville, the scholar's fantasy of using literature as a buttress for upper-class masculinity; Louis's fantasy of the 'binding power of poetry'), but the novel also, as I have been arguing, enacts and models the alternative processes of reading that

---

[210] Woolf, *The Waves*, pp. 160–2; Woolf, *Essays*, III, p. 486.
[211] Woolf, *The Waves*, p. 161.
[212] Woolf, *The Waves*, p. 160, p. 161.
[213] Woolf, *The Waves*, p. 160, p. 161.

it solicits (Neville's encounter with a difficult modernist poem; Rhoda's circular returns to a poem by Percy Bysshe Shelley). And yet, although *The Waves* does gesture towards its own attempts to enact an alternative to the dominant fantasies of reading in early-twentieth-century culture, it is also, as we have seen throughout this chapter, permeated by a sense of the dangers and the risks of literary identification, even as it seems to suggest the absolute necessity of such forms of literary and cultural experience for psychic survival in an often intolerable world. Although the novel does seek both to imagine and to enact alternatives to the fantasies of mastery that circulated within early-twentieth-century culture, at the same time *The Waves* doesn't quite hold out that celebratory vision of literature as a democratic 'common ground' that Woolf celebrates in her essays, presenting in its place an altogether more difficult portrait of the conflicting personal and political fantasies that shaped the scene of reading in the early twentieth century. In *The Years*, as we shall see in the next chapter, under the pressure of rising fascism, Woolf would place her own arguments about the politics and poetics of reading under further historical scrutiny.

4

'MONSTERS WITHIN AND WITHOUT', OR, 'FOREBODINGS ABOUT FASCISM': MARION MILNER READS VIRGINIA WOOLF

In her 1934 book *A Life of One's Own*, published under the penname Joanna Field, Marion Milner asked the apparently simple question: 'What do I like?'[1] *A Life of One's Own*, like Milner's later books, *An Experiment in Leisure* (1937) and *On Not Being Able to Paint* (1950), is a generic hybrid comprising fragments of life-writing, self-analysis, diary, doodles (see Figures 4.1 and 4.2), drawings, literary quotations, psychoanalytic theory, automatic writing, self-help book, mysticism and essay. As Vanessa Smith has observed, *A Life of One's Own* occupies 'a space athwart disciplinary and generic axioms'; it is 'impossible to pigeonhole; a text of radical discursive crossings':[2]

> It has elements of the confessional memoir, its gripping narrative of self-education puts it in the territory of the bildungsroman, it has been classed as both mysticism and detective fiction, it tells a story of a woman's development that elides the marriage plot. It sidles up to and then shies away from the two dominant discourses through which selfhood was rethought between the wars – psychoanalysis and Modernism. Its aleatory, stream

---

[1] Milner, *Life*, p. xxxiv. An earlier and shorter version of this chapter has been published as: Helen Tyson, '"Forebodings about Fascism": Marion Milner and Virginia Woolf', *Feminist Modernist Studies*, 4.1 (2021), 1–21, https://www.tandfonline.com/doi/abs/10.1080/2 4692921.2020.1848334.

[2] Vanessa Smith, 'Transferred Debts: Marion Milner's *A Life of One's Own* and the Limits of Analysis', *Feminist Modernist Studies*, 1–2 (2018), 96–111 (p. 96).

---

of consciousness style is reminiscent of Dorothy Richardson, but is presented as social-scientific rather than literary experimentation.[3]

Reviewing *A Life of One's Own* in *The Listener*, W. H. Auden found it 'as exciting as a detective story', singling out in particular Milner's refusal of the official scientific language of the 'case' study.[4] Milner would later train as a psychoanalyst – she qualified in 1943, and became a central and celebrated figure in British psychoanalysis until her death in 1998. And yet, although Milner was certainly knowledgeable about psychoanalysis in the 1930s, both *A Life of One's Own* and *An Experiment in Leisure* also keep psychoanalysis at bay: 'The psycho-analysts', she wrote, 'had always given me the feeling that they considered the unconscious mind as a sort of special preserve which no layman must tamper with.'[5] Milner hoped, she wrote in *A Life of One's*

Figure 4.1 A free drawing from Marion Milner, *A Life of One's Own* (1934) (Hove: Routledge, 2011), p. 64, by permission of the Marsh Agency Ltd, on behalf of the Estate of Marion Milner.

---

[3] Smith, 'Transferred Debts', p. 96.

[4] W. H. Auden, 'To Unravel Unhappiness', *The Listener*, 28 November 1934, reprinted in *Art, Creativity, Living*, ed. by Lesley Caldwell (London: Karnac, 2000), pp. 113–16 (p. 113); see also Stephen Spender, 'The Road to Happiness', *The Spectator*, 23 November 1934.

[5] Milner, *Life*, p. 160.

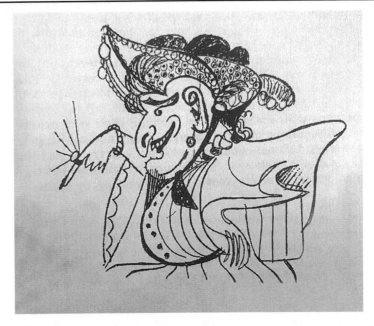

Figure 4.2 A free drawing from Marion Milner, *An Experiment in Leisure* (1937) (Hove: Routledge, 2011), p. 147, by permission of the Marsh Agency Ltd, on behalf of the Estate of Marion Milner.

Own, to 'devise a method which might be available for anyone, quite apart from whether opportunity or intellectual capacity inclined them to the task of wading through psycho-analytic literature or their income made it possible for them to submit themselves as a patient'.[6]

In *A Life of One's Own*, Milner set out to record, and reflect upon, her own experimental attempts to unearth 'what kinds of experience made me happy', ranging across diverse pleasures and desires, including her desire for a pair of red shoes, her feeling of 'delight' in front of a painting by Cézanne, and her 'thrill' at a football match.[7] One diary entry records having 'Exulted in my body and clothes and red skirt and freedom to do as I choose on Sunday morning', followed by 'Evening delight in Chapter I of *Ulysses*'. 'I want', Milner adds, 'to be carried in the stream because the stream is bigger than I am.'[8] Describing Milner's 'strange experimental quartet of books built around diary-keeping, diary reading and diary interpretation' as 'meta-diaries rather than diaries', Hugh Haughton

[6] Milner, *Life*, p. 159.
[7] Milner, *Life*, p. 16, p. 53, p. 21.
[8] Milner, *Life*, p. 18.

suggests that these books are 'not autobiographical documents so much as commentaries on autobiographical documents'.[9] In her 'Preface' to *A Life of One's Own*, Milner stated that

> The reason for publishing the book is that although what I found is probably peculiar to my own temperament and circumstances, I think the method by which I found it may be useful to others, even to those whose discoveries about themselves may be the opposite of my own. The need for such a method in these days is obvious, a method for discovering one's true likes and dislikes, for finding and setting up a standard of values that is truly one's own and not a borrowed mass-produced ideal.[10]

This experiment in pursuing the question 'What do I like?' is framed not as a record of solipsistic introspection, nor even, as in Freud's *The Interpretation of Dreams*, as a path on the 'royal road' to the interpretation of the unconscious, but, instead, as a new 'method' – a method that Milner offers up to her reader as a way of freeing himself or herself from the shackles of the 'borrowed mass-produced ideal[s]' foisted upon us in capitalist modernity.[11]

In a gesture that is characteristic of many of her modernist contemporaries, Milner rejects what she calls her 'Sunday paper mind' and attempts to cast off 'influence from custom, tradition, fashion', refusing to be 'swayed by standards uncritically accepted from my friends, my family, my countrymen, my ancestors'.[12] Echoing Virginia Woolf's description, in her 1924 essay 'Character in Fiction', of the 'smashing and crashing' of nineteenth-century traditions, Milner records that 'everywhere around me I saw old ways of doing things breaking down and proving inadequate'.[13] Not only, again like many modernist writers, does Milner feel 'dubious about trusting the dictates of a social tradition which had landed us in the war', *A Life of One's Own* also expresses a typically modernist anxiety about the pervasive and noxious influences of mass culture, refusing the 'standards' unconsciously picked up from 'romantic stories, plays, [and] films'.[14] Milner embarks, in this book, on an attempt to secure what she describes as her 'vacillating will' so that it is 'kept in the ways that I love', 'Instead of [being] pulled this way and that in response to the suggestion of the crowd'.[15]

[9] Hugh Haughton, 'The Milner Experiment: Psychoanalysis and the Diary', *British Journal of Psychotherapy*, 30.3 (2013), 349–62 (p. 350).

[10] Milner, *Life*, p. xxxiv.

[11] Freud, *The Interpretation of Dreams*, p. 608.

[12] Milner, *Life*, p. 5, p. 3, p. 5.

[13] Woolf, *Essays*, III, p. 433; Milner, *Life*, p. 5.

[14] Milner, *Life*, p. 5, p. 81.

[15] Milner, *Life*, p. 30.

If Milner's attitude to psychoanalysis is, in these early writings, characterised both by fascination and by hesitation, her relationship to literary modernism, and to Virginia Woolf in particular, is similarly complex. *A Life of One's Own* has, of course, been read as an unconscious echo of, or unacknowledged tribute to, Woolf's 1929 essay *A Room of One's Own*.[16] And yet, despite the echoes, in *A Life of One's Own* Milner doesn't refer directly to Woolf's feminist essay, but instead quotes a passage from Woolf's essay on Montaigne, describing the elusive, discordant and shifting nature of the 'soul' – a 'creature' that Woolf describes as 'so complex, so indefinite, corresponding so little to the version which does duty for her in public, that a man may spend his life in merely trying to run her to earth'.[17] In an act of 'common reading' that Woolf herself would surely have identified with, Milner remembers copying this quotation out on to a piece of paper at the very beginning of her 'experiment', and carrying it with her, talisman-like, crumpled up in her pocket at the time.[18] In *An Experiment in Leisure*, in a passage that I'll be discussing later, Woolf appears again in the form of a quotation from *Mrs Dalloway*, describing the 'brutal monster' of hatred that stalks the 'leaf-encumbered forest' of Mrs Dalloway's 'soul'.[19] Alongside these intertextual allusions to Woolf in Milner's published writings, we also know that Milner was connected both socially and professionally to the world of Bloomsbury modernism: she counted Woolf's brother and sister-in-law, the psychoanalysts Adrian and Karin Stephen, amongst her friends and colleagues, and her notebooks, housed at the Archives of the British Psychoanalytical Society, also reveal that, on at least one occasion, she attended the 1917 Club, which was founded by Leonard Woolf and frequented by numerous figures of Bloomsbury modernism.[20] 'The Milner archive', as Smith notes, 'certainly discloses side glances at Bloomsbury in general and Woolf in particular.'[21] A notebook entry for 8 September 1929 reveals Milner worrying 'That I'm no judge of poetry, my taste is uncertain, I often like things that other people jeer at: as sentimental etc.'; '"Taste"', Milner observes anxiously, 'is the God of the Bloomsbury school.' Another notebook entry for 22 January

---

[16] See Stonebridge, *The Destructive Element*, p. 144; Rachel Bowlby, 'Introduction', in Milner, *Life*, pp. xiii–xxxii (p. xxxii, p. xxxi); Ellmann, 'New Introduction', in Milner, *Experiment*, p. xiv.

[17] Milner, *Life*, p. 10; Virginia Woolf, 'Montaigne' (1925), in *Essays*, IV, pp. 71–81 (p. 73). On Milner's reading of Montaigne, see Ellmann, 'New Introduction', p. xxxiv.

[18] Milner, *Life*, p. 10.

[19] Milner, *Experiment*, p. 18.

[20] Emma Letley, *Marion Milner: The Life* (London: Routledge, 2014), p. 19, pp. 40–4; Marion Milner, 'Notebook', Marion Milner Collection, Archives of the British Psychoanalytical Society, P01/E/B/08.

[21] Smith, 'Transferred Debts', p. 103.

1929 reveals Milner meditating on the satirical mock-'Preface' to Woolf's *Orlando* (1928), and wondering, in relation to her own work in progress: 'Can the mood be like "Orlando"? Only when you can reconcile laughter enough to conquer the fear of the preface to Orlando, will it be safe to launch it.'[22] Focusing on Milner's complex negotiation of her evidently uneasy relationship to both modernist and psychoanalytic authorities, Smith argues that Milner's curious refusal to name *A Room of One's Own* as a literary antecedent to *A Life of One's Own* 'can be understood [. . .] not as unacknowledged debt', but 'as both jocular and shy homage to an author who has communicated to her the mood that enabled her to find her voice':

> In the spirit that she has assimilated from *Orlando*'s preface she cites and doesn't, joking with the writer who taught her to laugh at literary forebears.[23]

For Smith, Milner's determined refusal to cite both modernist and psychoanalytic sources constitutes a challenge to 'scholarship's reliance on models of authorial indebtedness'.[24] Indeed, the Milner archive reveals another shared interest with Woolf: Milner's determination to write for a figure that she, like Woolf, refers to as 'the common reader'.[25] '[I]t is an attempt', Milner writes of *A Life of One's Own*, 'to find a method by which the ordinary man can be himself, not dependent on experts.'[26]

Alongside the allusions to Woolf, Milner also refers, in both her published books and her unpublished notebooks, to Dorothy Richardson, James Joyce, T. S. Eliot, Ernest Hemingway, Joseph Conrad, Sylvia Townsend Warner, D. H. Lawrence, Vita Sackville-West, Roger Fry, Wyndham Lewis, H. G. Wells, Arnold Bennett and Aldous Huxley.[27] Milner's notebooks from the early 1930s reveal not only that she was a close observer of modernist experiments with form, but also that she consciously understood her own experiments in writing in relationship to modernist formal innovation. One diary entry from 1931 comments on the 'technique' of Richardson's *Pointed Roofs* ('no omniscient

---

[22] Marion Milner, Selection of diary notes in envelope marked 'M.O., 1929–', Marion Milner Collection, Archives of the British Psychoanalytical Society, P01/E/B/14, also cited by Smith, 'Transferred Debts', p. 104.

[23] Smith, 'Transferred Debts', p. 106, p. 104.

[24] Smith, 'Transferred Debts', p. 98.

[25] Milner, 'M.O., 1929–'.

[26] Milner, 'M.O., 1929–'.

[27] 'Personal Diaries and Notes', Marion Milner Collection, Archives of the British Psychoanalytical Society, P01/E/B.

observer'), while another entry from 1934, titled 'Next Book. (intimations of)', shows Milner comparing her own 'method' to *The Waste Land*:

> Isn't this, (ie my method) in a sense what T. S. Eliot was trying to do in his Waste Land? A series of emotionally important pictures . . . (organic symbols . . .) which he has tried (unsuccessfully?) to link, give coherence to, by a system of notes.[28]

As I have argued elsewhere, Milner's 1930s publications can both be read alongside contemporary modernist experiments with stream of consciousness writing by Virginia Woolf, Dorothy Richardson and May Sinclair.[29] Hugh Haughton has also drawn attention to the affinities between Woolf's epiphanic 'moments of being', James Joyce's epiphanies, and Milner's interest in capturing what she describes as enigmatic 'moments', when even 'the very simplest things', such as 'the glint of electric light on the water in my bath, gave me the most intense delight'.[30] There is, no doubt, more work to be done on the historical basis of this particular conversation between modernism and the early work of this celebrated British psychoanalyst, life-writer and artist.

My aim in this chapter, however, is not to trace the direct influences of Woolf on Milner, nor to track Milner's explicit borrowings from Woolf, but rather to think about Woolf's and Milner's shared – and deeply anxious – fascination with what Milner described, in her 1950 book *On Not Being Able to Paint*, as the 'Monsters within and without'.[31] In particular, I'll be tracking Woolf's and Milner's responses to the internal and external 'monsters' haunting 1930s Europe, showing how, for both writers, the historical vicissitudes of fascism traversed the terrains of psychic, cultural and political life, unsettling any easy distinction between the inside and outside of the mind.

---

[28] Marion Milner, 'Notebook', Marion Milner Collection, Archives of the British Psychoanalytical Society, P01/E/B/21; Marion Milner, 'Notebook', Marion Milner Collection, Archives of the British Psychoanalytical Society, P01/E/B/29. In 1964, Milner published a letter in the *Guardian* newspaper stating that she was 'making a study of Dorothy Richardson's twelve books which she called "Pilgrimage" and I would be glad if anyone who knew her personally would get in touch with me'. Richardson's friend Bernice Elliot and the poet Bryher wrote back to Milner. 'Two letters responding to a request by Marion Milner for information on Dorothy Richardson', Marion Milner Collection, Archives of the British Psychoanalytical Society, P01/D/C/51. My sincere thanks to Adam Guy for alerting me to the connection between Milner and Richardson.

[29] Helen Tyson, '"Catching Butterflies": Marion Milner and Stream of Consciousness Writing', *Literature Compass*, 17.6 (2020), https://doi.org/10.1111/lic3.12563.

[30] Haughton, 'The Milner Experiment', p. 357; Milner, *Life*, p. 46.

[31] Milner, *On Not Being Able to Paint*, p. 41.

Focusing on the portraits of reading in Woolf's 1937 novel *The Years*, alongside the portraits of leisure in Milner's 1937 book *An Experiment in Leisure*, I want to suggest that Woolf, like Milner, asks her readers to reflect upon the nature of our own personal and political investments in the act of reading books. For both Woolf and Milner, the question 'What do I like?' becomes freighted with anxiety in an era when individual desires were understood to be prey to the manipulations, not only of capitalist mass-deception, but also, increasingly in the late 1930s, of fascist demagogues. What might at first appear in Milner's writing as a whimsical project in self-analysis can in fact be read as a political project in extricating the self from the polluted desires of fascism. In the portraits of reading written into *The Years*, Woolf too explores the fear that entering into the pleasures of the text might leave the reader prey to the emotional manipulations of fascism. Woolf and Milner, I argue, are engaged in a similar endeavour to understand the entanglement of the psychic, social and political forces at work in everyday acts of leisure and reading. Their analyses of the drives that underpin our moments of everyday pleasure are informed, and haunted, by the history and politics of the 1930s. For both, there is a fragile border between rapturous forms of cultural abandon and the troubling psycho-politics of fascism.

Beginning with a discussion of *An Experiment in Leisure*, this chapter then moves on to an analysis of the troubled scenes of reading presented in *The Years*. I conclude by considering how Woolf and Milner solicit their readers to take up a method of self-reflective reading that anatomises the dominant 'mass-produced' fantasies of the early twentieth century, while resisting the 'monsters' that these writers trace inside and outside of the mind in 1930s Europe.

'FOREBODINGS ABOUT FASCISM': MARION MILNER'S *AN EXPERIMENT IN LEISURE* (1937)

In the 'Preface' to *An Experiment in Leisure*, Milner described her second book as an attempt 'to find out by simple observation just what this particular mind [. . .] seems to find most interesting'.[32] By 1937, however, the question with which Milner had begun *A Life of One's Own*, and the urgency of answering it, had shifted. Writing *An Experiment in Leisure* in Spain on the outbreak of the Spanish Civil War, Milner also recorded her responses to the 1930s hunger marches (including the 1936 Jarrow March), as well as Mussolini's aggressions in Ethiopia and the outbreak of the Abyssinian War. Milner's 1937 book was marked by a newfound sense of urgency in her endeavour to disentangle personal desires from those thrust upon us amidst the crowd. Out of the question 'What do I like?' grew a second question: 'Is this feeling of liking something

---

[32] Milner, *Experiment*, p. xliii.

trustworthy at all, is feeling a safe guide?'[33] 'I had been driven', Milner writes, 'to ask the second question because for a long time I had suffered from a growing uneasiness over the anti-intellectual trends of modern life':

> This uneasiness was not entirely disinterested, it grew from the knowledge that I myself had always been more guided by feeling than by reason; although loving the clear precision of science and rational exposition I had always felt it to be slightly foreign and a little dangerous, too clear to be true—and also too difficult for the ordinary business of living. But now I was continually reading accounts of how the uncritical exaltation of feeling seemed to be leading to manifestations which with my whole soul I loathed: to intolerance and ruthless tyranny over individual freedom of thought. Particularly did the distortion of facts for the sake of arousing and exploiting the feelings of the masses make me feel physically sick, as though the ground had fallen away under my feet. I had decided therefore that my experiment with leisure interests might also provide a way for studying certain feelings and might show me under what circumstances they were to be trusted, if at all.[34]

Milner had, as she pointed out in *A Life of One's Own*, 'a First Class Honour Degree in Psychology' from University College London; she had worked with Cyril Burt (the infamous father of IQ testing) at the National Institute of Industrial Psychology; she had lectured on psychology for the Workers' Educational Association; and in 1927 she was awarded a Laura Spelman Rockefeller Scholarship to study industrial psychology at the Harvard Business School.[35] The ambivalence, in both of these early books, to the 'clear precision of science' is, therefore, by no means a simplistic opposition of reason and feeling. And yet, writing against the backdrop of a rising current of fascism and 'ruthless tyranny' across Europe and in Britain, there is a new urgency, for Milner in 1937, in understanding the ease with which not only Hollywood movie makers but now also European dictators might manipulate individual desires, 'exploiting the feelings of the masses' for their own ends.[36]

Beginning this study of 'leisure interests' and 'feelings' by exploring 'pleasant memories' from childhood, Milner takes her reader on a journey of self-observation, tracking the threads of association between her memories, pastimes and pleasures, as recorded in diaries, fragments of automatic writing,

---

[33] Milner, *Experiment*, p. xliii.
[34] Milner, *Experiment*, pp. xliii–xliv.
[35] Letley, *Marion Milner*, pp. 17–19.
[36] Milner, *Experiment*, p. 82, p. xliv.

doodles and drawings.[37] Considering her attraction to English landscapes marked by pagan history – places like Stonehenge, Dartmoor and Wychwood Forest – Milner records that one day she found this 'thread of allurement to places had become entangled with ideas that I remembered from books'.[38] Milner describes the experience of lying in bed after the birth of her son, free associating:

> I found I was repeating the name of a book of short stories that I had just read; *The Runagates Club* [by John Buchan]. It was so persistent that finally I let go all my absorption with immediate purposes and simply watched my thoughts; as I did so a vague fear grew round the name, and with it the memory of a passage in another book that I had just been reading [*Mrs Dalloway*]:
>
> > It rasped her, though, to have stirring about in her this brutal monster! To hear twigs cracking and feel hooves planted down in the depths of that leaf-encumbered forest, the soul; never to be content quite, or quite secure, for at any moment the brute would be stirring, this hatred . . .
>
> and then my thoughts jumped to a rough sketch I had myself made at the Zoo [see Figure 4.3]. Spontaneously this thought with its vague fear took the name of 'the Green Wildebeste'.[39]

The fearful 'Green Wildebeste', the 'brutal monster' that rasps Mrs Dalloway, the 'hooves' that she feels 'planted down in the depths' of her soul – all these lead Milner on to another set of free associations: from her memories of the pains of childbirth, to the mythological figure of Pan, a drawing with 'a pair of great horns', and an English folk dance called 'The Horn Dance of Abbots Bromley'.[40] 'Certainly', Milner observes, 'the theme of horns and hoofs seemed to be cropping up rather frequently. But I could not see any reason for this, so I went on following up the clues of interest.'[41] The 'clues of interest' (this is Milner in detective mode) lead from Woolf's 'brutal monster', the 'horns and hoofs' of Pan and English folk dancing, on to Milner's attraction to witchcraft, other forms of pagan ritual, Wagner's *Ring* cycle and Spanish bullfighting.

---

[37] Milner, *Experiment*, p. 1.
[38] Milner, *Experiment*, p. 17.
[39] Milner, *Experiment*, pp. 17–18.
[40] Milner, *Experiment*, p. 19.
[41] Milner, *Experiment*, p. 19.

Figure 4.3 The sketch from the zoo. Marion Milner, *An Experiment in Leisure* (1937) (Hove: Routledge, 2011), p. 22, by permission of the Marsh Agency Ltd, on behalf of the Estate of Marion Milner.

Tracking her own interest in the imagery and ideas of witchcraft (a fascination that Milner shares, as she notes, with Sylvia Townsend Warner's novel about a witch, *Lolly Willowes*), Milner describes her fascination with R. L. Thompson's *The History of the Devil* (1929), noting the book's emphasis on reading 'popular views of witchcraft' as 'decadent survivals, distorted by ignorant imaginations, of what had once been a deeply serious pagan ritual and belief'.[42] Linking the 'conventional picture of the Devil with horns, hoofs and a tail, and the Greek idea of Pan, great god of flocks and shepherds', Milner is struck by Thompson's assertion that 'those dark ceremonies in the depths of the forest which had so allured me, were the central mysteries of an older religion, that the god they worshipped was not really a personification of evil, but the best symbol they knew for the forces of life'.

'I was not', Milner writes, 'concerned with whether this view corresponded with historical fact, but only with the particular images it suggested.'[43] Recalling her own childhood entrancement with 'the Norse myths of the struggle between the giants and the gods of Valhalla', Milner begins to see 'the theme of the horned beast and the horned god cropping up everywhere in my life', remembering how,

[42] Milner, *Experiment*, p. 152, p. 21.
[43] Milner, *Experiment*, p. 21.

in adolescence, she had 'made little surreptitious flower offerings to Pan'.[44] 'But', she asks,

> granted so many interests pointed in the same directions, what was there at the end of the road? Pan, the Devil, the elder gods, fertility rites, dark ceremonies in forests—and what was I to do about it? The implications seemed a little awkward. Was I to hunt for a present-day company of devil-worshippers and join their ranks?[45]

Milner contemplates what she thinks 'Freud would say', noting the intensity with which these themes preoccupied her in the aftermath of childbirth and wondering whether her interest in 'the dark powers of the earth' might not be 'only a roundabout way of being preoccupied with physical sex'. But she brushes the Freudian interpretation off, noting that although her interest in witchcraft may not be 'entirely explained by physical sex', it nonetheless had 'to do with relations to people—and to myself'.[46] Following a mysterious encounter with an unnamed person who fills her like a shell, Milner writes:

> Suddenly I thought I knew what witchcraft had meant to me. It was obvious that one had a deep instinct to submit oneself to the best one knew, an insatiable instinct to adore which would find heroes by hook or by crook, often making one build fantasies round people who could never bear such a weight of the ideal. But here was something else, a darker instinct; for to worship what one thought to be 'the good' was only half the picture. It could not bring complete submission, for there was still some of one's own will left in the choice of 'the good'.[47]

Concluding that she is possessed by a desire for submission, Milner comments: 'To submit yourself to an alien force that wishes to destroy you, this seems the only ultimate security.'[48]

Milner traces this urge 'to submit' in her other 'leisure interests', noting that while 'the theme melody of the impending doom of the gods from *The Ring* had haunted me for weeks', she had also become fascinated by similar accounts of the 'ceremony of the killing of the god' in James Frazer's *The Golden Bough* (which she goes on to quote from at length).[49] In *A Life of One's Own*, Milner had described her aesthetic experiences of music, sculptures, architecture, paintings

[44] Milner, *Experiment*, pp. 21–2.
[45] Milner, *Experiment*, p. 23.
[46] Milner, *Experiment*, p. 24.
[47] Milner, *Experiment*, p. 25.
[48] Milner, *Experiment*, p. 25.
[49] Milner, *Experiment*, p. 28.

and books as linked to a desire to 'lose myself in the thing perceived'.[50] This form of self-abandonment is described, in both books, as an intensely pleasurable but also fearful experience: 'Sometimes in listening to music', Milner writes, 'I would feel myself being carried away until neither I nor anything else existed but only sound, and in spite of the delight I would clutch wildly at some wandering thought to bring me back to the familiar world of bored self-consciousness.'[51] Looking at sculpture (a 'form of art' which she 'had always found rather puzzling'), Milner finds that 'by keeping very still and forgetting everything I had been told, I could slip down into a world of dark tensions, stresses and strains that forged themselves into an obscure but deep satisfaction'.[52] And yet, in Westminster Abbey, when she applies this attempt to 'break through the fog of associations and to escape from my preconceived ideas of boredom in churches', Milner finds that although she manages 'to strip my mind clean of all its ideas and to feel through the decoration to the bare structure of the building and to growing lines of stone', she also experiences 'an echo of terror', 'the dread of annihilation merging into a deep delight'.[53] For Milner, it's not so much that certain types of artwork take us over, but that the only true way of experiencing aesthetic pleasure is in a form of self-abandonment where the ego dissolves into the artwork.

Part of the pleasure, for Milner, of self-abandonment is that she views what she calls the 'internal act of the wiping out of myself' as a crucial aspect of creativity, for both the creator and the reader or spectator.[54] For Milner, a 'ritual sacrifice' of personal worries is a method of overcoming intellectual and creative inhibition: repeating, as a kind of mantra, 'I am nothing, I know nothing, I want nothing', she describes a process of 'wip[ing] away all sense of my own existence'.[55] As a result, Milner observes, 'my mind would begin, entirely of itself, throwing up useful ideas on the very problem which I had been struggling with'.[56] Describing her desire for 'emotional abandon' as a 'symbolic way of thinking about' this 'internal act of the wiping out of myself', Milner interprets her obsession with witchcraft and pagan rituals as a symbolic way of understanding her own path to creativity and aesthetic experience.[57]

And yet, while, on the one hand, Milner interprets her desire for 'emotional abandon' as a key to creative endeavour, there is, on the other hand, something

---

[50] Milner, *Life*, p. 151. For more on how *A Life of One's Own* examines aesthetic experience, see Tyson, '"Catching Butterflies"'.

[51] Milner, *Life*, p. 150.

[52] Milner, *Life*, p. 150.

[53] Milner, *Life*, p. 151.

[54] Milner, *Experiment*, pp. 30–1.

[55] Milner, *Experiment*, p. 31.

[56] Milner, *Experiment*, p. 31.

[57] Milner, *Experiment*, p. 31.

more disturbing about her Wagnerian 'interests' in rituals of submission and abandon.[58] As Maud Ellmann has written, Milner 'offers few particulars about the crises of her times'.[59] And yet, *An Experiment in Leisure* is nonetheless saturated by what Milner describes as her 'forebodings about Fascism'.[60] In the sections of the book that address her present-day diaries and notebooks, Milner records her journey to Spain in 1936, where she rented an attic room in Malaga and wrote much of her book on the eve of the Spanish Civil War. In the diary entries recording her journey across Europe, Milner finds herself troubled by 'thoughts of political brutalities', 'obsessed' by 'preoccupations with cruelty'.[61] In Spain, Milner dwells on 'those preoccupations of the past months which had been an undercurrent in all my living, preoccupations with the renewed outburst of cruelty and assertive destroying power in the world, and also with illness and the lives of the poor'.[62] In her 1987 book *Eternity's Sunrise: A Way of Keeping a Diary*, Milner reflects that '*An Experiment in Leisure* was written during the time of the 1930s hunger marches' and suggests that her concern for the poor 'pointed to the fact that, unless we do manage to solve the problem of how to share the world's resources, the horror-struck face' in what she calls her 'Holocaust picture' (a painting she made following a visit to what she calls 'the Holocaust Museum' in Israel in 1975) 'could become a reality'.[63] In *An Experiment in Leisure*, Milner also notes her tendency to 'see red' when she hears about 'political atrocities'.[64] Recalling her response to Eisenstein's 1933 film *Thunder Over Mexico*, 'in which the rulers trample three peasant boys to death with horses', Milner describes her 'dull rage', which grew 'to a fierce throbbing in my stomach and I had longed to murder and utterly destroy those triumphant horsemen—while at the same time I felt resentment against Eisenstein for so exploiting my emotions'.[65] Registering the daily news of dictators, military aggression and creeping war, Milner's diaries record the feelings of despair that accompany her 'every time I go out in the streets these days, or look at a newspaper'.[66] 'Not long ago', she writes in one notebook entry, 'it was—"MACHINE-GUNS IN VIENNA"' that blared out from newspaper headlines; 'Now', following Mussolini's aggressions against Ethiopian troops in 1935, it is '"MASSACRE OF ABYSSINIANS"'.[67] Milner records a

---

[58] Milner, *Experiment*, p. 32.

[59] Ellmann, 'New Introduction', p. xxxvii.

[60] Milner, *Experiment*, p. 82.

[61] Milner, *Experiment*, p. 82, p. 87.

[62] Milner, *Experiment*, p. 86.

[63] Marion Milner, *Eternity's Sunrise: A Way of Keeping a Diary* (Hove: Routledge, 2011), p. 194.

[64] Milner, *Experiment*, p. 86.

[65] Milner, *Experiment*, pp. 86–7.

[66] Milner, *Experiment*, p. 87.

[67] Milner, *Experiment*, p. 87.

'dead weight of foreboding over international affairs', and describes her feelings of impotent rage concerning 'the pain of the common people everywhere, poverty and oppression', the 'dead weight of pain over the world's troubles'.[68] Milner is, therefore, horrified to discover that the rituals of submission she finds so enthralling also take centre stage within the propaganda stalking fascist and totalitarian Europe.

In her 'Summing Up' to *An Experiment in Leisure*, Milner writes:

> The discovery of the power of these half-pictured ideas that drew me like a magnet had certainly been surprising. I had been so bred up in the belief in argument and purposes that this other way of living seemed impossibly vague and spineless. Also I had often been filled with a kind of horror to observe how the opinions of groups of people could be stampeded by an image, particularly an image with the word 'red' attached. [. . .] I had been most shocked when I found that some of those images which had seemed to grow out of my most intimate and private experience, and that I had thought represented for me the kernel of the problem of escape from the narrow focus of egoism, were being used by others to foster what seemed to me that most sinister form of egoism—jingoistic nationalism. For I had read in the newspapers that pagan rituals were being revived in Germany, as part of the movement to glorify violence and to discredit the teachings of Christ. When I first read this I had been tempted to throw over my whole enterprise, I thought that all this time I must have been following a will-o'-the-wisp, that images in their double-facedness were false gods after all.[69]

Milner describes a feeling of horror, as she recognises that her own desire for a form of emotional surrender to a fantasy world dominated by images of witches, horned devils, bullfights, Wagnerian mythology and sacrificial gods bears a disturbing resemblance to the fascist appeals to the iconography, and forms, of pagan ritual.

As Ellmann notes, Milner's lengthy discussion of her awe at Spanish bull-fighting (she describes it as 'the most satisfying religious ceremony of my life') is tempered by her unease at the possible fascist connotations of a nationalist ritual that Franco would quickly promote 'as a symbol of Spanish national unity'.[70] The reference to the revival of 'pagan rituals' in Germany also suggests Milner's awareness of the Nazi adoption of Wagnerian mythology.[71] Milner was

---

[68] Milner, *Experiment*, p. 88.

[69] Milner, *Experiment*, p. 166.

[70] Milner, *Experiment*, p. 86; Ellmann, 'New Introduction', p. xxx.

[71] Milner, *Experiment*, p. 166.

fascinated by Wagnerian mythology, recording, in both *A Life of One's Own* and *An Experiment in Leisure*, her 'haunting' returns to *Götterdämmerung*, as well as her interest in the *Nibelungenlied*.[72] And yet, by 1937, Milner seems, like many others (including Virginia Woolf), to have been worrying about the Nazi adoption of Wagnerian mythology in propaganda such as Leni Riefenstahl's *Triumph of the Will*, the 1935 film of the Nuremberg Rally, in which Hitler is seen to descend from the sky like the Germanic god Wotan.[73] Milner may also have 'read in the newspaper', specifically in *The Times* in May 1936, about 'Herr Hitler's May Day', when, as the newspaper correspondent described, Hitler delivered a speech to the masses next to 'a large Maypole [. . .] decorated with swastikas and fir branches'.[74] For Milner, what is most disturbing is not simply that she uncovers a shared fascination with the icons of European fascism, but that these magnetic 'images' also, in Milner's interpretation, represent her own 'most intimate and private' desire for a form of emotional surrender of the ego – a form of individual surrender that bears a striking resemblance to the forms of emotional surrender demanded by fascism. Being 'carried in the stream' might, for Milner, represent 'the kernel of the problem of escape from the narrow focus of egoism'.[75] But such a form of self-obliteration may also, when deployed to sweep up the individual into the fascist crowd, be used 'to foster [. . .] that most sinister form of egoism—jingoistic nationalism', and much worse.

Milner's response to this recognition is initially, she records, one of shock. And yet, she insists, the prevailing insistence that we must fight totalitarian irrationalism with democratic reason seems to have failed. 'We are continually

---

[72] Milner, *Experiment*, p. 28; Milner, *Life*, pp. 113–14.

[73] On this, see Roger Eatwell, *Fascism: A History* (London: Pimlico, 2003), p. 145; on Woolf's response to the Nazi appropriation of Wagner, see Emma Sutton, *Virginia Woolf and Classical Music* (Edinburgh: Edinburgh University Press, 2013), pp. 126–33.

[74] 'Herr Hitler's May Day', *The Times*, 2 May 1936, p. 14, cited by Iain Boyd Whyte, 'Berlin, 1 May 1936', in *Fascism: Fascism and Culture*, ed. by Roger Griffin and Matthew Feldman (Basingstoke: Palgrave Macmillan, 2004), pp. 292–306 (p. 292). Roger Griffin writes: 'the entire event was deliberately staged through the creation of a liturgical space, choreography of the crowds, and the enactment of a ritual invented for the occasion in order to superimpose onto a spring festival of seasonal regeneration a Nazi concept of national renewal. For this to happen, ancient pagan customs had to be reshaped into what the art historian Hans Weigert, in 1934, called "the deepest maternal foundations of blood and soil". The Nazis' act of mythic appropriation and subversion is epitomised by the huge swastika crowning the maypole. The painting subsequently recording the festival completed the transfiguration of a stage-managed piece of political propaganda transformed into the icon of a transcendental moment in the history of the reborn *Volk*.' Roger Griffin, *A Fascist Century: Essays by Roger Griffin*, ed. by Matthew Feldman (Basingstoke: Palgrave Macmillan, 2008), p. 17.

[75] Milner, *Life*, p. 18; Milner, *Experiment*, p. 166.

reading', Milner writes in her conclusion, 'of how democracy demands that all of us should think more clearly, reason more adequately, about public affairs.'[76] 'But', she notes, 'it has in recent years been proved that the inborn reasoning capacity of most of us is not very high.'[77] Citing a review by Aldous Huxley of 'a book which expounded the racial beliefs of Nazi Germany' (the book was Lothar G. Tirala's 1935 publication *Rasse, Geist und Seele*), Milner draws out the ways in which the dogged insistence on democratic 'reason' merely leaves a gaping hole for the raging passions of modern nationalism to burn.[78] Struck by Huxley's observation that 'the attempt to replace passion and prejudice by reason' is, in the face of 'Modern nationalists', 'absurd', Milner asks:

> Was it not possible that Freud was right, and that man's discovery of reason had, so to speak, gone to his head, with the result that many reformers assumed it should be possible to make everybody live by reason all the time, when actually the great majority of people can never live by reason, but only by habit and by faith?[79]

The illusion that we might banish the irrational fantasy components of social and political life through the simple appeal to 'reason', Milner implies, may drive those irrational elements further underground – and, of course, like any good student of Freud, Milner recognises that the attempt to drive unreason underground only results in its more violent re-emergence.

Attempting to distinguish between her own fascination with rituals of self-abandon and the image of submission to 'an absolute father-god-dictator' within Nazi propaganda, Milner develops, or at least attempts to develop, a crucial distinction between the inward psychological meanings of images, and the ideological manipulation of such symbols in 'public life'.[80] Acknowledging the power of images in 'controlling a people's mood', Milner writes:

> My own experience seemed to show that such images were really outward and visible signs of inward experience, and I thought that their power in controlling mood must lie in the fact that, unlike abstract ideas and reasoning, their outwardness was deeply rooted in simple sensation, in the concreteness of colour and shape and texture and sound and movement. Yet this very source of their power was also the source of their danger; for [. . .] the double meaning of the image so easily got

[76] Milner, *Experiment*, p. 165.
[77] Milner, *Experiment*, p. 165.
[78] Milner, *Experiment*, p. 166.
[79] Milner, *Experiment*, pp. 166–7; Milner cites Aldous Huxley, 'Race', *New Statesman and Nation*, 11.272 (9 May 1936), 716, 718 (p. 718).
[80] Milner, *Experiment*, p. 168, p. 167.

lost, the whole matter got transferred into the outside world. Instead of vehicles for the communication of inner private immediate experience, they had been taken as real in their own right, because to believe in the innerness of experience was difficult, but to cling to a concrete statement of apparent external fact was easy.[81]

The appeal, Milner insists, of 'primitive images' is that they speak powerfully to the individual's inner psychological needs – but in political and cultural life this potent imagery is manipulated so that it will be confused, by readers, spectators and consumers, with a direct representation of 'external fact'. 'In democratic countries', Milner writes,

> the most powerful manipulators of vital images seemed to be the film-producers, the advertisers and the popular press; and these on the whole manipulated them quite irresponsibly for their own financial advantage, though at times of national stress and in elections they were also used politically. Under dictatorships, vital images seemed used more deliberately for political purposes, primitive images of blood-brotherhood, of blood sacrifice for one's country, of an absolute father-god-dictator at the head of the nation.[82]

The danger resides, Milner insists, in 'taking images literally', in confusing the outer symbol of one's inner needs with external 'fact':

> For if you lived recognising only the outer half of the facts, taking images literally, as many people did, then the ignored inner facts, the demands of the inner organization of desire, took their revenge by distorting your external vision, and you would read with gusto the lies of atrocity-mongers and pass them on to your friends as if they were the external truth.[83]

Once taken as a 'truth of external fact' (rather than as a figure that symbolically satisfies internal needs), such imagery becomes 'the instrument of all kinds of exploitation—lustful, political, social, the instrument of the crudest infantile desire to be king of the castle and to prove that others are dirty rascals'.[84]

[81] Milner, *Experiment*, p. 168.

[82] Milner, *Experiment*, pp. 167–8.

[83] Milner, *Experiment*, p. 169.

[84] Milner, *Experiment*, p. 168. Milner, as Maud Ellmann notes, provides few 'practical examples of this principle', but, Ellmann suggests, 'perhaps she is thinking of the fascist image of the Jew, in which an inner fear—of the inhuman, the excremental, the abject, the uncanny—is mistaken for an outer menace, justifying all atrocities against this bugbear'. Ellmann, 'New Introduction', p. xxxi.

Milner's anxiety about her own emotional susceptibility to the irrational appeals of totalitarianism does not dissipate. But, in the final pages of *An Experiment in Leisure*, she does describe what she sees as a way 'to pass sagely between this Scylla and Charybdis' of 'reason' and 'passion', suggesting that her 'method' of self-observation and analysis might itself become what Maud Ellmann describes as a 'program for resisting fascism'.[85] Milner argues that the process of cultivating and observing one's own interests and desires might itself be a method of avoiding the blind adherence to those she describes as the 'public exploiters of furtive emotion—the politicians, the atrocity-mongers, the popular press'. Wondering 'whether the problem of the education of opinion towards public affairs might not be approached from a different angle', Milner writes:

> instead of trying to teach people to reason better, which is very likely beyond the inborn capacity of most of us, why not teach us to understand our feelings better, to know what we really want, so that we would be less at the mercy of unscrupulous exploiters [. . .]?[86]

In both *A Life of One's Own* and *An Experiment in Leisure*, Milner emphasises the need for a method of self-observation that might allow the individual not only to understand their own pleasures and desires, but also to cultivate these individual desires in opposition to the 'unscrupulous exploiters' of capitalist and fascist modernity. 'I do not mean', she acknowledges, 'that we should all try to join the ranks of minor poets or exhibit at local art shows, but that each of us should realise that the act of welding, by means of words or shape or musical sounds or colour—into some sort of tangible form—a single moment of lived experience, is action [. . .] real and effective.'[87] For Milner, the act of crafting, of 'welding' 'raw lived experience' into 'some sort of tangible form', is a form of what she calls 'expressive action' – an active creative process of resisting the widespread surrender to fascism.[88] Unreason, Milner argues, cannot be simply tamed by appeal to the court of reason, but by seeking, through her method of self-observation, 'to understand our feelings better', we might be 'less at the mercy of unscrupulous exploiters'.

Reading the Reader in *The Years*

In *An Experiment in Leisure*, Marion Milner charts the perils of a desire for different forms of cultural abandon within the social and political world of

---

[85] Ellmann, 'New Introduction', p. xxxvii.
[86] Milner, *Experiment*, p. 164.
[87] Milner, *Experiment*, pp. 148–9.
[88] Milner, *Experiment*, pp. 148–9, p. 153.

1930s Europe. In *The Years* – published, like Milner's *Experiment*, in 1937 – Virginia Woolf similarly offers up an analysis of the psychic and political perils of cultural abandon in an age of fascism. In *The Years*, Woolf stages a series of scenes of reading that place questions about the psychic, social and political life of reading at the heart of the novel. In these portraits of reading, Woolf offers up a thrilling account of the pleasures, for women in particular, that reside in reading books. Nonetheless, I want to argue, Woolf does not rest in any easy celebration of the pleasures and enchantments of reading. Like Milner, who tracks the political dangers of her own desire to immerse herself in rituals of self-abandon (whether in the form of pagan ritual or aesthetic absorption in a book, a painting or a piece of music), Woolf traces a similar anxiety about the proximity between moments of aesthetic self-abandon and the reader's self-abandonment to fascism. Just as Milner is fearful of the ways in which her pleasures might be co-opted by the 'unscrupulous exploiters' of fascism, Woolf too reveals how the reader's pleasure in reading might leave her vulnerable prey to fascist ideology.

In a crucial, and much-revised, scene from the 1907 section of *The Years*, Sara Pargiter, who suffers from what we are told in the final text is a 'very slight deformity', has been instructed by her doctor to 'Lie straight, lie still', and so remains alone at home in bed, while her older sister and parents are out at a ball.[89] 'A faded brown book lay on her bed; as if she had been reading':

> 'And he says,' she murmured, 'the world is nothing but . . .' She paused. What did he say? Nothing but thought, was it? [. . .] Well [. . .] she would let herself *be* thought. It was easier to act things than to think them. Legs, body, hands, the whole of her must be laid out passively to take part in this universal process of thinking which the man said was the world living. She stretched herself out. Where did thought begin?
>
> 'In the feet?' she asked. There they were, jutting out under the single sheet. They seemed separated, very far away. She closed her eyes. Then against her will something in her hardened. It was impossible to act thought. She became something; a root; lying sunk in the earth; veins seemed to thread the cold mass; the tree put forth branches; the branches had leaves.[90]

Abandoning the 'dull' and 'faded brown book' of philosophy, Sara gazes out of her bedroom window to watch the guests from a neighbour's dance mingling

---

[89] Woolf, *The Years*, p. 108, p. 125. When drafting what was, in 1933, still part of her 'Essay-Novel' *The Pargiters*, Woolf described this scene as 'the turn of the book'. Woolf, *Diary*, IV, p. 129, p. 149; Anna Snaith, 'Introduction', in Woolf, *The Years*, pp. xxxix–xcix (p. lxvi).
[90] Woolf, *The Years*, p. 118.

in the garden, and reaches 'her hand above her head' for 'another book' – this time for her cousin Edward's translation of Sophocles' *Antigone*.

Taking down *Antigone* from the shelf, 'Her lip raised [. . .] like that of a horse that is going to bite', Sara opens 'the book at random', but, at the same time, her eye is 'caught by one of the couples who were still sitting out in the garden'.[91] As she reads, Sara moves seamlessly between different imaginative and psychic spaces, turning over the pages of the ancient tragedy while simultaneously making up her own romantic story about the couple in the garden, and lingering over romantically tinged memories of her cousin in Oxford. Eschewing the impersonal, disinterested, scholarly modes of reading practised by the male scholars in Woolf's novels (including an earlier scene in *The Years* that depicts Edward reading and translating Sophocles), Sara indulges, like Mrs Ramsay in *To the Lighthouse*, in Woolf's preferred mode of reading 'at random'.[92] In this densely interwoven portrait of Sara's inner life, the operations of perception, sensation, daydreaming, memory, fantasy and imagination all blur and intermingle, shaping and reshaping the contents of Sara's mind. Although to begin with Sara's attention moves, almost imperceptibly, distractedly between the garden, her daydream, memories and the words on the page, increasingly Sara finds herself absorbed within the scenes from ancient Greece:

> She skipped through the pages. At first she read a line or two at random; then, from the litter of broken words, scenes rose, quickly, inaccurately, as she skipped. The unburied body of a murdered man lay like a fallen tree-trunk, like a statue, with one foot stark in the air. Vultures gathered. Down they flopped on the silver sand. With a lurch. With a reel, the top-heavy birds came waddling; with a flap of the grey throat swinging, they hopped—she beat her hand on the counterpane as she read—to that lump there. Quick, quick, quick with repeated jerks they struck the mouldy flesh. Yes. She glanced at the tree outside in the garden. The unburied body of the murdered man lay on the sand. Then in a yellow cloud came whirling—who? She turned the page quickly. Antigone? She came whirling out of the dust-cloud to where the vultures were reeling and flung white sand over the blackened foot. [. . .] Then behold! [. . .]

---

[91] Woolf, *The Years*, p. 119, p. 120.

[92] In *To the Lighthouse*, Mrs Ramsay opens a book 'and began reading here and there at random, and as she did so she felt that she was climbing backwards, upwards, shoving her way up under petals that curved over her, so that she only knew this is white, or this is red' (Woolf, *To the Lighthouse*, p. 96). Later in *The Years*, Peggy picks up Guy de Maupassant's *Sur l'eau* (1888) and opens it 'at random' (Woolf, *The Years*, pp. 345–6). In 1940, when Woolf began to write a book about reading, she called it *Reading at Random* and, later, *Turning the Page*. '"Anon" and "The Reader"', p. 356.

the horsemen leapt down; she was seized; her wrists were bound with withies; and they bore her, thus bound—where?

There was a roar of laughter from the garden. She looked up. Where did they take her? she asked. The garden was full of people. She could not hear a word that they were saying. The figures were moving in and out.

'To the estimable court of the respected ruler?' she murmured, picking up a word or two at random, for she was still looking out into the garden. The man's name was Creon. He buried her. [. . .] The man in the loincloth gave three sharp taps with his mallet on the brick. She was buried alive. The tomb was a brick mound. There was just room for her to lie straight out. Straight out in a brick tomb, she said. And that's the end, she yawned, shutting the book.

She laid herself out, under the cold smooth sheets, and pulled the pillow over her ears. The one sheet and the one blanket fitted softly round her.[93]

After she has discarded the 'ugly little brown volume' of philosophy, Sara's reading of *Antigone* is breathless, imaginative and embodied, producing a vivid imagining of the scenes from the play.[94] Woolf offers a dramatic evocation of the power with which scenes rise up from the page, conjured, as if by magic, out of a 'litter of broken words'.[95] The short sentences convey the excited rapidity with which Sara reads, 'turn[ing] the page quickly', while the slippage and blurring of the ambiguous third-person pronoun suggests Sara's identification with Antigone. 'She' comes to describe both the reader and the protagonist in this passage – 'she', Sara, in the process of reading Sophocles' account of Antigone being 'seized' and 'bound' by Creon's henchmen, is herself 'seized', 'bound', gripped by the words on the page.[96]

Placed alongside Woolf's critique of institutionalised forms of masculine, disinterested scholarly reading, it is tempting to read this scene from *The Years* as a counter-celebration of feminine pleasure in reading 'at random' – a celebration of the forms of embodied and affective identification outlawed by a masculine scholarly taboo on personal emotion within the scene of reading.[97] It's tempting to read Sara's pleasure in reading as an example of the forms of rapturous delight that Milner tracks in her experiments in leisure. Not only, however, might we want to read this scene in *The Years* as a portrait of feminine pleasure in reading, we might also want to read it, as other critics have,

---

[93] Woolf, *The Years*, pp. 121–2.
[94] Woolf, *The Years*, p. 119, p. 124.
[95] Woolf, *The Years*, p. 121.
[96] Woolf, *The Years*, p. 121.
[97] On Woolf's hostility to institutionalised, scholarly methods of reading see Chapter 3, and Cuddy-Keane, *Virginia Woolf*, pp. 68–75.

alongside Woolf's analysis of *Antigone* in *Three Guineas*, and to argue that Sara enacts the form of feminist reading that Woolf modelled in what she called her 'Anti fascist Pamphlet'.[98]

In *Three Guineas*, Woolf summoned Sophocles' *Antigone* as a lens through which to examine her contemporary historical moment.[99] Exhorting her readers to go to the 'public libraries', Woolf held out the example of *Antigone* and asked her readers to 'Consider the character of Creon':

> There you have a most profound analysis by a poet, who is a psychologist in action, of the effect of power and wealth upon the soul. Consider Creon's claim to absolute rule over his subjects. That is a far more instructive analysis of tyranny than any our politicians can offer us. [. . .] Consider Antigone's distinction between the laws and the Law. That is a far more profound statement of the duties of the individual to society than any our sociologists can offer us. Lame as the English rendering is, Antigone's five words are worth all the sermons of all the archbishops.[100]

Tracing the egotistical cry of the patriarchs and dictators issuing from the 1930s wireless back to the cry of 'Creon, the dictator' in ancient Greece, Woolf tracked the parallels between Creon's dictatorship and the dictatorships of 1930s Europe:

> As we listen to the voices we seem to hear an infant crying in the night, the black night that now covers Europe, and with no language but a cry, Ay, ay, ay, ay . . . But it is not a new cry, it is a very old cry. Let us shut off the wireless and listen to the past. We are in Greece now; Christ has not been born yet, nor St Paul either. But listen:
> 'Whomsoever this city may appoint, that man must be obeyed, in little things and great, in just things and unjust . . . disobedience is the

---

[98] Woolf, *Diary*, IV, p. 202. On the relationship between the 'Essay-Novel' that Woolf began under the title *The Pargiters*, the novel that became *The Years*, and the essay *Three Guineas*, see Alice Wood, *Virginia Woolf's Late Cultural Criticism: The Genesis of 'The Years', 'Three Guineas' and 'Between the Acts'* (London: Bloomsbury, 2013).

[99] Woolf, *Three Guineas*, p. 162. As Emily Dalgarno has argued, Woolf's 'reading of *Antigone* is part of a larger twentieth-century European criticism in which new approaches to the interpretation of classical texts criticised by implication Fascist policies'. Emily Dalgarno, *Virginia Woolf and the Migrations of Language* (Cambridge: Cambridge University Press, 2012), p. 41, p. 46.

[100] Woolf, *Three Guineas*, p. 162. In the footnotes, Woolf gives R. C. Jebb's translation of Antigone's 'five words': "'Tis not my nature to join in hating, but in loving. [. . .] To which Creon replied: "Pass, then, to the world of the dead, and, if thou must needs love, love them. While I live, no woman shall rule me"' (p. 239, n. 40).

worst of evils . . . We must support the cause of order, and in no wise suffer a woman to worst us . . . They must be women, and not range at large. Servants take them within.' That is the voice of Creon, the dictator. To whom Antigone, who was to have been his daughter, answered, 'Not such are the laws set among men by the justice who dwells with the gods below.' But she had neither capital nor force behind her. And Creon said: 'I will take her where the path is loneliest, and hide her, living, in a rocky vault.' And he shut her not in Holloway or in a concentration camp, but in a tomb. And Creon we read brought ruin on his house, and scattered the land with the bodies of the dead. It seems, Sir, as we listen to the voices of the past, as if we were looking at the photographs again, at the picture of dead bodies and ruined houses that the Spanish Government sends us almost weekly. Things repeat themselves it seems. Pictures and voices are the same today as they were 2,000 years ago.[101]

For Woolf, Antigone not only appears as a feminist critic of patriarchal and fascist power, but she also exposes the inseparable connections between the 'public and private worlds', reinforcing Woolf's argument in *Three Guineas* that the 'tyrannies and servilities of the one are the tyrannies and servilities of the other'.[102] Anticipating a number of later twentieth-century interpretations of *Antigone*, Woolf offers a reading of Antigone not only as a feminist critic of Creon's patriarchal dictatorship, but also as a figure who, in Gillian Rose's words, performs an 'act of justice' that serves to 'reinvent the political life of the community'.[103] For Woolf, in *Three Guineas*, Antigone stands as a model for Woolf's own argument about the figure of the 'outsider', who is uniquely empowered, through her marginal position, to offer up a critique, and a potential reimagining, of the reigning structures of patriarchal, imperialist and fascist oppression.

Returning to the scene of Sara reading *Antigone* in *The Years*, we might imagine that, on the basis of her identification with Antigone, Sara too will be empowered to perform a similar critique of twentieth-century patriarchs and dictators. Making this link between the interpretation of *Antigone* in *Three Guineas* and the scene of Sara reading in *The Years*, Emily Dalgarno suggests

---

[101] Woolf, *Three Guineas*, pp. 213–14.

[102] Woolf, *Three Guineas*, p. 214.

[103] Gillian Rose, *Mourning Becomes the Law: Philosophy and Representation* (Cambridge: Cambridge University Press, 1996), pp. 35–6; see also Madelyn Detloff, '"'Tis Not my Nature to Join in Hating, But in Loving": Toward Survivable Public Mourning', in *Modernism and Mourning*, ed. by Patricia Rae (Lewisburg: Bucknell University Press, 2007), pp. 50–68 (p. 53); Judith Butler, *Antigone's Claim: Kinship between Life and Death* (New York: Columbia University Press, 2002).

that Sara's identification with Antigone 'makes intelligible to [Woolf's] reader the deathlike life of a female in the Victorian family'.[104] Lying 'herself out' in her bed, echoing and mirroring Antigone lying 'straight out' in her 'brick tomb', Sara presents us with one of Woolf's archetypal images of female imprisonment within the Victorian home – a form of imprisonment which, in this novel as in *Three Guineas*, is implicitly linked to the tyrannies and impositions of the fascist state. Again, the slippage in Woolf's use of the third-person pronoun encourages us as readers to consider the ways in which 'She', Sara, might identify with Antigone: 'She', Sara, is metaphorically 'buried alive' within the patriarchal household.[105] Reading Sara reading *Antigone*, therefore, we might be tempted to hope that, on the basis of her identification with Antigone, Sara too will be empowered to perform a similar 'outsider's' critique of twentieth-century dictators.[106]

The portrait of Sara reading certainly forms part of Woolf's valorisation of the pleasures of imaginative, leisurely reading, and I do think that this scene is linked to Woolf's claim, in *Three Guineas*, that reading *Antigone* in a public library (or in bed) might inspire the 'common reader' to perform her own outsider's critique of patriarchal fascism. And yet, nonetheless, I also want to argue that there is something in this scene of Sara reading that exceeds both of these arguments. There's something disturbing in the breathless anticipation with which Sara confronts the body of the dead brother, 'beat[ing] her hand on the counterpane as she read[s]', mirroring, enacting the vultures, 'Quick, quick, quick', as they strike the 'lump' of 'mouldy flesh'. There's something troubling about that 'Yes' that follows on from the image of the 'mouldy flesh'. In R. C. Jebb's translation of *Antigone* (the parallel text translation that Woolf read and quoted from in *Three Guineas*), this scene is narrated by a guard who describes how 'suddenly a whirlwind lifted from the earth a storm of dust'.[107] The dust clears to reveal Antigone 'wailing', before she scatters dust over 'the corpse bare'.[108] Sara echoes the description of a 'whirlwind', but, although the guard's description does refer to the 'dank body' and its 'smell', it is only later in the play that Sophocles employs the image of Polyneices' body as carrion

[104] Dalgarno, *Virginia Woolf*, p. 56.

[105] See also Diana L. Swanson, 'An Antigone Complex? Psychology and Politics in *The Years* and *Three Guineas*', in *Virginia Woolf: Texts and Contexts: Selected Papers from the Fifth Annual Conference on Virginia Woolf*, ed. by Beth Rigel Daugherty and Eileen Barrett (New York: Pace University Press, 1996), pp. 35–9 (p. 37).

[106] Woolf, *Three Guineas*, p. 183. See Julia Briggs, *Virginia Woolf: An Inner Life* (London: Allen Lane, 2005), p. 307.

[107] Sophocles, *The Plays and Fragments, Part III: Antigone*, trans. by R. C. Jebb (Cambridge: Cambridge University Press, 1888), p. 85.

[108] Sophocles, *The Plays and Fragments*, p. 87, p. 86.

for birds of prey.[109] Later in the play, Teireseus warns Creon: 'the altars of our city and of our hearths have been tainted, one and all, by birds and dogs, with carrion from the hapless corpse, the son of Oedipus.'[110] The birds, 'screaming with dire, feverish rage', no longer give any 'clear sign' to the seer, 'for they have tasted the fatness of a slain man's blood'.[111] Teireseus forewarns that a 'tumult of hatred against thee stirs all the cities whose mangled sons had the burial-rite from dogs, or from wild beasts, or from some winged bird that bore a polluting breath to each city that contains the hearths of the dead'.[112] Reading rapidly, and 'at random', rather than with the slow methodical accuracy of the scholar, Sara is possessed by the image of the corpse, seizing disparate parts of the text which come together to form this feverish scene within her mind. Sara doesn't appear only to identify with Antigone, but gets caught up in, bound up in, the actions of the vultures pecking at the dead brother's 'unburied body'.

Sara's imagining of this scene is, as George Steiner notes in his account of the many Antigones that haunt Western culture, 'the most hallucinatory, the most knowing in its macabre sexuality'.[113] There is, in Sara's feverish and even 'macabre' bedtime reading, something that exceeds both the interpretation of this scene as a tribute to feminine pleasure in reading and the interpretation of this scene as a potential route to feminist critique. Furthermore, as we'll see in my second scene of reading from *The Years*, despite Woolf's apparent insistence in *Three Guineas* that Antigone might provide a model for women to speak out against the perverted patriarchal laws of totalitarian Europe, the deeply eccentric and troubling character of Sara does not appear to carry such values across from her reading of *Antigone* into her present-day life or politics. Just as Milner's *Experiment in Leisure* describes a fearfulness that individual pleasures might be co-opted by noxious political ideologies, Woolf too forces us to confront the ways in which the individual's pleasure in reading might get caught up in some of the most troubling political ideologies of 1930s Europe.

'DELICIOUS SOLITUDE'

In the 'Present Day' 1930s section of *The Years*, Sara's cousin North recites Andrew Marvell's 'The Garden' to her in a darkened room in an East London boarding house. Their 'delicious solitude' is interrupted by Sara's disturbingly

---

[109] Woolf, *The Years*, p. 121; Sophocles, *The Plays and Fragments*, p. 83.

[110] Sophocles, *The Plays and Fragments*, p. 183.

[111] Sophocles, *The Plays and Fragments*, p. 179, p. 183.

[112] Sophocles, *The Plays and Fragments*, p. 191.

[113] George Steiner, *Antigones* (Oxford: Clarendon Press, 1984), p. 141.

antisemitic outburst when she hears a person she describes as 'the Jew' running a bath in the shared bathroom of the boarding house:

> As he spoke the words out into the semi-darkness they sounded extremely beautiful, he thought, because they could not see each other, perhaps.
>
> He paused at the end of the verse.
>
> 'Go on,' she said.
>
> He began again. The words going out into the room seemed like actual presences, hard and independent; yet as she was listening they were changed by their contact with her. But as he reached the end of the second verse—
>
> > Society is all but rude—
> > To this delicious solitude . . .
>
> he heard a sound. Was it in the poem or outside of it, he wondered? Inside, he thought, and was about to go on, when she raised her hand. He stopped. He heard heavy footsteps outside the door. [. . .]
>
> 'The Jew,' she murmured.
>
> 'The Jew?' he said. They listened. He could hear quite distinctly now. Somebody was turning on taps; somebody was having a bath in the room opposite.
>
> 'The Jew having a bath,' she said.
>
> 'The Jew having a bath?' he repeated.
>
> 'And tomorrow there'll be a line of grease round the bath,' she said.
>
> 'Damn the Jew!' he exclaimed. The thought of a line of grease from a strange man's body on the bath next door disgusted him.
>
> 'Go on—' said Sara: 'Society is all but rude,' she repeated the last lines, 'to this delicious solitude.'
>
> 'No,' he said.[114]

This, one of the most disturbing scenes in Woolf's writing, quickly develops into a barely intelligible frenzied rant from Sara, in which she describes herself, upon hearing the 'unemployed singing hymns under the window', as having 'rushed out in a rage' on to a bridge to cry: 'Am I a weed, carried this way, that way, on a tide that comes twice a day without a meaning?'[115] Evoking T. S. Eliot's deathlike crowd flowing over London Bridge, Sara describes 'people passing' with a horror for the passive urban masses of modernity, recalling them as 'the strutting; the tiptoe-ing; the pasty; the ferret-eyed; the bowler-hatted, servile innumerable army of workers'.[116] 'Must I join your conspiracy?' Sara

---

[114] Woolf, *The Years*, pp. 305–6.
[115] Woolf, *The Years*, p. 307.
[116] Woolf, *The Years*, p. 307.

demands. 'Stain the hand, the unstained hand [. . .] and sign on, and serve a master; all because of a Jew in my bath [. . .]?'[117] Recounting her trip to a newspaper office to seek work, Sara spuriously displaces her rage at her own material downfall on to her Jewish neighbour.[118] But, even as Sara claims a desire not to be subservient to group behaviour, even as she claims to reject the passive 'servility' of the masses, she nonetheless reveals her own subscription to the antisemitic groupthink of the 1930s. Towards the end of the passage Woolf describes Sara sitting up and laughing, 'excited by the sound of her own voice which had run into a jog-trot rhythm'.[119] Sara is – and I am arguing that Woolf wants us to recognise this – caught up in the mass mind and the 'jog-trot rhythm' of British fascism.

For some of Woolf's critics, this controversial and much-discussed scene is not only evidence of Woolf's own antisemitism, it also reveals the way that her antisemitism was bound up in a specifically modernist desire for a lyrical and historically evasive culture of redemption. For Maren Linett, Sara's and North's desire for the 'delicious solitude' of the lyric poet expresses Woolf's own feeling of being under pressure, in part from the political position of her Jewish husband (who, unlike Woolf, advocated sanctions against Italy), 'to abandon her pacifism and sacrifice her modernism of interiority and "vision"' for the sordid world of historical fact.[120] And yet, as David Bradshaw has pointed out, Woolf carefully frames this particular scene in a way that critically exposes rather than endorses Sara's antisemitism – not only does Sara live on a road chalked up with the same British Union of Fascists graffiti that Woolf herself had noted with concern in London in 1935, but she also lives in a part of East London that was the site of repeated and violent attacks on the Jewish community,

---

[117] Woolf, *The Years*, p. 307.

[118] Anna Snaith cites an extended version of this passage from the galley proofs for *The Years* in which Woolf much more explicitly links 'journalism, prostitution and anti-semitism'. Snaith, 'Introduction', pp. lxxxiii–lxxxiv.

[119] Woolf, *The Years*, p. 307.

[120] Maren Linett, 'The Jew in the Bath: Imperilled Imagination in Woolf's *The Years*', *Modern Fiction Studies*, 48.2 (2002), 341–61 (p. 349). For Phyllis Lassner, similarly, the antisemitism in this scene is bound up in Woolf's use of a specifically modernist 'mythic method'. Phyllis Lassner, '"The Milk of Our Mother's Kindness Has Ceased to Flow": Virginia Woolf, Stevie Smith, and the Representation of the Jew', in *Between 'Race' and Culture: Representations of 'The Jew' in English and American Literature*, ed. by Bryan Cheyette (Stanford: Stanford University Press, 1996), pp. 129–44 (p. 136). On Woolf and antisemitism, see Phyllis Lassner and Mia Spiro, 'A Tale of Two Cities: Virginia Woolf's Imagined Jewish Spaces and London's East End Jewish Culture', *Woolf Studies Annual*, 19 (2013), 58–82 (p. 69); Briggs, *Virginia Woolf*, pp. 305–10; Lara Trubowitz et al., 'Responses', *Woolf Studies Annual*, 19 (2013), 16–25 (p. 17).

including the 1936 Battle of Cable Street.[121] Alongside this historical framing, I also think it's significant that Sara's antisemitic outburst appears within a carefully staged scene of reading lyric poetry. Far from reading this scene as a symptom of Woolf's own desire for retreat, I want to suggest that it is, on the contrary, part of Woolf's own self-conscious indictment of the very idea that lyric poetry might offer the reader a form of redemption from historical and political reality.

In this scene, Woolf reveals how North and Sara turn to the 'beautiful' poetry of 'solitude' as part of an attempt to bolster fascist fantasies about the contaminating presence of 'the Jew' in British society, showing how they prop up a racist fantasy of solitude via the act of reading lyric poetry. Following his arrival at Sara's East End boarding house, North repeatedly expresses his disgust at the 'dirty', 'sordid', 'low-down' street that Sara lives on, expressing his frustration at the perpetual interruptions of the sounds from the street, while meditating on the question of 'society or solitude; which is best'.[122] North, who has, as Sara observes, 'been alone all these years', writing lyrical letters from his farm in colonial Africa, appears firmly on the side of 'solitude'. North's turn to poetry is clearly framed as part of his desire to escape from the 'rude' eruptions from the street. As he reads aloud to Sara, North takes pleasure in the feeling of solitude conveyed by the 'semi-darkness', observing that the words 'sounded extremely beautiful [. . .] because they could not see each other, perhaps'.[123] 'The words going out into the room seemed like actual presences, hard and independent', suggesting North's fantasy of poetry as autonomous, impervious to the 'sordid' nature of his surroundings. And 'yet', as Sara listens, the words are 'changed by their contact with her'.[124] Despite North's fantasy of solitude and poetic autonomy, Woolf's description of this scene as a pointedly social scene (North reading poetry aloud to his cousin, rather than sitting alone in silence with a book) also insists upon the irreducibly social nature of poetic language, implicitly criticising Sara's and North's desire for an uncontaminated solitude, and challenging their own antisocial impulses. 'Words', as Woolf put it in her radio broadcast on 'Craftsmanship', 'have been out and about, on people's lips, in their houses, in the streets, in the fields, for so many centuries.'[125]

---

[121] Woolf, *The Years*, pp. 279–80; David Bradshaw, 'Hyams Place: *The Years*, the Jews and the British Union of Fascists', in *Women Writers of the 1930s: Gender, Politics and History*, ed. by Maroula Joannou (Edinburgh: Edinburgh University Press, 1999), pp. 179–91 (p. 182). On 4 September 1935, Woolf had written in her diary: 'In London yesterday. Writings chalked up all over the walls. "Don't fight for foreigners. Briton should mind her own business." Then a circle with a symbol in it. Fascist propaganda, L. said. Mosley active again.' Woolf, *Diary*, IV, p. 337.

[122] Woolf, *The Years*, p. 280, p. 285.

[123] Woolf, *The Years*, p. 306.

[124] Woolf, *The Years*, p. 306.

[125] Virginia Woolf, 'Craftsmanship', in *Essays*, VI, pp. 91–102 (p. 95).

As Judith Allen has noted, there is a striking parallel between Woolf's description of the shifting, sociable nature of language and Mikhail Bakhtin's theory of language: 'As a living, socio-ideological concrete thing, as heteroglot opinion, language, for the individual consciousness, lies on the borderline between oneself and the other,' wrote Bakhtin. 'The word in language is half someone else's.'[126] In Woolf's portrait of North reading to Sara, words lie 'on the borderline' between speaker and listener, changing as they move between 'oneself and the other', ironising and undercutting North's fantasy of poetic autonomy.

In this scene, the uncomfortable juxtaposition of the seductive lyricism of Marvell's reflection on 'delicious solitude' with Sara's and North's antisemitism reveals how violent antisocial fantasies about solitude might be bolstered via the reading of poetry. In Marvell's poem, despite the luscious temptations of solitude, the speaker finds that "twas beyond a mortal's share / To wander solitary there'.[127] But, despite Sara's attempts to goad North to 'Go on' with his reading of the poem, they never reach this line, remaining caught up in the fantasy of an unattainable 'delicious solitude'. This intimate, charged, but also deeply uneasy portrait of reading offers a self-reflective meditation on, and critique of, the very idea of 'delicious solitude', subtly ironising North's and Sara's attempt to use poetry in order to build up a protective barrier against the imagined corruptions of the modern city. Although both North and Sara may seek to use the poem to prop up a fantasy of retreat from the 'Polluted city', nonetheless, Woolf's framing of the scene refuses to grant them the kind of lyric escape that they desire, their longing for solitude repeatedly disrupted by the interruptions from the street and the boarding house.

Later in the scene, following Sara's antisemitic rant, North switches on the electric light and Sara picks up a book again: this time, Shakespeare. First, Sara alights on *Macbeth*, but when she hands the book to North, he opens it 'at random' on *The Tempest*.[128] In the manuscript drafts of this scene, in the passages following Elvira's outburst, George takes 'the book open at the Tempest' and begins to read, while Elvira lies 'back without a book, trying to remember [. . .] what scene it would be': 'The storm was over: there was music in the air, & [. . .] the shipwrecked crew, rubbed the sleep from their eyes. She put her knuckles to her own face; & sighed. Acting the past [part?].'[129] George

---

[126] M. M. Bakhtin, *The Dialogic Imagination: Four Essays by M. M. Bakhtin*, ed. by Michael Holquist, trans. by Caryl Emerson and Michael Holquist (Austin: University of Texas Press, 1981), p. 291, cited by Judith Allen, *Virginia Woolf and the Politics of Language* (Edinburgh: Edinburgh University Press, 2010), p. 29, pp. 42–3.

[127] Andrew Marvell, 'The Garden', in *The Complete Poems*, ed. by Elizabeth Story Donno (London: Penguin, 2005), p. 101.

[128] Woolf, *The Years*, p. 312.

[129] Virginia Woolf, *The Pargiters: The Novel-Essay Portion of The Years*, ed. Mitchell A. Leaska (New York and London: Harcourt Brace Jovanovich, 1977), p. 12, p. 14.

finds that 'the words acted upon him as if they opened something in his mind, set it free':[130]

> The two were on an [. . .] island; couched on the yellow sand, there was faint music, & the boom of the breaker, receding, slowly, for the storm was over, & [. . .] moment by moment the howl & the storm was hushed, before the voice spoke. [. . .] & now, a light, made her turn: what wonderful apparition. [. . .]—She said: Are you in the play or not? [. . .] she asked. A woman stood there in white.[131]

In the published text, Woolf describes this scene in similar terms:

> He opened it at random.
> 'The scene is a rocky island in the middle of the sea,' he said. He paused.
> Always before reading he had to arrange the scene; to let this sink; that come forward. A rocky island in the middle of the sea, he said to himself—there were green pools, tufts of silver grass, sand, and far away the soft sigh of waves breaking. He opened his mouth to read. Then there was a sound behind him; a presence—in the play or in the room? He looked up.
> 'Maggie!' Sara exclaimed.[132]

In these passages, George and Elvira, later North and Sara, seek refuge in the solitude of Shakespeare's 'rocky island', entering a kind of dreamscape in which they struggle to distinguish what is 'in the play or in the room'. Similarly, when North recites Marvell, he hesitates about whether the sound he hears is 'in the poem or outside of it', revealing his immersion within the world of the poem. But this striking metaphor of the poem as a container with uncertain and permeable borders itself exposes the limitations in North's and Sara's fantasy of the scene of reading as an island of retreat. In these scenes of North and Sara reading, Woolf reveals how their alluring fantasies of poetic solitude are shot through with troublingly antisocial and antisemitic impulses, while at the same time challenging the idea of poetry as retreat and demanding something different from her own readers.

In *Three Guineas*, Woolf argued that reading *Antigone* might solicit a recognition of the 'duties of the individual to society'.[133] In a footnote to *Three*

---

[130] Woolf, *The Pargiters*, p. 15.
[131] Woolf, *The Pargiters*, p. 15.
[132] Woolf, *The Years*, p. 312.
[133] Woolf, *Three Guineas*, p. 162.

Guineas, Woolf comments on the ease with which *Antigone* might be made into what she describes as 'anti-Fascist propaganda':

> Antigone herself could be transformed either into Mrs Pankhurst, who broke a window and was imprisoned in Holloway; or into Frau Pommer [a Prussian woman imprisoned and charged with 'slandering the State and the Nazi movement']. Antigone's [. . .] words [. . .] could be spoken either by Mrs Pankhurst, or by Frau Pommer; and are certainly topical. Creon, again, [. . .] is typical of certain politicians in the past, and of Herr Hitler and Signor Mussolini in the present.[134]

In this footnote, we find Woolf pushing at the more disturbing dimensions of our mobile and multi-layered investments in literary texts. Reading *Antigone*, we might, like Woolf, identify the heroine with a Mrs Pankhurst or a Frau Pommer, and thereby translate Antigone's fight against tyranny into a contemporary articulation of resistance against patriarchal fascism. But beneath Woolf's faith in the transformative possibilities of the outsider's identification with Antigone lurks a more troubling possibility – that we might 'when the curtain falls [. . .] sympathise [. . .] even with Creon himself'. Although it may be easy to 'squeeze' characters from ancient Greece 'into up-to-date dress', it is, Woolf insists, 'impossible to keep them there': the reader's sympathies might take them to the darkest of places.[135] As we saw in Sara's reading of *Antigone*, we cannot be certain that the reader will identify herself only in the figure of the feminist critic of totalitarian patriarchal rule. At the close of that scene, despite her apparently powerful identification with Antigone, Sara yawns and falls asleep.

'SUMMING UP'

In *An Experiment in Leisure*, Marion Milner doesn't offer a historical analysis of why, in the 1920s and 1930s, people became so acutely vulnerable to the appeals of fascist propaganda. There is, however, a striking link between Milner's analysis of the process through which fascist propaganda appeals to 'the demands of the inner organization of desire', and Hannah Arendt's analysis, in *The Origins of Totalitarianism*, of the totalitarian method of 'dominating and terrorizing human beings from *within*'.[136] In her account of the rise of totalitarianism, Arendt describes a shift from what she calls the 'extroverted Chauvinism' of the older, nineteenth-century nationalisms, to the 'introverted'

---

[134] Woolf, *Three Guineas*, p. 238, n. 39.

[135] Woolf, *Three Guineas*, p. 238, n. 39.

[136] Milner, *Experiment*, p. 169; Hannah Arendt, *The Origins of Totalitarianism* (New York: Schocken, 2004), p. 431, my emphasis.

appeal of the new 'tribal nationalism' that arose across Europe at the beginning of the twentieth century.[137] 'In psychological terms,' Arendt writes, 'the chief difference between even the most violent chauvinism and this tribal national-ism is that the one is extroverted, concerned with visible spiritual and mate-rial achievements of the nation, whereas the other, even in its mildest forms (for example, the German youth movement) is introverted.'[138] Like the 'vital' imagery that Milner describes as making an appeal to the 'inner organization of desire', this new 'introverted' nationalism 'concentrates', in Arendt's words, 'on the individual's own soul'.[139] For Arendt, it was the increasingly atom-ised nature of post-war society that rendered Europe so ripe for the ideologi-cal manipulations of fascist demagogues. The boom in statelessness (and its consequent rightlessness) in the wake of the First World War, the breakdown of traditional class structures across Europe, and an increasing 'alienation of the masses from government' all coincided, in Arendt's analysis, to produce a population of alienated, atomised, lonely individuals who, 'in the first helpless-ness of their new experience', were uniquely prey to the rise of an 'especially violent', 'introverted' nationalism propagated by mass leaders for 'purely dem-agogic reasons'.[140] For Milner too, the power of Nazi propaganda resides in its appeal to the 'inner organization of desire', distorting the individual's 'external vision' and becoming, in the process, the 'instrument of all kinds of exploi-tation—lustful, political' and 'social'.[141] Both Milner and Arendt describe, in different ways, the process through which fascist ideology makes its appeal to the inner psychological needs of the atomised modern individual, in order to manipulate, as Milner puts it, his or her 'external vision' of political and historical reality.[142]

In Arendt's analysis, the 'self-abandonment into the mass' was precipitated by the social atomisation that she describes as the condition of totalitarian rule: 'Isolation', she writes, 'may be the beginning of terror; it certainly is its most fertile ground; it always is its result.'[143] For Arendt,

> Isolation is that impasse into which men are driven when the political sphere of their lives, where they act together in the pursuit of a com-mon concern, is destroyed. Yet isolation, though destructive of power and the capacity for action, not only leaves intact but is required for all so-called productive activities of man. Man insofar as he is *homo faber*

[137] Arendt, *Origins*, p. 292.
[138] Arendt, *Origins*, p. 292.
[139] Milner, *Experiment*, p. 169; Arendt, *Origins*, p. 292.
[140] Arendt, *Origins*, p. 328, p. 421.
[141] Milner, *Experiment*, p. 169, p. 168.
[142] Milner, *Experiment*, p. 169.
[143] Arendt, *Origins*, p. 421, p. 611.

tends to isolate himself with his work, that is to leave temporarily the world of politics. Fabrication (*poiesis*, the making of things), as distinguished from action (*praxis*) on one hand and sheer labor on the other, is always performed in a certain isolation from common concerns, no matter whether the result is a piece of craftsmanship or of art. In isolation, man remains in contact with the world as the human artifice; only when the most elementary form of human creativity, which is the capacity to add something of one's own to the common world, is destroyed, isolation becomes altogether unbearable.[144]

In the final pages of *The Origins of Totalitarianism*, Arendt traces the similarities, and the crucial differences, between experiences of isolation, solitude and loneliness. Although, for Arendt, the loneliness of the uprooted modern masses renders those individuals ripe for totalitarian rule, there is also, in these final pages, the faint glimmer of an alternative in the creative possibilities of solitude and the activity of thinking. In the activity of thinking, the individual performs what Arendt describes as 'a dialogue between me and myself; but this dialogue of the two-in-one does not lose contact with the world of my fellow-men because they are represented in the self with whom I lead the dialogue of thought'.[145]

For Arendt, the task faced in the post-1945 world was to wrest the capacity for thinking back from the abyss of totalitarianism. For Marion Milner, writing in 1937, a process of creative experiment and self-reflection represented a risky, yet vital, form of action in response to the lies of dictators. In the 'Summing Up' to *An Experiment in Leisure*, Milner writes:

> My conclusion was that there was a psychological necessity to pay deliberate homage to something since if it is not deliberate it will be furtive, but none the less powerful and at the mercy of public exploiters of furtive emotion—the politicians, the atrocity-mongers, the popular press; and also the psychological necessity to find your own pantheon of vital images, a mythology of one's own, not the reach-me-down mass-produced mythology of Hollywood, of the newspapers, or the propaganda of dictators.[146]

Milner's endeavour to separate her personal desires from the mass-produced fantasies of twentieth-century cultural and political life is precarious. As Lyndsey Stonebridge has noted, Milner's attempts to insert a 'frontier which differentiates what is inside from what is outside a self' founders on a 'paradoxical logic' that is repeatedly imperilled by Milner's own discovery that the boundary between

---

[144] Arendt, *Origins*, pp. 611–12.
[145] Arendt, *Origins*, p. 613.
[146] Milner, *Experiment*, p. 174.

individual and political fantasies is porous and slippery.[147] Milner does not, as Stonebridge adds, offer her reader 'a fence to sit on, or a line which would neatly demarcate the space between personal desires and identifications and those of a wider political scenario'.[148] 'Instead', Stonebridge argues, Milner 'point[s] uncompromisingly to the fragility of this line of severance'.[149] Despite her fearfulness that this need to 'pay deliberate homage to something' bears an uncomfortable resemblance to the forms of homage and individual surrender demanded under totalitarian rule, Milner nonetheless insists that it is a 'psychological necessity'.[150] For Milner, this need for emotional surrender is, in fact, at its most dangerous when the emotion is forced to become 'furtive', where it becomes prey to the 'public exploiters of furtive emotion—the politicians, the atrocity-mongers, the popular press' and the 'dictators'.[151] Milner, as I've argued in this chapter, insists that the only way to guard against the passive adherence to the 'monsters' of 1930s Europe is through the very process of cultivating, observing and analysing one's own interests and desires. The 'method' of cultivating and analysing one's own pleasures that Milner models in *An Experiment in Leisure* itself becomes a fragile attempt to insure individual desires against the unconscious acceptance of the 'reach-me-down mass-produced mythology of Hollywood, of the newspapers, or the propaganda of dictators'.

If Milner, to quote Stonebridge once again, refuses to offer us 'a line which would neatly demarcate the space between personal desires and identifications and those of a wider political scenario', then Woolf too reveals the fragile border between rapturous identification and the troubling psycho-politics of the group. In *The Years*, Woolf charts the perilous proximity between the individual reader's pleasure in a literary fantasy of 'delicious solitude' and fascist groupthink fantasies about the contaminating presence of 'the Jew' in British society. Submitting herself to the pleasures of the literary text, the reader might discover herself in the figure of Antigone, but, like Sara, she might also find herself submitting to the 'jog-trot' rhythms of fascism. She might find herself sympathising 'with Creon himself', or, in Sara's case, repeating the racist tropes of Oswald Mosley. In presenting us with these self-reflexive scenes of reading, Woolf encourages her readers to confront the more troubling fantasies at work within modernist culture about the role of the literary text in psychic, social and political life. Woolf's portraits of reading also provide a sharp riposte to the age-old and recently much-trumpeted claim that empathetic identification in the act of reading is, in itself, a moral or political good. As Lyndsey

---

[147] Stonebridge, *The Destructive Element*, p. 156.
[148] Stonebridge, *The Destructive Element*, p. 171.
[149] Stonebridge, *The Destructive Element*, p. 171.
[150] Milner, *Experiment*, p. 174.
[151] Milner, *Experiment*, p. 174.

Stonebridge and Rachel Potter write in the context of literature and human rights, 'Few [. . .] have questioned the assumption that rights writing should produce empathy, or that empathy is somehow intrinsically good for rights outcomes.'[152] And yet, they cite Arendt, 'Pity taken as the spring of virtue, has proved to possess a greater capacity for cruelty than cruelty itself.'[153] Woolf's deeply ambivalent portraits of Sara and North reading, when read alongside the footnote about *Antigone* in *Three Guineas*, demonstrate that the reader's process of identification with a literary text can be as politically compromised as it can be politically liberating.

Although, in *Three Guineas*, Woolf imagines the scene of reading as an enactment of feminist solidarity with the 'Outsiders' Society', in *The Years*, she depicts literary encounters that do not always transform into the kind of outsider's critique inspired by her reading of *Antigone* in *Three Guineas*. In *The Years*, literature – be it Sophocles' *Antigone*, Marvell's 'The Garden' or Shakespeare's *The Tempest* – won't necessarily yield the reader a safe position outside of the fantasies and structures that dominated Europe in the 1930s. In *Three Guineas*, Woolf exhorted women to read and write with 'their own tongue', to 'practise the profession of reading and writing in the interests of culture and intellectual liberty'.[154] But, just as Antigone models a form of outsider's critique while simultaneously tracing the messy overlaps between women's political and psychic lives, so, in *The Years*, Woolf reveals that the scene of reading requires a risky form of identification that doesn't guarantee the reader a safe position outside of the structures that she might wish to criticise. Like Milner, who struggles, in *An Experiment in Leisure*, to insert what Stonebridge describes as a 'frontier which differentiates what is inside from what is outside a self', in both *Three Guineas* and *The Years*, Woolf comes up against the difficulty of inserting boundaries both within and between individual minds.[155]

And yet, where Milner encourages her reader to take up her 'method' of cultivating, observing and analysing her individual pleasures, Woolf too, as I have been arguing throughout this book, asks her reader to develop a similar self-reflexive 'method' of analysing her own literary pleasures and identifications. In *The Years*, Woolf embeds within her writing a series of self-reflexive scenes of reading that work to foreground, and also to challenge, the fantasies that shape our understanding of the function of literature in individual psychic, social and political life. Although, formally, *The Years* is strikingly

---

[152] Rachel Potter and Lyndsey Stonebridge, 'Writing and Rights', *Critical Quarterly*, 56.4 (2014), 1–16 (p. 6).

[153] Hannah Arendt, *On Revolution* (Harmondsworth: Penguin, 1977), cited by Potter and Stonebridge, 'Writing and Rights', p. 7.

[154] Woolf, *Three Guineas*, p. 168, p. 169.

[155] Stonebridge, *The Destructive Element*, p. 156.

distinct from the first-person soliloquies and poetry of *The Waves*, the scenes of reading enacted within *The Years* function in a similar way to the scenes of reading staged in the earlier novel, soliciting Woolf's own reader to reflect not only on the process of reading such a vast, formally complex and multi-layered text (Woolf described it as 'facts, as well as the vision [. . .] The Waves going on simultaneously with Night & Day'), but also on the fantasies that shape, and overdetermine, his or her own scene of reading.[156] In a diary entry for 1934, while working on what, at that stage, she was calling 'Here & Now', Woolf notes 'An idea about Sh[akespea]re':

> That the play demands coming to the surface—hence insists upon a reality wh. the novel need not have, but perhaps should have. Contact with the surface. Coming to the top. This is working out my theory of the different levels in writing, & how to combine them: for I begin to think the combination necessary. [. . .] Idea that one cd work out a theory of fiction &c on these lines: how many levels attempted.[157]

When North sits down to read Shakespeare, Woolf describes how 'Always before reading he had to arrange the scene; to let this sink; that come forward'.[158] In *The Years*, Woolf asks her own readers to engage in a similar process of 'let[ting] this sink; that come forward'. In the scenes of reading depicted in the novel, Woolf asks her own readers to reflect on their own process of reading. These portraits of reading, like Milner's *Experiment*, demand that we, as readers, reflect more seriously on, and develop an analysis of, the individual, social and political fantasies that shape our own pleasures, desires and identifications as readers. In performing such an analysis we might better understand the ways in which such pleasures and identifications can become captive to toxic political ideologies. And, as we will see in my conclusion, it's only by understanding such desires – today in the twenty-first century as much as in the 1930s – that we might mobilise them for an alternative to the fantasies that have shaped the scene of reading in this book.

---

[156] Woolf, *Diary*, IV, pp. 151–2. On the relationship between experimental modernism and realism in *The Years*, see Anna Snaith, '*The Years* and Contradictory Time', in *A Companion to Virginia Woolf*, ed. by Jessica Berman (Oxford: Wiley Blackwell, 2016), pp. 137–50 (p. 142); Anna Snaith, 'Late Virginia Woolf', *Oxford Handbooks Online*, 2015, https://www.oxfordhandbooks.com/view/10.1093/oxfordhb/9780199935338.001.0001/oxfordhb-9780199935338-e-28 (accessed 27 October 2023).

[157] Woolf, *Diary*, IV, p. 207.

[158] Woolf, *The Years*, p. 312.

CONCLUSION: READING MODERNISM'S READERS TODAY

In his 1992 book *Being a Character*, Christopher Bollas writes about books as 'transformational objects', objects that allow their readers to process, and to transform, their own inner lives.[1] For Bollas, through a 'particular type of projective identification', we secrete parts of ourselves within the object world and are in turn 'substantially metamorphosed by the structure of objects; internally transformed by objects that leave their traces within us, whether it be the effect of a musical structure, a novel, or a person'.[2] Having completed his PhD thesis on Herman Melville, Bollas believes that the paradigmatic transformational object is *Moby Dick*:

> I know that by choosing Melville's book I selected an object that allowed me to be dreamed by it, to elaborate myself through the many experiences of reading it. In some ways its mental spaces, its plot, its characters, allowed me to move elements of my idiom into collaboration with the text and hence into being. Selecting it [. . .] was an intuitive choice [. . .] based on my knowing (yet not knowing why) that this book—rather than, say, Hawthorne's *The Scarlet Letter*—would bring something of

---

[1] Christopher Bollas, *Being a Character: Psychoanalysis and Self Experience* (London: Routledge, 1992). See also Christopher Bollas, *The Shadow of the Object: Psychoanalysis of the Unthought Known* (London: Free Association Books, 1987).
[2] Bollas, *Being a Character*, p. 20, p. 59.

me into expression. I did not think at the time that it connected to an episode at the age of eleven when I was swimming some hundred yards off the shore of my favorite cove in my hometown when I saw what initially looked to me like a large reef moving in my direction. In fact, it was a whale and it passed me by so closely that although it did not touch me I could still feel it. It was a profoundly upsetting moment and linked in the unconscious, I believe, to an experience at the age of nine of riding up over a wave to collide with the bloated body of a woman who must have been dead at sea for some time—an experience whose memory I repressed, but which 'resurfaced' some years after writing the dissertation when I incorrectly assumed that it was pure fantasy. Although I subsequently discovered its authenticity, it nonetheless collected to it, like a screen memory, many factors in my psyche which had then organized into a repression. Thus in choosing to work on *Moby Dick* [. . .] I selected an object that I could use to engage in deep unconscious work, an effort that enabled me to experience and articulate something of myself.[3]

Like Proust's narrator's rediscovery of his childhood favourite *François le Champi* in *Time Regained*, or Rhoda's reading of Shelley in *The Waves*, the novel works as a magnet for deeply buried memories from childhood. While Proust's narrator at first dismisses the childhood self resurrected within him by *François le Champi* as a 'stranger', Bollas at first responds to the resurfacing of childhood memory as an intrusion, 'pure fantasy'; but, like Proust's narrator, he comes to accept the 'authenticity' of the repressed memory, brought back to life within him, made available to thought, by his work on Melville's novel. *Moby Dick*, Bollas notes, is 'the exception': for the most part, our transformational objects remain 'ahermeneutic', or uninterpretable.[4] Although we feel a '*jouissance*' in the encounter with such objects, the roots of this feeling remain inscrutable and illegible.[5]

Bollas stages his work as a return to the 'truth' of the unconscious: to its irreducible and ineluctable slippage. Like the early modernist critics of psychoanalysis, for whom the pathologising propensities of the psychoanalyst represented an insidious and sovereign claim to delimit unconscious processes that are not amenable to such forms of interpretation, Bollas maintains a scepticism towards certain strands of contemporary psychoanalysis, asking: 'Has psychoanalysis discarded an early effort to be lost in thoughts, to be inside

---

[3] Bollas, *Being a Character*, pp. 57–8.
[4] Bollas, *Being a Character*, p. 58; Proust, *Time Regained*, pp. 239–40.
[5] Bollas, *Being a Character*, p. 53.

the complexity of subjectivity by concentrating attention on the identifiable samples of psychic life: the symptom, the obvious character trait, the narrated history?'[6] Proposing 'a different fate—or at least a more complex fate—for the human subject than is suggested by the ego-psychological ideal of a progressive adaptation to reality', Bollas suggests that 'the self *is* unconsciousness' and that our uniquely 'private idiom' deposits in each of us 'a substantial part of our-self somehow deeply known (profoundly us) yet unthought'.[7] 'Above all,' he asserts, 'our itness, or our idiom, is our mystery.'[8] It is this 'itness', this irreducibly private idiom, this 'deeply known' but 'unthought' residue, that is at work in the encounter with a transformational object.

There is a crucial political drive in Bollas's insistence on the need to remain alert to the irreducibly unconscious aspects of human experience. The political vein here is thrown into sharp relief in an essay in the same collection on 'The Fascist State of Mind', in which, drawing on Hannah Arendt, Bollas describes the prerequisite for the fascist state of mind as the inability to tolerate 'doubt' and the expulsion of all 'uncertainty' from the mind in order to achieve 'totality' and 'maintain ideological certainty'.[9] For Bollas, the encounter with a transformational object, like the encounter with a modernist text, brings the reader up against the 'unthought known' of psychic life, forcing us to let go of the potentially totalising claims to self-knowledge and textual mastery that Woolf too, as we have seen, viewed as dangerously close to the totalitarian mindset.[10]

As we've seen throughout this book, the modernist scene of reading is often depicted as a site of transformation. For Proust, Woolf, Freud, Klein and Milner, the scene of reading offers moments in which the boundaries between reader and book begin to dissolve, granting the reader access to powerful fantasies of literature as a source of pleasure, a form of consolation, a source of communal belonging, and a site of reparation. And yet, as I've been arguing throughout this book, the scene of reading in modernist literature and psychoanalysis is also fraught with the political perils of the 1920s and 1930s: from fears about the standardising effects of mass culture, to the 'forebodings about Fascism' that haunted writers in the 1930s.[11] In this conclusion, I turn to two final scenes of reading, one from Woolf's last novel, *Between the Acts*, published in 1941, and the other from Eimear McBride's 2013 novel *A Girl Is a Half-formed*

[6] Bollas, *Being a Character*, p. 49.

[7] Bollas, *Being a Character*, pp. 50–1.

[8] Bollas, *Being a Character*, p. 51.

[9] Bollas, *Being a Character*, pp. 200–1. On the politico-ethical ramifications of Bollas's writing, see Josh Cohen, *The Private Life: Why We Remain in the Dark* (London: Granta, 2013), pp. 6–8, pp. 196–7.

[10] Bollas, *The Shadow of the Object*, p. 4, pp. 13–40.

[11] Milner, *Experiment*, p. 87.

Thing. Reading these scenes of reading in light of recent arguments about the contemporary uses of literature, I consider the legacies of the modernist scene of reading today, and ask: what kind of reading might be adequate, or necessary even, in an age of 'fake news' and 'alternative facts'?

*   *   *

In the opening scenes of *Between the Acts* (1941), Isa finds herself standing in the library, running her eyes along the bookshelves:

> 'The library's always the nicest room in the house,' she quoted, and ran her eyes along the books. 'The mirror of the soul' books were. *The Faerie Queen* and Kinglake's *Crimea*: Keats and the *Kreutzer Sonata*. There they were, reflecting. What? What remedy was there for her at her age—the age of the century, thirty-nine—in books? Book-shy she was, like the rest of her generation; and gun-shy too. Yet as a person with a raging tooth runs her eye in a chemist's shop over green bottles with gilt scrolls on them lest one of them may contain a cure, she considered: Keats and Shelley; Yeats and Donne. Or perhaps not a poem; a life. The life of Garibaldi. The life of Lord Palmerston. Or perhaps not a person's life; a country's. *The Antiquities of Durham*; *The Proceedings of the Archaeological Society of Nottingham*. Or not a life at all, but science—Eddington, Darwin, or Jeans.
>
> None of them stopped her toothache. For her generation the newspaper was a book; and, as her father-in-law had dropped *The Times*, she took it and read: 'A horse with a green tail . . .' which was fantastic. Next, 'The guard at Whitehall . . .' which was romantic, and then, building word upon word she read: 'The troopers told her the horse had a green tail; but she found it was just an ordinary horse. And they dragged her up to the barrack room where she was thrown upon a bed. Then one of the troopers removed part of her clothing, and she screamed and hit him about the face. . . .' That was real; so real that on the mahogany door panels she saw the Arch in Whitehall; through the Arch the barrack room; in the barrack room the bed, and on the bed the girl was screaming and hitting him about the face, when the door (in fact it was a door) opened and in came Mrs. Swithin carrying a hammer.[12]

In *Between the Acts*, the characters are haunted by the fragments of poetry, books and newspapers that echo and reverberate within their minds. Mr Oliver quotes Byron ('She walks in beauty like the night') and Swinburne ('Swallow,

[12] Woolf, *Between the Acts*, pp. 14–15.

my sister, O sister swallow'), his sister, Mrs Swithin, finds herself stalked by the 'mammoths, mastodons, and prehistoric birds' described in her 'Outline of History', and Isa (who is also a poet) repeatedly finds herself muttering scraps of poetry from Swinburne, Keats and Shelley.[13] And yet, in this scene, Isa reads about a violent gang rape in the morning newspaper – a scene that sticks with her and becomes bound up with the fragments of poetry that echo round her mind over the course of the summer's day.

Scenes of reading, like the scenes from Miss La Trobe's pageant, run around inside the characters' heads in *Between the Acts*. When William Dodge stumbles across Isa murmuring lines of poetry to herself, she tells him: 'It's the play [. . .] The play keeps running in my head.'[14] In this, her final novel, Woolf sets up an analogy between the scene of reading and the village pageant (which is itself a kind of patchwork of English literature), encouraging her own readers to reflect on the parallels between the act of reading and the act of attending the community play. And yet, although *Between the Acts* certainly encodes Woolf's own longing for an art form capable of fostering forms of collective belonging, it does not present either the village pageant or the scene of reading as a straightforwardly reparative or democratic affair.[15] In *Between the Acts*, the central characters, the villagers, and even Miss La Trobe herself may express a desire for a form of collective unity, but, at the same time, this novel also expresses Woolf's ambivalence about the politics of any such form of collective identification in the political context of the late 1930s.

Throughout the novel Woolf underscores the appeal of moments that seem to express 'some inner harmony'.[16] Following Miss La Trobe's 'experiment' in exposing the audience to 'ten mins. of present time', a rain shower falls suddenly to her rescue, creating a powerful collective experience:

> No one had seen the cloud coming. There it was, black, swollen, on top of them. Down it poured like all the people in the world weeping. Tears. Tears. Tears.
>
> 'Oh that our human pain could here have ending!' Isa murmured. Looking up she received two great blots of rain full in her face. They trickled down her cheeks as if they were her own tears. But they were all people's tears, weeping for all people.[17]

---

[13] Woolf, *Between the Acts*, p. 4, p. 80, p. 156.

[14] Woolf, *Between the Acts*, p. 76.

[15] See Jed Esty, *A Shrinking Island: Modernism and National Culture in England* (Princeton: Princeton University Press, 2004), pp. 54–107; Marina McKay, '*Between the Acts*: Novels and Other Mass Media', in *A Companion to Virginia Woolf*, ed. by Jessica Berman (Oxford: Wiley Blackwell, 2016), pp. 151–62.

[16] Woolf, *Between the Acts*, p. 87.

[17] Woolf, *Between the Acts*, p. 129.

As the rain ceases and the 'voice that was no one's voice' resumes its nursery rhyme, Isa's experience of the pageant is described in terms of a religious experience:

> 'Oh that my life could here have ending,' Isa murmured (taking care not to move her lips). Readily would she endow this voice with all her treasure if so be tears could be ended. The little twists of sound could have the whole of her. On the altar of the rain-soaked earth she laid down her sacrifice. . . .[18]

And yet, although Woolf celebrates Isa's experience of ecstatic group feeling, the pageant itself also serves as a critical commentary on the forms of togetherness enshrined in English imperialism, while Miss La Trobe's Brechtian finale is a striking rejection of the 'Grand Ensemble, round the Union Jack' expected by Mrs Mayhew.[19] Although early on in the pageant Miss La Trobe longs for the moments in which 'The tick, tick, tick seemed to hold them together, tranced', the novel's references to fascism in Europe render the villagers' vulnerability to this form of entrancement politically suspect.[20] Miss La Trobe may feel a form of triumph in the moments when 'for one moment she held them together', but when she turns the mirrors on the audience she introduces a form of Brechtian alienation that breaks up the experience of unity and togetherness.[21]

In these scenes, Woolf's own readers are solicited to identify with the audience at the pageant, but also to reflect critically on the fantasies of solace, community and togetherness underpinning our own acts of reading. When the 'pilgrims' appear on stage, 'each declaim[ing] some phrase or fragment from their parts', the reader is also presented with a patchwork of 'orts, scraps and fragments' from the pageant, from literature, and nursery rhyme:

> I am not (said one) in my perfect mind . . . Another, Reason am I . . . And I? I'm the old top hat. . . . Home is the hunter, home from the hill . . . Home? Where the miner sweats, and maiden faith is rudely strumpeted. . . . Sweet and low; sweet and low, wind of the western sea . . . Is that a dagger that I see before me? . . . The owl hoots and the ivy mocks tap-tap-tapping on the pane. . . . Lady I love till I die, leave thy chamber and I come . . . Where the worm weaves its winding sheet . . . I'd be a butterfly. I'd be a butterfly. . . . In thy will is our peace. . . . Here, Papa, take your book and read aloud. . . . Hark, hark, the dogs do bark and the beggars . . .[22]

---

[18] Woolf, *Between the Acts*, p. 130.
[19] Woolf, *Between the Acts*, p. 114.
[20] Woolf, *Between the Acts*, p. 60.
[21] Woolf, *Between the Acts*, p. 70.
[22] Woolf, *Between the Acts*, pp. 132–3.

In these final passages, Woolf's prose is permeated by a deep tension between the appeal to rhythmic unity and collective experience, and a counter-current of critical anxiety about the political significance of such forms of collective experience in the late 1930s.[23] Although the 'megaphontic [sic], anonymous, loud-speaking' voice exhorts the audience to 'break the rhythm and forget the rhyme', Woolf's own prose continues to be propelled by the rhythms of the pageant, offering Woolf's own readers the seductive appeal of collective identification even as it offers up a critique of the political abuses of such forms of collective identification in 1930s Britain and Europe.[24]

In the final pages of the novel, the central characters sit down to read letters, newspapers and books, and Mrs Swithin reflects on the local vicar's 'interpretation' of the play: 'Did you feel', she asks Isa, 'what he said: we act different parts but are the same?'[25] 'Yes,' says Isa, affirming Mrs Swithin's characteristically redemptive interpretation of the pageant; but then 'No':

> It was Yes, No. Yes, yes, yes, the tide rushed out embracing. No, no, no, it contracted. The old boot appeared on the shingle.
> 'Orts, scraps and fragments,' she quoted what she remembered of the vanishing play.[26]

As Mrs Swithin settles down once more with her 'Outline of History', Isa watches 'the pageant fade', Bartholomew's newspaper 'crackle[s]', and the story from the morning's newspaper plays over once more in Isa's mind: 'The girl had gone skylarking with the troopers. She had screamed. She had hit him. . . . What then?'[27] This scene of violent sexual assault – rooted in an actual newspaper account of a teenage girl who was gang raped by soldiers in Whitehall in 1938 – haunts Isa throughout the novel, muddled up amongst the fragments of poetry that circle within her head, casting a shadow over any attempt to find redemption in this scene of reading.[28]

[23] On rhythm in *Between the Acts*, see Stonebridge, *The Destructive Element*, pp. 79–107.
[24] Woolf, *Between the Acts*, p. 134.
[25] Woolf, *Between the Acts*, p. 154.
[26] Woolf, *Between the Acts*, p. 154.
[27] Woolf, *Between the Acts*, p. 155.
[28] Mark Hussey notes: '*The Times* reported for several days in July 1938 on the trial of Sir Aleck Bourne, who had performed an abortion on a teenage girl who had been raped at the barracks of the Royal Horse Guards earlier that year. The soldiers had lured the girl by asking if she would like to see a horse with a green tail. The rape itself was reported on in *The Times*, 28 June 1938 ("Three Troopers on Trial", II), and 29 June 1938 ("Two Troopers found 'Guilty'", II). The article on 29 June reported that the girl "screamed and tried to push him away and punched him, and he said he would hit her back and hurt her"; the girl was then "dragged upstairs to the barrack room and thrown on a bed and was again assaulted".' Mark Hussey, 'Explanatory Notes', in *Between the Acts*, p. 173, n. 15: 3–10.

In this, Woolf's final novel, the scenes of reading express Woolf's longing for a form of democratic community, but they also explore the limits in the vision of literature as a democratic 'common ground', forcing Woolf's own readers up against the darker side of this vision. In Isa's troubled encounter with a newspaper story about gang rape, Woolf reminds her readers of her own analysis of the violence at the heart of patriarchal group formations, challenging any simple idealisation of the scene of reading as a site of collective reparation.

*   *   *

Following its publication in 2013, Eimear McBride's *A Girl Is a Half-formed Thing* has been celebrated as a twenty-first-century return to the experimental audacity of modernist writing. In this novel, narrated in a halting, traumatised, yet deeply and unnervingly intimate form of first-person monologue, the reader is placed inside the mind of a girl who, upon being raped by her uncle at thirteen, is propelled into a series of violent, shame-riddled and abject sexual encounters with her uncle and other men. Beginning inside the womb, the unnamed protagonist recounts her life from earliest infancy through to her brother's death from a brain tumour and her own suicide by drowning in her early twenties. Reviewers and critics have compared McBride's intense, half-formed and halting sentences with Molly Bloom's monologue at the end of *Ulysses*, with the stuttering syntax of Samuel Beckett's *Not I*, with the prose of Ernest Hemingway and Gertrude Stein, and with the interior monologues and representation of female consciousness in Dorothy Richardson, May Sinclair and Virginia Woolf.[29] McBride herself proudly claims her allegiance to modernist writing, declaring James Joyce as her 'hero' and citing *Ulysses* as a decisive influence on the book.[30]

---

[29] See for example Adam Mars-Jones, 'All your walkmans fizz in tune', *London Review of Books*, 35.15 (8 August 2013), 31–2; James Wood, 'Useless Prayers', *The New Yorker*, 29 September 2014, http://www.newyorker.com/magazine/2014/09/29/useless-prayers (accessed 8 October 2021); John Sutherland, 'Eimear McBride's novel doesn't fit any terms we use to categorise writing', *The Guardian*, 6 June 2014, http://www.theguardian.com/commentisfree/2014/jun/06/eimear-mcbride-novel-terms-writing-consciousness (accessed 8 October 2021); Jacqueline Rose, 'From the Inside Out', *London Review of Books*, 38.18 (22 September 2016), https://www.lrb.co.uk/the-paper/v38/n18/jacqueline-rose/from-the-inside-out (accessed 8 October 2021); Paige Reynolds, 'Bad Girls: Modernism and Sexual Ethics in Contemporary Irish Fiction', in *Modernism and Close Reading*, ed. by David James (Oxford: Oxford University Press, 2020), pp. 173–90.

[30] See Eimear McBride, 'My Hero: Eimear McBride on James Joyce', *The Guardian*, 6 June 2014, https://www.theguardian.com/books/2014/jun/06/my-hero-eimear-mcbride-james-joyce (accessed 8 October 2021); Eimear McBride, cited by Kira Cochrane, 'Eimear McBride: There are serious readers who want to be challenged', *The Guardian*, 5 June 2014, http://www.theguardian.com/books/2014/jun/05/eimear-mcbride-serious-readers-challenged-baileys-womens-prize (accessed 8 October 2021).

Like the modernist writers encountered in this book, McBride also stages her own scenes of reading. As teenage girls the protagonist and her best friend 'read and read. Quote quotes back forth. [. . .] Correct each other's grammar. Chew gum and talk and think of sex.'[31] Reading, for these teenage girls in rural Ireland, involves an escape to vast fantasy landscapes:

> And we go on travels. Great worlds to our minds, like interrail from here to there. Slum it downtown Bucharest eat cheese in Paris fall in love. Take boats in Venice to Constantinople by the train. Where speak good Russian Portuguese. Know people. Flit around the world to New York parties. Kandahar. We don't know the world but want and want and on the very tip of tongue I'd fly away if I could. With her. It is our love affair. How we'd be. Who we think we are beneath royal blue jerseys and pleated skirts. [. . .] Read Milton and feeling moved discuss the heavens and the earth and film stars we'd do with a chance.[32]

In these scenes, literature offers the teenage girls a source of fantasy and escape, acting as a potent vehicle for trying on different identities:

> And I am reading Scott Fitzgerald know that I must drop the F. Think American twenties just divine and I'd be Zelda if I could. Think suffering's worth it. To be mad a fine exciting thing to be for those short times in those mad years. Wearing pearls and drink champagne and bob my hair and show my knees. Be daring darling simply wild. I'd be if I had a chance I'd be. She. Feeling more pre-Raphaelite has dyed her hair an orange red and keeps Rossetti in her bag for reference always to be inspired by love and nature and dying young. Her choice is poor compared to me I think but nod and smile along at every quote. Think her a little behind and all that cheap to be admired.[33]

At first, these scenes of adolescent fantasy and identification appear at odds with the kind of reading that McBride's own novel appears to demand. McBride has been quoted saying that, despite the publishing industry's perpetuation of the 'myth that readers like a very passive experience, that all they want is a beach novel', *A Girl Is a Half-formed Thing* proves that 'There are serious readers who want to be challenged, who want to be offered something else, who don't mind being asked to work a little bit to get there'.[34] And yet, by invoking the

[31] Eimear McBride, *A Girl Is a Half-formed Thing* (London: Faber and Faber, 2014), p. 63.
[32] McBride, *A Girl*, pp. 63–4.
[33] McBride, *A Girl*, p. 66.
[34] McBride, cited by Cochrane, 'There are serious readers who want to be challenged'.

forms of close identification at work in adolescent fantasy, these scenes of reading also draw attention to the more difficult forms of intimacy and identification
demanded by McBride's own writing.

In writing *A Girl*, McBride was, she has commented, 'attempting to tell a
story from a point so far back in the mind that it is completely experiential,
completely gut-reactive and balancing on the moment just before language
becomes formatted thought'.[35] Describing Gertrude Stein's *The Making of
Americans* and Joyce's *Finnegans Wake* as 'important' experiments but ultimately 'kamikaze missions leaving no viable legacy for the next generation',
McBride has argued that

> In trying to find a new origin of perspective and coercing the language
> into working in a way that might plausibly suggest it, I was attempting
> to take what I considered to be the successes of that era, then turn them
> inside out to achieve the opposite effect. So while [. . .] the non-specialist
> reader finds those books obtuse and alienating, I wanted mine to go in
> as close as the reader would reasonably permit. I wanted the simplicity
> of the vocabulary to allow the more complex construction to slip in
> under the radar so that the decoding would take place within the readers
> themselves, almost as though they were experiencing the story from the
> inside rather than the outside in.[36]

In *A Girl*, the reader is solicited to experience the protagonist's most intimate,
traumatic and abject experiences 'from the inside'. The girl might imagine herself
as Zelda Fitzgerald, indulging in the 'champagne' and 'pearls' of the jazz age,
but McBride asks her own readers to perform an identification with the protagonist that goes much further than the wish-fulfilments of teenage fantasy. As
Paige Reynolds has commented, 'At no point is [McBride's] protagonist's tale so
romanticized that it invites readers to desire its replication, though the narrative
is emotionally affecting, and even sexually titillating.'[37] In this novel, where other
characters are referred to by the pronouns 'you', 'she' and 'he' rather than by
proper names, we, as readers, are absorbed into the girl's mind, experiencing with
her the struggle to find the boundaries between one self and another. Although
McBride distinguishes this aspect of her writing from the modernist experiments
of Stein and Joyce, the scenes of reading in *A Girl Is a Half-formed Thing* in
fact highlight, and take further, the forms of close, troubled identification enacted

---

[35] Eimear McBride, cited by David Collard, 'Interview with Eimear McBride', *The White
Review* (May 2014), online exclusive, http://www.thewhitereview.org/interviews/interview-
with-eimear-mcbride/ (accessed 8 October 2021).

[36] McBride, cited by Collard, 'Interview with Eimear McBride'.

[37] Reynolds, 'Bad Girls', p. 169.

within the scenes of reading that I've been examining in this book. As McBride argues, this is not a form of modernism that alienates the reader, but a kind of writing that 'go[es] in as close as the reader would reasonably permit', asking the reader to perform troubling and intimate forms of identification with the darkest underside of modern femininity.

* * *

In recent years, a number of writers and critics have suggested that we are now living in what is sometimes described as a 'post-critical' moment, that we are, in Charles Altieri's words, 'disenchanted with disenchantment'.[38] In this so-called 'post-truth' world, it might seem that we need, more than ever, to arm ourselves, and others, with a vigilant hermeneutics of suspicion in order to protect ourselves against the seductive blandishments of globalised digital mass culture, of 'fake news', populist myths and 'alternative facts'. For Eve Kosofsky Sedgwick, Rita Felski, Bruno Latour and others, however, the pervasive paranoia, suspicion and cynicism of present-day society means that we all already know that we inhabit illusions on a daily basis: the idea, in such a political climate, that it is the special role of the literary critic to demystify, unveil and disillusion feels somewhat absurd, even quaint, or perhaps downright dangerous.[39] The relentlessly paranoid faith in exposure may, as Sedgwick argued, run us into dead ends.[40] Paranoia may breed more paranoia. Despite its potency as the driving force of social critique, suspicion also, as Felski notes, takes the form of 'right-wing populism, hostility toward big government, grassroots opposition to multiculturalism and a scapegoating of migrants, disdain for out-of-touch intellectuals and an energetic debunking of their scholarly credentials'.[41] 'We are', Felski writes, 'sorely in need of richer and deeper accounts of how selves interact with texts.'[42] Drawing on Melanie Klein's account of reparation, Sedgwick wrote that

> For Klein's infant or adult, the paranoid position—understandably marked by hatred, envy, and anxiety—is a position of terrible alertness to the dangers posed by the hateful and envious part-objects that one

---

[38] Charles Altieri, 'Afterword: Are Aesthetic Models the Best Way to Talk About the Artfulness of Literary Texts?', in *American Literature's Aesthetic Dimensions*, ed. by Cindy Weinstein and Christopher Looby (New York: Columbia University Press, 2012), pp. 393–404 (p. 394).

[39] Sedgwick, 'Paranoid Reading and Reparative Reading', p. 141; Felski, *The Limits of Critique*, p. 45; Bruno Latour, 'Why Has Critique Run Out of Steam? From Matters of Fact to Matters of Concern', *Critical Inquiry*, 30.2 (Winter 2004), 225–48.

[40] Sedgwick, 'Paranoid Reading and Reparative Reading'.

[41] Felski, *The Limits of Critique*, p. 45.

[42] Felski, *The Uses of Literature*, p. 11.

defensively projects into, carves out of, and ingests from the world around one. By contrast, the depressive position is an anxiety-mitigating achievement that the infant or adult only sometimes, and often only briefly, succeeds in inhabiting: this is the position from which it is possible in turn to use one's own resources to assemble or 'repair' the murderous part-objects into something like a whole—though, I would emphasize, *not necessarily like any preexisting whole*. Once assembled to one's own specifications, the more satisfying object is available both to be identified with and to offer nourishment and comfort in turn.[43]

For Sedgwick – who emphasised the fragile, often temporary, and risky nature of Kleinian reparation – the turn to reparative reading meant a shift towards a form of reading in which 'selves and communities succeed in extracting sustenance from the objects of a culture—even of a culture whose avowed desire has often been not to sustain them'.[44]

In the scenes of reading that I've been examining in this book, the writers depict the multiple, overdetermined, and often conflicting fantasies that shaped the scene of reading for readers in the first part of the twentieth century. In the 1920s and 1930s, the scene of reading was shaped by nostalgic memories about the pleasures and intimacies of childhood reading, by potent post-war fantasies about the reparative balm of poetry in the wake of death and destruction, by deep-rooted longings for escape from the day-to-day realities of modernity, and by seductive ideas about the capacity of literature to confer feelings of belonging and togetherness in an age of mass alienation. These portraits of reading offer a more nuanced and subtle account of the scene of reading than has so often appeared in modernist literary criticism, foregrounding what Rita Felski has described as the 'messy, blurred, compounded, and contradictory' forms of engagement that characterise individual acts of reading.[45] And yet, as I've been arguing throughout this book, although these scenes are attentive to the many psychological and social uses of reading, they are also imbued with, and draw attention to, some of the political risks of literary identification in the 1920s and 1930s.

Although many writers and psychoanalysts were deeply invested in the idea of literature as a form of reparation, these writers and psychoanalysts also depicted the scene of reading as a site of overdetermined, conflicting and ambivalent fantasies in which literature appears not only as a potential source of solace or reparation, but also, as we have seen, as a source of imperialist

---

[43] Sedgwick, 'Paranoid Reading and Reparative Reading', p. 128.
[44] Sedgwick, 'Paranoid Reading and Reparative Reading', pp. 150–1.
[45] Felski, *The Uses of Literature*, p. 132.

masculine authority, a repository of proto-fascist community, and as a buttress of antisemitic fantasies about literary solitude. As we saw in Chapters 3 and 4, writers like Virginia Woolf, Melanie Klein and Marion Milner were fascinated by the idea of reading as a form of reparation, but, for all three writers, the scene of reading was also shot through with forms of psychic, social and historical violence. Not only do these scenes complicate some of our contemporary discussions about reparative reading, but they also present a challenge to more widespread assumptions about the humanising power of literary empathy and identification.

Responding to arguments that seek to celebrate literature on the basis of its capacity to promote empathy and compassion, Lyndsey Stonebridge has recently argued that we need now, in the twenty-first century, 'to embrace ways of thinking about literature that go beyond the trading of moral sentiments; and that [. . .] means taking literature more seriously than as a desideratum for a compassion so violently lacking in the real world'.[46] Writing about Samuel Beckett, Stonebridge describes how, although 'Beckett consistently demanded that his readers put themselves in another's place', he also 'makes identification difficult', setting himself 'against the consolations of easy sympathy'.[47] This, for Stonebridge, puts us on the path to thinking 'seriously about political solidarity' rather than simply celebrating the scene of reading as a site of compassionate identification.[48] In *A Girl Is a Half-formed Thing*, McBride asks her readers to experience the protagonist's trauma 'from the inside', challenging the boundaries between inside and outside of the mind. This novel rejects the 'consolations of easy sympathy' while nonetheless demanding a troubling form of identification that is at once intimate and critical, forcing us intimately and painfully up against the psychic devastation of the protagonist, while also offering a striking critique of the brutalising effects of sexual violence.[49]

In the portraits of reading that I've been exploring in this book, Woolf, Proust and Milner reveal that the scene of reading is fraught with the perils of risky forms of literary identification that are frequently shaped as much by politically dubious fantasies of communal oneness as by fantasies of personal

[46] Lyndsey Stonebridge, 'Once More, With Feeling', *New Humanist*, 8 June 2017, https://www.eurozine.com/once-more-with-feeling/ (accessed 8 October 2021). For a more detailed critique of what Stonebridge describes as 'literary humanism' in relationship to modernism, see Lyndsey Stonebridge, *Placeless People: Writing, Rights, and Refugees* (Oxford: Oxford University Press, 2018), p. 12. See also Lyndsey Stonebridge, *Writing and Righting: Literature in the Age of Human Rights* (Oxford: Oxford University Press, 2021), pp. 21–43.
[47] Stonebridge, *Placeless People*, p. 136.
[48] Stonebridge, *Placeless People*, p. 136.
[49] Stonebridge, *Placeless People*, p. 136.

and collective reparation. And yet, just as Milner encourages her reader to take up her 'method' of cultivating, observing and self-reflexively analysing her individual pleasures, so the staged scene of reading in modernist texts demands that we, as readers, reflect on, and analyse, the personal and political fantasies that shape our own pleasures, desires and identifications as readers. As we read about Louis's fantasy of literature as a form of collective belonging, or Neville's fantasy of poetry as a buttress of masculine authority, or Sara's and North's fantasy of literature as a source of refuge and 'delicious solitude', we, as readers, are encouraged to reflect on the fantasies that underpin our own acts of reading modernist literature today. In *The Years*, Woolf reveals that, despite its attractions, the fantasy of literary solitude might also fall directly into line with the violent fantasies that animated British fascism in the 1930s. Although, like Louis, Neville, Rhoda and Bernard, today's reader might find genuine forms of comfort and solace in the rhythms of Woolf's writing, the scenes of reading depicted in these novels also encourage us, as readers, to reflect more seriously on how our literary pleasures and identifications can become captive to toxic political ideologies.[50] 'For the desire to read,' wrote Woolf in an essay on Thomas Browne, 'like all the other desires which distract our unhappy souls, is capable of analysis.'[51]

---

[50] For examples of what could be seen as 'reparative' readings of Woolf, see Katharine Smyth, *All the Lives We Ever Lived: Seeking Solace in Virginia Woolf* (London: Atlantic Books, 2019); Kate Zambreno, *Heroines* (Los Angeles: Semiotext(e), 2012).

[51] Virginia Woolf, 'Sir Thomas Browne', in *Essays*, III, pp. 368–9.

BIBLIOGRAPHY

ARCHIVAL SOURCES

British Psycho-Analytical Society, *The Minute Book of the Scientific Proceedings of the British Psycho-Analytical Society from November Sixth 1929*, Society and Institute Records, Archives of the British Psychoanalytical Society S/B/01/A/01

Dell, Ethel M., Autograph MS of *The Way of an Eagle*, 1909–1912, Add MS 45743, British Library Manuscript Collections

Milner, Marion, Milner Collection, Archives of the British Psychoanalytical Society

Woolf, Virginia, Holograph Reading Notebooks, Virginia Woolf Collection of Papers, Henry W. and Albert A. Berg Collection of English and American Literature, New York Public Library, Astor, Lenox and Tilden Foundations

PUBLISHED TEXTS

Abel, Elizabeth, 'Spaces of Time: Virginia Woolf's Life-Writing', in *Modernism and Autobiography*, ed. by Maria DiBattista and Emily O. Wittman (New York: Cambridge University Press, 2014), pp. 55–66

—— *Virginia Woolf and the Fictions of Psychoanalysis* (Chicago: University of Chicago Press, 1989)

Adorno, Theodor, *Aesthetic Theory*, trans. by Robert Hullot-Kentor, ed. by Gretel Adorno and Rolf Tiedemann (London: Continuum, 2009)

—— 'On the Fetish-Character in Music and the Regression of Listening', in *Essays on Music*, trans. by Susan H. Gillespie, ed. by Richard Leppert (Berkeley: University of California Press, 2002), pp. 288–317

—— 'Trying to Understand Endgame', in *Notes to Literature: Volume One*, trans. by Shierry Weber Nicholsen, ed. by Rolf Tiedemann (New York: Columbia University Press, 1991), pp. 241–75

—— 'Why Is the New Art So Hard to Understand?', in *Essays on Music*, trans. by Susan H. Gillespie, ed. by Richard Leppert (Berkeley: University of California Press, 2002), pp. 127–34

—— and Max Horkheimer, *Dialectic of Enlightenment*, trans. by John Cumming (London: Verso, 1997)

Alexander, Sally, 'D. W. Winnicott and the Social Democratic Vision', in *Psychoanalysis in the Age of Totalitarianism*, ed. by Matt ffytche and Daniel Pick (London: Routledge, 2016), pp. 114–30

—— 'Psychoanalysis in Britain in the Early Twentieth Century: An Introductory Note', *History Workshop Journal*, 45 (1998), 135–44

—— and Barbara Taylor, eds, *Psyche and History: Culture, Psychoanalysis, and the Past* (London: Palgrave, 2012)

Allen, Judith, *Virginia Woolf and the Politics of Language* (Edinburgh: Edinburgh University Press, 2010)

Altieri, Charles, 'Afterword: Are Aesthetic Models the Best Way to Talk About the Artfulness of Literary Texts?', in *American Literature's Aesthetic Dimensions*, ed. by Cindy Weinstein and Christopher Looby (New York: Columbia University Press, 2012), pp. 393–404

—— 'Modernist Innovations: A Legacy of the Constructed Reader', in *Modernism*, ed. by Astradur Eysteinsson and Vivian Liska, 2 vols (Amsterdam and Philadelphia: John Benjamins, 2007), I, pp. 67–86

Arendt, Hannah, 'Letter to Gershom Scholem', in *The Jewish Writings*, ed. by Jerome Kohn and Ron H. Feldman (New York: Schocken, 2007), p. 471

—— *On Revolution* (Harmondsworth: Penguin, 1977)

—— *The Origins of Totalitarianism* (New York: Schocken, 2004)

Armstrong, Isobel, *The Radical Aesthetic* (Oxford: Blackwell, 2000)

Auden, W. H., 'To Unravel Unhappiness', *The Listener*, 28 November 1934, reprinted in *Art, Creativity, Living*, ed. by Lesley Caldwell (London: Karnac, 2000), pp. 113–16

Bahun, Sanja, *Modernism and Melancholia: Writing as Countermourning* (Oxford: Oxford University Press, 2014)

—— 'Woolf and Psychoanalytic Theory', in *Virginia Woolf in Context*, ed. by Jane Goldman and Bryony Randall (Cambridge: Cambridge University Press, 2012), pp. 92–109

Bakhtin, M. M., *The Dialogic Imagination: Four Essays by M. M. Bakhtin*, ed. by Michael Holquist, trans. by Caryl Emerson and Michael Holquist (Austin: University of Texas Press, 1981)

Baldick, Chris, *The Social Mission of English Criticism 1848–1932* (Oxford: Clarendon Press, 1983)

Banfield, Ann, *The Phantom Table: Woolf, Fry, Russell and the Epistemology of Modernism* (Cambridge: Cambridge University Press, 2000)

Bar-Haim, Shaul, Elizabeth Coles and Helen Tyson, 'Introduction: Wild Analysis', in *Wild Analysis: From the Couch to Cultural and Political Life*, ed. by Shaul Bar-Haim, Elizabeth Coles and Helen Tyson (London: Routledge, 2021) pp. xxi–xlvi

Barnes, Djuna, 'How It Feels to Be Forcibly Fed', *New York World Magazine*, 6 September 1914, reprinted in *Djuna Barnes's New York*, ed. by Alyce Barry (London: Virago, 1990), pp. 174–9

Barrie, J. M., *Peter and Wendy* (1911), in *Peter Pan*, ed. by Jack Zipes (London: Penguin, 2004), pp. 1–153

Beauman, Nicola, *A Very Great Profession: The Woman's Novel 1914–39*, 2nd edn (London: Persephone, 2008)

Beer, Gillian, *Virginia Woolf: The Common Ground* (Edinburgh: Edinburgh University Press, 1996)

Bell, Clive, *Art* (London: Chatto & Windus, 1914)

—— 'Dr. Freud on Art', *Nation and Athenaeum*, 35.23 (6 September 1924), 690–1

Bell, Quentin, *Virginia Woolf: A Biography*, 2 vols (London: Hogarth Press, 1972)

Bell, Vanessa, *Selected Letters of Vanessa Bell*, ed. by Regina Marler (London: Bloomsbury, 1993)

Benjamin, Walter, 'A Glimpse into the World of Children's Books' (1926), trans. by Rodney Livingstone, in *Selected Writings: Volume 1, 1913–1926*, ed. by Marcus Bullock and Michael W. Jennings (Cambridge, MA: Belknap Press of Harvard University Press, 2004), pp. 435–43

—— 'Toys and Play' (1928), trans. by Rodney Livingstone, in *Selected Writings: Volume 2, Part 1, 1927–1930*, ed. by Michael W. Jennings, Howard Eiland and Gary Smith (Cambridge, MA: Belknap Press of Harvard University Press, 2005), pp. 117–21

—— *Understanding Brecht*, trans. by A. Bostock (London: Verso, 1998)

Berman, Jessica, *Modernist Fiction, Cosmopolitanism, and the Politics of Community* (Cambridge: Cambridge University Press, 2011)

Bersani, Leo, *The Culture of Redemption* (Cambridge, MA: Harvard University Press, 1990)

—— and Ulysse Dutoit, *Arts of Impoverishment: Beckett, Rothko, Resnais* (Cambridge, MA: Harvard University Press, 1993)

Bloom, Clive, *Bestsellers: Popular Fiction Since 1900*, 2nd edn (Basingstoke: Palgrave Macmillan, 2008)

Boll, Theophilus, 'May Sinclair and the Medico-Psychological Clinic of London', *Proceedings of the American Philosophical Society*, 106 (1962), 310–26

Bollas, Christopher, *Being a Character: Psychoanalysis and Self Experience* (London: Routledge, 1992)

—— *The Shadow of the Object: Psychoanalysis of the Unthought Known* (London: Free Association Books, 1987)

Borch-Jacobsen, Mikkel, *The Freudian Subject*, trans. by Catherine Porter (London: Macmillan, 1989)

Bowen, Elizabeth, 'James Joyce' (1941), in *People, Places, Things: Essays by Elizabeth Bowen*, ed. by Allan Hepburn (Edinburgh: Edinburgh University Press, 2008), pp. 239–47

—— 'Outrageous Ladies' [n.d.], in *People, Places, Things: Essays by Elizabeth Bowen*, ed. by Allan Hepburn (Edinburgh: Edinburgh University Press, 2008), pp. 379–83

Bowie, Malcolm, *Proust Among the Stars* (London: HarperCollins, 1998)

Bowlby, Rachel, *Freudian Mythologies: Greek Tragedy and Modern Identities* (Oxford: Oxford University Press, 2009)

—— 'Introduction', in Marion Milner, *A Life of One's Own* (Hove: Routledge, 2011), pp. xiii–xxxii

—— *Shopping with Freud* (London and New York: Routledge, 1993)

Bradshaw, David, 'Beneath *The Waves*: Diffusionism and Cultural Pessimism', *Essays in Criticism*, 63.3 (2013), 317–43

—— 'Hyams Place: *The Years*, the Jews and the British Union of Fascists', in *Women Writers of the 1930s: Gender, Politics and History*, ed. by Maroula Joannou (Edinburgh: Edinburgh University Press, 1999), pp. 179–91

—— 'Introduction', in *The Waves*, ed. by David Bradshaw (Oxford: Oxford University Press, 2015), pp. xi–xxxix

—— '"Vanished, Like Leaves": The Military, Elegy and Italy in *Mrs Dalloway*', *Woolf Studies Annual*, 8 (2002), 107–25

Brewster, Ben, 'From Shklovsky to Brecht: A Reply', *Screen*, 15.2 (1974), 82–102

Briggs, Julia, *Virginia Woolf: An Inner Life* (London: Allen Lane, 2005)

Brooks, Peter, *The Melodramatic Imagination: Balzac, Henry James, Melodrama, and the Mode of Excess* (1976), 2nd edn (New Haven and London: Yale University Press, 1995)

—— *Reading for the Plot: Design and Intention in Narrative* (Oxford: Clarendon Press, 1984)

Butler, Judith, *Antigone's Claim: Kinship Between Life and Death* (New York: Columbia University Press, 2002)

—— *Precarious Life: The Powers of Mourning and Violence* (London: Verso, 2006)

Carey, John, *The Intellectuals and the Masses: Pride and Prejudice Among the Literary Intelligentsia, 1880–1939* (London: Faber and Faber, 1992)

Caselli, Daniela, 'Attack of the Easter Bunnies: Walter Benjamin's Youth Hour', *Parallax*, 22.4 (2016), 459–79

—— 'Eerie Changelings', *New Formations*, 74.1 (2012), 122–9

—— 'Kindergarten Theory: Childhood, Affect, Critical Thought', *Feminist Theory*, 11 (2010), 241–54

Cloud, Henry, *Barbara Cartland: Crusader in Pink* (London: Weidenfeld & Nicolson, 1979)

Cochrane, Kira, 'Eimear McBride: There are serious readers who want to be challenged', *The Guardian*, 5 June 2014, http://www.theguardian.com/books/2014/jun/05/eimear-mcbride-serious-readers-challenged-baileys-womens-prize (accessed 8 October 2021)

Cohen, Josh, *The Private Life: Why We Remain in the Dark* (London: Granta, 2013)

Collard, David, 'Interview with Eimear McBride', *The White Review*, May 2014, online exclusive, http://www.thewhitereview.org/interviews/interview-with-eimear-mcbride/ (accessed 8 October 2021)

Conkling, Hilda, *Poems by a Little Girl* (New York: Frederick A. Stokes Co., 1922)

Cuddy-Keane, Melba, *Virginia Woolf, the Intellectual, and the Public Sphere* (Cambridge: Cambridge University Press, 2003)

Dalgarno, Emily, *Virginia Woolf and the Migrations of Language* (Cambridge: Cambridge University Press, 2012)

Damon, S. Foster, 'The Odyssey in Dublin', in *James Joyce: Two Decades of Criticism*, ed. by Seon Givens (New York: Vanguard Press, 1948), pp. 203–42

Daugherty, Beth Rigel, '"You see you kind of belong to us, and what you do matters enormously": Letters from Readers to Virginia Woolf', *Woolf Studies Annual*, 12 (2006), 1–12

—— ed., 'Letters from Readers to Virginia Woolf', *Woolf Studies Annual*, 12 (2006), 13–212

Davidson, Arnold I., 'How to Do the History of Psychoanalysis: A Reading of Freud's *Three Essays on the Theory of Sexuality*', *Critical Inquiry*, 13.2 (1987), 252–77

Dell, Ethel M., *Charles Rex* (London: Hurst and Blackett, 1969)

—— *The Juice of the Pomegranate* (London: Cassell & Co., 1941)

—— *The Knave of Diamonds* (London: Ernest Benn Ltd, 1954)

—— *The Way of an Eagle* (London: Virago, 1996)

Dell, Penelope, *Nettie and Sissie: The Biography of Ethel M. Dell and her Sister Ella* (London: Hamish Hamilton, 1977)

Derrida, Jacques, *Of Grammatology*, trans. by Gayatri Chakravorty Spivak (Baltimore: Johns Hopkins University Press, 1976)

—— *Writing and Difference*, trans. by Alan Bass (Abingdon: Routledge, 2001)

Detloff, Madelyn, '"'Tis Not my Nature to Join in Hating, But in Loving": Toward Survivable Public Mourning', in *Modernism and Mourning*, ed. by Patricia Rae (Lewisburg: Bucknell University Press, 2007), pp. 50–68

Diepeveen, Leonard, *The Difficulties of Modernism* (London: Routledge, 2003)

Dixon, jay [*sic*], *The Romance Fiction of Mills & Boon 1909–1990s* (London: UCL Press, 1999)

Dusinberre, Juliet, *Alice to the Lighthouse: Children's Books and Radical Experiments in Art* (Basingstoke: Macmillan, 1987)

Dyhouse, Carol, *Heartthrobs: A History of Women and Desire* (Oxford: Oxford University Press, 2017)

Eastman, Max, 'The Cult of Unintelligibility', *Harper's Monthly Magazine*, 518 (April 1929), 632–86

Eatwell, Roger, *Fascism: A History* (London: Pimlico, 2003)

Edelman, Lee, *No Future: Queer Theory and the Death Drive* (Durham, NC: Duke University Press, 2004)

Eliot, T. S., *The Complete Poems and Plays of T. S. Eliot* (London: Faber and Faber, 2004)

—— *The Letters of T. S. Eliot*, ed. by Valerie Eliot, Hugh Haughton and John Haffenden, 5 vols (London: Faber and Faber, 1988–2009)

—— 'London Letter: August 1922', *Dial*, 73 (September 1922), 329–31

—— *Selected Prose of T. S. Eliot*, ed. by Frank Kermode (London: Faber and Faber, 1975)

Ellmann, Maud, 'Failing to Fail', *Essays in Criticism*, 65.1 (1995), 84–92

—— *The Hunger Artists: Starving, Writing and Imprisonment* (London: Virago, 1993)

—— *The Nets of Modernism: Henry James, Virginia Woolf, James Joyce, and Sigmund Freud* (Cambridge: Cambridge University Press, 2010)

—— 'New Introduction: The Thing that Lives Us', in Marion Milner, *An Experiment in Leisure* (Hove: Routledge, 2011), pp. xiii–xlii

—— 'On Not Being Able to Paint: *To the Lighthouse* via Psychoanalysis', in *Virginia Woolf*, ed. by James Acheson (London: Palgrave, 2017), pp. 106–24

—— 'A Passage to the Lighthouse', in *A Companion to Virginia Woolf*, ed. by Jessica Berman (Oxford: John Wiley & Sons, 2016), pp. 95–108

—— *The Poetics of Impersonality: T. S. Eliot and Ezra Pound* (Brighton: Harvester, 1987)

—— ed., *Psychoanalytic Literary Criticism* (London: Longman, 1994)

Esty, Jed, *A Shrinking Island: Modernism and National Culture in England* (Princeton: Princeton University Press, 2004)

—— *Unseasonable Youth: Modernism, Colonialism, and the Fiction of Development* (Oxford: Oxford University Press, 2014)

Felman, Shoshana, 'To Open the Question', *Yale French Studies*, 55/56 (1977), 5–10

—— 'Turning the Screw of Interpretation', *Yale French Studies*, 55/56 (1977), 94–207

Felski, Rita, *The Limits of Critique* (Chicago: University of Chicago Press, 2015)

—— *The Uses of Literature* (Oxford: Blackwell, 2008)

ffytche, Matt, 'The Modernist Road to the Unconscious', in *The Oxford Handbook of Modernisms*, ed. by Peter Brooker et al. (Oxford: Oxford University Press, 2010), pp. 410–28

Fletcher, John, *Freud and the Scene of Trauma* (New York: Fordham University Press, 2013)

Flint, Kate, 'Reading Uncommonly: Virginia Woolf and the Practice of Reading', *The Yearbook of English Studies*, 26 (1996), 187–98

—— *The Woman Reader 1837–1914* (Oxford: Oxford University Press, 1993)

Forrester, John, and Laura Cameron, *Freud in Cambridge* (Cambridge: Cambridge University Press, 2017)

Fox, Alice, *Virginia Woolf and the Literature of the English Renaissance* (Oxford: Clarendon Press, 1990)

Franklin, Marjorie, 'Barbara Low', *International Journal of Psychoanalysis*, 37 (1956), 473–4

Freud, Anna, 'British Psycho-Analytical Society: First Quarter, 1930', *Bulletin of the International Psycho-Analytical Association*, 11 (1930), 352–3

Freud, Sigmund, *Beyond the Pleasure Principle* (1920), in *The Standard Edition of the Complete Psychological Works of Sigmund Freud*, trans. and ed. by James Strachey et al., 24 vols (London: Hogarth Press and the Institute of Psycho-Analysis, 1953–74), XVIII, pp. 1–64

—— *Civilization and Its Discontents* (1930), *Standard Edition*, XXI, pp. 57–146

—— *The Complete Letters of Sigmund Freud to Wilhelm Fliess (1887–1904)*, trans. and ed. by J. M. Masson (Cambridge, MA: Belknap Press of Harvard University Press, 1985)

—— 'Creative Writers and Day-Dreaming' (1908 [1907]), *Standard Edition*, IX, pp. 141–53

—— 'Female Sexuality' (1931), *Standard Edition*, XXI, pp. 221–44

—— *From the History of an Infantile Neurosis* (1918), *Standard Edition*, XVII, pp. 1–123

—— *Group Psychology and the Analysis of the Ego*, trans. by James Strachey (London: International Psycho-Analytical Press, 1922)

—— *The Interpretation of Dreams* (1900–1901), *Standard Edition*, IV–V

—— *Introductory Lectures on Psycho-Analysis: A Course of Twenty-Eight Lectures Delivered at the University of Vienna*, trans. by Joan Riviere (London: George Allen & Unwin and International Psycho-Analytical Institute, 1922)

—— 'Mourning and Melancholia' (1917 [1915]), *Standard Edition*, XIV, pp. 237–60

—— *New Introductory Lectures on Psycho-Analysis* (1933 [1932]), *Standard Edition*, XXII, pp. 1–182

—— 'On Dreams' (1901), *Standard Edition*, V, pp. 629–86

—— 'On Transience' (1916 [1915]), *Standard Edition*, XIV, pp. 303–7

—— 'Screen Memories' (1899), *Standard Edition*, III, pp. 299–322

—— 'Thoughts for the Times on War and Death' (1915), *Standard Edition*, XIV, pp. 273–300

—— *Three Essays on the Theory of Sexuality* (1905), *Standard Edition*, VII, pp. 123–245

—— '"Wild" Psycho-Analysis' (1910), *Standard Edition*, XI, pp. 219–28

—— and Josef Breuer, *Studies on Hysteria* (1893–95), *Standard Edition*, II, pp. 135–81

—— and Ernest Jones, *The Complete Correspondence of Sigmund Freud and Ernest Jones 1908–1939*, ed. by R. Andrew Paskauskas (Cambridge, MA: Belknap Press of Harvard University Press, 1993)

Frosh, Stephen, 'Psychoanalysis in Britain: "The Rituals of Destruction"', in *A Concise Companion to Modernism*, ed. by David Bradshaw (Malden: Blackwell Publishing, 2003), pp. 116–37

Frost, Laura, *The Problem with Pleasure: Modernism and Its Discontents* (New York: Columbia University Press, 2013)

Froula, Christine, *Virginia Woolf and the Bloomsbury Avant-Garde: War, Civilization, Modernity* (New York: Columbia University Press, 2005)

Fry, Roger, *The Artist and Psycho-Analysis* (London: Hogarth Press, 1924)

—— 'Children's Drawings' (1917), in *A Roger Fry Reader*, ed. by Christopher Reed (Chicago: University of Chicago Press, 1996)

—— *Vision and Design* (Harmondsworth: Penguin, 1937)

Gifford, Dennis, 'The Early Memoirs of Maurice Elvey', *Griffithiana*, 60/61 (1997), 76–125

Glendinning, Victoria, *Leonard Woolf: A Biography* (New York: Free Press, 2006)

Glover, Edward, 'Notes on Oral Character Formation', *International Journal of Psycho-Analysis*, 6 (1925), 131–54

—— 'On the Aetiology of Drug-Addiction', *International Journal of Psycho-Analysis*, 13 (1932), 298–328

—— 'The Significance of the Mouth in Psycho-Analysis', *The British Journal of Medical Psychology*, 4.2 (1924), 134–55

Glover, James, 'Freud and His Critics: I', *Nation and Athenaeum*, 38.5 (31 October 1925), 180–2

—— 'Freud and His Critics: II', *Nation and Athenaeum*, 38.7 (14 November 1925), 242, 259

Goldman, Jane, *The Feminist Aesthetics of Virginia Woolf: Modernism, Post Impressionism, and the Politics of the Visual* (Cambridge: Cambridge University Press, 1998)

—— 'To the Lighthouse's Use of Form', in *The Cambridge Companion to To the Lighthouse*, ed. by Allison Pease (Cambridge: Cambridge University Press, 2015), pp. 30–46

—— and Bryony Randall, eds, *Virginia Woolf in Context* (Cambridge: Cambridge University Press, 2012)

Goldstein, Jan Ellen, 'The Woolfs' Response to Freud: Water Spiders, Singing Canaries, and the Second Apple', in *Literature and Psychoanalysis*, ed. by Edith Kurzweil and William Phillips (New York: Columbia University Press, 1983), pp. 232–55

Graham, Philip, *Susan Isaacs: A Life Freeing the Minds of Children* (London: Karnac, 2009)

Grensted, Laurence William, 'Appendix I: Certain Psychological and Physiological Considerations', in *The Ministry of Women, Report of the Archbishops' Commission on The Ministry of Women* (London: Church Literature Association, 1936), pp. 79–87

Griffin, Roger, *A Fascist Century: Essays by Roger Griffin*, ed. by Matthew Feldman (Basingstoke: Palgrave Macmillan, 2008)

Grosskurth, Phyllis, *Melanie Klein: Her World and Her Work* (London: Karnac, 1987)

Hammond, Claudia, 'Does reading fiction make us better people?', BBC, 3 June 2019, https://www.bbc.com/future/article/20190523-does-reading-fiction-make-us-better-people (accessed 27 October 2023)

Harris, Ed, *Britain's Forgotten Film Factory: The Story of Isleworth Film Studios* (Stroud: Amberley Publishing, 2012)

Harvey, Benjamin, 'Woolf, Fry and the Psycho-Aesthetics of Solidity', in *Virginia Woolf's Bloomsbury, Volume 1: Aesthetic Theory and Literary Practice*, ed. by Gina Potts and Lisa Shahriari (Basingstoke: Palgrave Macmillan, 2010), pp. 104–20

Haughton, Hugh, 'The Milner Experiment: Psychoanalysis and the Diary', *British Journal of Psychotherapy*, 30.3 (2013), 349–62

Hilliard, Christopher, *English as a Vocation: The 'Scrutiny' Movement* (Oxford: Oxford University Press, 2012)

Hinshelwood, R. D., *A Dictionary of Kleinian Thought*, 2nd edn (Northvale: Aronson, 1991)

—— 'The Elusive Concept of "Internal Objects" (1934–1943): Its Role in the Formation of the Klein Group', *International Journal of Psycho-Analysis*, 78 (1997), 877–97

—— 'Psychoanalysis in Britain: Points of Cultural Access, 1893–1918', *International Journal of Psycho-Analysis*, 76 (1995), 135–51

Hipsky, Martin, *Modernism and the Women's Popular Romance in Britain, 1885–1925* (Ohio: Ohio University Press, 2011)

Howarth, Peter, *The Cambridge Introduction to Modernist Poetry* (Cambridge: Cambridge University Press, 2012)

—— 'Close Reading as Performance', in *Modernism and Close Reading*, ed. by David James (Oxford: Oxford University Press, 2020), pp. 45–68

—— 'Eliot in the Underworld: The Politics of Fragmentary Form', *Textual Practice*, 20.3 (2006), 441–62

Huxley, Aldous, 'Race', *New Statesman and Nation*, 11.272 (9 May 1936), 716, 718

Huyssen, Andreas, *After the Great Divide: Modernism, Mass Culture, Postmodernism* (Bloomington: Indiana University Press, 1986)

Jacobus, Mary, *The Poetics of Psychoanalysis: In the Wake of Klein* (Oxford: Oxford University Press, 2005)

—— *Psychoanalysis and the Scene of Reading* (Oxford: Oxford University Press, 1999)

James, David, *Discrepant Solace: Contemporary Literature and the Work of Consolation* (Oxford: Oxford University Press, 2019)

—— ed., *Modernism and Close Reading* (Oxford: Oxford University Press, 2020)

James, Emily, 'Virginia Woolf and the Child Poet', *Modernist Cultures*, 7.2 (2012), 279–305

James, Henry, *The Turn of the Screw and Other Stories*, ed. by T. J. Lustig (Oxford: Oxford University Press, 2008)

Jones, Clara, *Virginia Woolf: Ambivalent Activist* (Edinburgh: Edinburgh University Press, 2016)

—— 'Virginia Woolf and "The Villa Jones" (1931)', *Virginia Woolf Studies Annual*, 22 (2016), 75–95

Jones, Ernest, *Sigmund Freud: Life and Work*, 3 vols (London: Hogarth Press, 1955)

Joyce, James, *A Portrait of the Artist as a Young Man*, ed. by Seamus Deane (London: Penguin, 2000)

—— *The Restored Finnegans Wake* (1923–39), ed. by Danis Rose and John O'Hanlon (London: Penguin, 2010)

—— *Ulysses*, ed. by Jeri Johnson (Oxford: Oxford University Press, 1993)

Kaplan, Alice, *Reproductions of Banality* (Minneapolis: University of Minnesota Press, 1986)

Kaplan, Cora, '*The Thorn Birds*: Fiction, Fantasy, Femininity', in *Sea Changes: Essays on Culture and Feminism* (London: Verso, 1986), pp. 117–46

Kappa, 'Life and Politics', *Nation and Athenaeum*, 37.23 (5 September 1925), 672

Kinkead-Weekes, Mark, *D. H. Lawrence: Triumph to Exile 1912–1922* (Cambridge: Cambridge University Press, 2011)

Klein, Melanie, *Envy and Gratitude and Other Works 1946–1963* (London: Vintage, 1997)

—— *Love, Guilt and Reparation and Other Works 1921–1945* (London: Vintage, 1998)

—— *The Psycho-Analysis of Children*, trans. by Alix Strachey, rev. by H. A. Thorner (London: Vintage, 1997)

Knights, Ben, 'English on Its Borders', in *English Studies: The State of the Discipline, Past, Present, and Future*, ed. by Niall Gildea, Helena Goodwyn, Megan Kitching and Helen Tyson (Basingstoke: Palgrave Macmillan, 2015), pp. 15–24

—— 'Outlaws and Misfits: The Identities of Modernist Criticism', *Modernist Cultures*, 14.3 (2019), 337–56

—— *Pedagogic Criticism: Reconfiguring University English Studies* (Basingstoke: Palgrave, 2017)

—— 'Reading as a Man: Women and the Rise of English Studies in England', in *Gendered Academia: Wissenschaft und Geschlechterdifferenz 1890–1945*, ed. by Miriam Kauko, Sylvia Mieszkowski and Alexandra Tischel (Gottingen: Wallstein Verlag, 2005), pp. 65–81

Kristeva, Julia, *Melanie Klein*, trans. by Ross Guberman (New York: Columbia University Press, 2001)

—— *Revolution in Poetic Language*, trans. by Margaret Waller (New York: Columbia University Press, 1984)

—— *Time and Sense: Proust and the Experience of Literature*, trans. by Ross Guberman (New York: Columbia University Press, 1996)

Laplanche, Jean, and J. B. Pontalis, 'Fantasy and the Origins of Sexuality', *International Journal of Psycho-Analysis*, 49 (1968), 1–18

—— *The Language of Psychoanalysis*, trans. by Donald Nicholson-Smith (London: Karnac, 1988)

Lassner, Phyllis, '"The Milk of Our Mother's Kindness Has Ceased to Flow": Virginia Woolf, Stevie Smith, and the Representation of the Jew', in *Between 'Race' and Culture: Representations of 'The Jew' in English and American Literature*, ed. by Bryan Cheyette (Stanford: Stanford University Press, 1996), pp. 129–44

—— and Mia Spiro, 'A Tale of Two Cities: Virginia Woolf's Imagined Jewish Spaces and London's East End Jewish Culture', *Woolf Studies Annual*, 19 (2013), 58–82

Latour, Bruno, 'Why Has Critique Run Out of Steam? From Matters of Fact to Matters of Concern', *Critical Inquiry*, 30.2 (Winter 2004), 225–48

Lawrence, D. H., *The Letters of D. H. Lawrence, Volume II: 1913–1916*, ed. by George J. Zytaruk and James T. Boulton, 2nd edn (Cambridge: Cambridge University Press, 2002)

Lawrie, Alexandra, *The Beginnings of University English: Extramural Study, 1885–1910* (Basingstoke: Palgrave, 2014)

Lazarus, Neil, *The Postcolonial Unconscious* (Cambridge: Cambridge University Press, 2011)

Lear, Jonathan, *Open Minded: Working Out the Logic of the Soul* (Cambridge, MA: Harvard University Press, 1998)

Leavis, F. R., *The Great Tradition* (Harmondsworth: Penguin, 1972)

—— 'Mass Civilization and Minority Culture' (1930), in *Education and the University: A Sketch for an 'English School'*, 2nd edn (Cambridge: Cambridge University Press, 2011), pp. 141–71

Leavis, Q. D., 'Caterpillars of the Commonwealth Unite!', *Scrutiny*, 7.2 (1938), 203–14

—— *Fiction and the Reading Public* (London: Chatto & Windus, 1932)

Lee, Hermione, *Virginia Woolf* (London: Vintage, 1997)

Letley, Emma, *Marion Milner: The Life* (London: Routledge, 2014)

Lewis, Wyndham, 'The Revolutionary Simpleton', *Enemy*, 1 (January 1927)

Liddle, Helen Gordon, *The Prisoner: An Experience of Forcible Feeding: A Sketch* (Letchworth: Garden City Press Ltd, 1911)

Light, Alison, *Forever England: Femininity, Literature and Conservatism between the Wars* (Abingdon: Routledge, 1991)

—— *Mrs Woolf and the Servants* (London: Penguin, 2007)

—— '"Returning to Manderley": Romance Fiction, Female Sexuality and Class', *Feminist Review*, 16 (April 1984), 7–25

Linett, Maren, 'The Jew in the Bath: Imperilled Imagination in Woolf's *The Years*', *Modern Fiction Studies*, 48.2 (2002), 341–61

Lowell, Amy, 'Preface', in Hilda Conkling, *Poems by a Little Girl* (New York: Frederick A. Stokes Co., 1922)

Lurz, John, *The Death of the Book: Modernist Novels and the Time of Reading* (New York: Fordham University Press, 2016)

Lytton, Constance, *Prisons and Prisoners: Some Personal Experiences* (London: William Heinemann, 1914)

McAleer, Joseph, *Passion's Fortune: The Story of Mills & Boon* (Oxford: Oxford University Press, 1999)

—— *Popular Reading and Publishing in Britain 1914–1950* (Oxford: Clarendon Press, 1992)

McBride, Eimear, *A Girl Is a Half-formed Thing* (London: Faber and Faber, 2014)

—— 'My Hero: Eimear McBride on James Joyce', *The Guardian*, 6 June 2014, https://www.theguardian.com/books/2014/jun/06/my-hero-eimear-mcbride-james-joyce (accessed 8 October 2021)

MacGibbon, Jean, *There's the Lighthouse: A Biography of Adrian Stephen* (London: James & James Publishers Ltd, 1997)

McIntire, Gabrielle, 'Heteroglossia, Monologism, and Fascism: Bernard Reads *The Waves*', *Narrative*, 13.1 (2005), 29–45

McKay, Marina, '*Between the Acts*: Novels and Other Mass Media', in *A Companion to Virginia Woolf*, ed. by Jessica Berman (Oxford: Wiley Blackwell, 2016), pp. 151–62

McLoughlin, Kate, 'Woolf's Crotchets: Textual Cryogenics in *To The Lighthouse*', *Textual Practice*, 28.6 (2014), 949–67

Mahaffey, Vicki, *Modernist Literature: Challenging Fictions* (Oxford: Blackwell, 2007)

Mansfield, Katherine, *The Collected Letters of Katherine Mansfield*, ed. by Vincent O'Sullivan and Margaret Scott, 5 vols (Oxford: Oxford University Press, 1984–2008)

Mao, Douglas, *Fateful Beauty: Aesthetic Environments, Juvenile Development, and Literature 1860–1960* (Princeton: Princeton University Press, 2008)

Marcus, Jane, *Hearts of Darkness: White Women Write Race* (New Brunswick: Rutgers University Press, 2003)

—— 'Introduction', in *Suffrage and the Pankhursts*, ed. by Jane Marcus (London: Routledge & Kegan Paul, 1987), pp. 1–17

—— '*The Years* as Greek Drama, Domestic Novel, and *Götterdämmerung*', *Bulletin of the New York Public Library*, 80 (1977), 276–301

—— ed., *Suffrage and the Pankhursts* (London: Routledge & Kegan Paul, 1987)

Marcus, Laura, *Dreams of Modernity: Psychoanalysis, Literature, Cinema* (Cambridge: Cambridge University Press, 2014)

—— and Ankhi Mukherjee, eds, *A Concise Companion to Psychoanalysis, Literature, and Culture* (Oxford: Wiley, 2014)

Marcus, Steven, 'Freud and Dora: Story, History, Case History', in *Representations: Essays on Literature and Society* (New York: Random House, 1976), pp. 247–310

Mars-Jones, Adam, 'All your walkmans fizz in tune', *London Review of Books*, 35.15 (8 August 2013), 31–2

Martindale, Philippa, '"Against all hushing up and stamping down": The Medico-Psychological Clinic of London and the Novelist May Sinclair', *Psychoanalysis and History*, 6.2 (2004), 177–200

Marvell, Andrew, *The Complete Poems*, ed. by Elizabeth Story Donno (London: Penguin, 2005)

Masson, Jeffrey, *The Assault on Truth: Freud's Suppression of the Seduction Theory* (London: Faber, 1984)

Mavor, Carol, *Reading Boyishly: Roland Barthes, J. M. Barrie, Jacques Henri Lartigue, Marcel Proust, and D. W. Winnicott* (Durham, NC: Duke University Press, 2007)

Mehlman, Jeffrey, *Walter Benjamin for Children: An Essay on His Radio Years* (Chicago: University of Chicago Press, 1993)

Meisel, Perry, 'Woolf and Freud: The Kleinian Turn', in *Virginia Woolf in Context*, ed. by Jane Goldman and Bryony Randall (Cambridge: Cambridge University Press, 2012), pp. 332–41

Mepham, John, *Virginia Woolf: A Literary Life* (London: Macmillan, 1991)

Miller, Tyrus, *Late Modernism: Politics, Fiction, and the Arts Between the World Wars* (Berkeley: University of California Press, 1999)

Milner, Marion, *Eternity's Sunrise: A Way of Keeping a Diary* (Hove: Routledge, 2011)

—— *An Experiment in Leisure* (Hove: Routledge, 2011)

—— *A Life of One's Own* (Hove: Routledge, 2011)

—— *On Not Being Able to Paint* (Hove: Routledge, 2010)

Mitchell, Juliet, *Psychoanalysis and Feminism* (London: Penguin, 1990)

Mitchell, Stanley, 'From Shklovsky to Brecht: Some Preliminary Remarks towards a History of the Politicisation of Russian Formalism', *Screen*, 15.2 (1974), 74–81

Modleski, Tania, *Loving with a Vengeance: Mass-Produced Fantasies for Women* (London: Methuen, 1984)

Monroe, Harriet, 'Two Child Poets', *Poetry: A Magazine of Verse*, 16.4 (1922), 222–7

Moody, Alys, *The Art of Hunger: Aesthetic Autonomy and the Afterlives of Modernism* (Oxford: Oxford University Press, 2018)

Morris, Nathalie, 'Pictures, Romance and Luxury: Women and British Cinema in the 1910s and 1920s', in *British Women's Cinema*, ed. by Melanie Bell and Melanie Williams (Abingdon: Routledge, 2010), pp. 19–33

Mulhern, Francis, *The Moment of 'Scrutiny'* (London: Verso, 1981)

Mullaney, Steven, *The Reformation of Emotions in the Age of Shakespeare* (Chicago: University of Chicago Press, 2015)

Mulvey, Laura, *Visual and Other Pleasures* (Basingstoke: Macmillan, 1989)

Ngai, Sianne, *Our Aesthetic Categories: Zany, Cute, Interesting* (Cambridge, MA: Harvard University Press, 2012)

Nicholsen, Shierry Weber, '*Aesthetic Theory*'s Mimesis of Walter Benjamin', in *Exact Imagination, Late Work: On Adorno's Aesthetics* (Cambridge, MA: MIT Press, 1997), pp. 137–80

Nussbaum, Martha, *Love's Knowledge: Essays on Philosophy and Literature* (Oxford: Oxford University Press, 1990)

—— *Upheavals of Thought: The Intelligence of the Emotions* (Cambridge: Cambridge University Press, 2001)

Orwell, George, 'Bookshop Memories' (1936), in *The Collected Essays, Journalism and Letters of George Orwell*, ed. by Sonia Orwell and Ian Angus, 4 vols (Harmondsworth: Penguin, 1970), I, pp. 273–7

—— 'The Cost of Letters' (1946), in *The Collected Essays, Journalism and Letters of George Orwell*, ed. by Sonia Orwell and Ian Angus, 4 vols (Harmondsworth: Penguin, 1970), IV, pp. 236–8

—— 'In Defence of the Novel' (1936), in *The Collected Essays, Journalism and Letters of George Orwell*, ed. by Sonia Orwell and Ian Angus, 4 vols (Harmondsworth: Penguin, 1970), I, pp. 281–7

——'Inside the Whale' (1940), in *The Collected Essays, Journalism and Letters of George Orwell*, ed. by Sonia Orwell and Ian Angus, 4 vols (Harmondsworth: Penguin, 1970), I, pp. 540–78

—— *Keep the Aspidistra Flying* (London: Penguin, 2000)

Pankhurst, Sylvia, 'Forcibly Fed: The Story of My Four Weeks in Holloway Gaol', *McClure's Magazine*, August 1913, 87–93

Phillips, Adam, *The Beast in the Nursery* (London: Faber and Faber, 1998)

—— 'Bombs Away', *History Workshop Journal*, 39.45 (1998), 183–98

—— *Promises, Promises: Essays on Literature and Psychoanalysis* (London: Faber and Faber, 2000)

Phillips, Kathy J., *Virginia Woolf Against Empire* (Knoxville: University of Tennessee Press, 1994)

Pick, Daniel, 'Freud's *Group Psychology* and the History of the Crowd', *History Workshop Journal*, 40.1 (1995), 39–62

Pollock, Griselda, *After-affects/After-images: Trauma and Aesthetic Transformation in the Virtual Feminist Museum* (Manchester: Manchester University Press, 2013)

Potter, Rachel, and Lyndsey Stonebridge, 'Writing and Rights', *Critical Quarterly*, 56.4 (2014), 1–16

Proust, Marcel, *À la recherche du temps perdu*, ed. by Jean-Yves Tadié et al., 4 vols (Paris: Gallimard, 1987–89)

—— *In Search of Lost Time*, trans. by C. K. Scott Moncrieff and Terence Kilmartin, rev. by D. J. Enright, 6 vols (London: Vintage, 2000–5)

—— *On Reading*, trans. and ed. by Damion Searls (London: Hesperus, 2011)

—— *Swann's Way*, trans. by C. K. Scott Moncrieff and Terence Kilmartin, rev. by D. J. Enright (London: Vintage, 2005)

—— *Time Regained*, trans. by Andreas Mayor and Terence Kilmartin, rev. by D. J. Enright (London: Vintage, 2000)

Radway, Janice, *Reading the Romance: Women, Patriarchy, and Popular Culture*, 2nd edn (London: Verso, 1987)

Raitt, Suzanne, 'Early British Psychoanalysis and the Medico-Psychological Clinic', *History Workshop Journal*, 58.1 (2004), 63–85

Rapp, Dean, 'The Early Discovery of Freud by the British General Educated Public, 1912–1919', *Social History of Medicine*, 3.2 (1990), 217–43

—— 'The Reception of Freud by the British Press: General Interest and Literary Magazines, 1920–1925', *Journal of the History of the Behavioural Sciences*, 24 (1988), 191–201

Revesz, Rachael, 'Donald Trump's presidential counsellor Kellyanne Conway says Sean Spicer gave "alternative facts" at first press briefing', *The Independent*, 22 January 2017, https://www.independent.co.uk/news/world/americas/kellyanne-conway-sean-spicer-alternative-facts-lies-press-briefing-donald-trump-administration-a7540441.html (accessed 27 October 2023)

Reynolds, Paige, 'Bad Girls: Modernism and Sexual Ethics in Contemporary Irish Fiction', in *Modernism and Close Reading*, ed. by David James (Oxford: Oxford University Press, 2020), pp. 173–90

Richards, I. A., *Practical Criticism: A Study of Literary Judgement*, ed. by John Constable (Abingdon: Routledge, 2011)

—— *Principles of Literary Criticism* (Abingdon: Routledge, 2001)

Ricœur, Paul, *Freud and Philosophy: An Essay on Interpretation*, trans. by Denis Savage (New Haven: Yale University Press, 1970)

Riley, Denise, *War in the Nursery: Theories of the Child and Mother* (London: Virago, 1983)

Riviere, Joan, 'The Inner World in Ibsen's *Master Builder*', *International Journal of Psycho-Analysis*, 33 (1952), 173–80

—— 'On the Genesis of Psychical Conflict in Earliest Infancy', *International Journal of Psycho-Analysis*, 17 (1936), 395–422

—— 'Symposium on Child-Analysis', *International Journal of Psycho-Analysis*, 8 (1927), 370–7

—— 'The Unconscious Phantasy of an Inner World Reflected in Examples from English Literature', *International Journal of Psycho-Analysis*, 33 (1952), 160–72

Rose, Gillian, *Mourning Becomes the Law: Philosophy and Representation* (Cambridge: Cambridge University Press, 1996)

Rose, Jacqueline, *The Case of Peter Pan, or The Impossibility of Children's Fiction* (Basingstoke: Macmillan, 1984)

—— 'From the Inside Out', *London Review of Books*, 38.18 (22 September 2016), https://www.lrb.co.uk/the-paper/v38/n18/jacqueline-rose/from-the-inside-out (accessed 8 October 2021)

—— 'Introduction', in Sigmund Freud, *Mass Psychology and Other Writings*, trans. by J. A. Underwood (London: Penguin, 2004), pp. vii–xlii

—— *On Not Being Able to Sleep: Psychoanalysis and the Modern World* (London: Vintage, 2004)

—— *Proust Among the Nations: From Dreyfus to the Middle East* (London: University of Chicago Press, 2011)

—— *Sexuality in the Field of Vision*, 2nd edn (London: Verso, 2005)

—— *Why War? Psychoanalysis, Politics and the Return to Melanie Klein* (Oxford: Blackwell, 1993)

Rose, Jonathan, *The Intellectual Life of the British Working Classes* (London: Yale University Press, 2001)

Russo, John Paul, *I. A. Richards: His Life and Work*, 2nd edn (Abingdon: Routledge, 2015)

Ryan, Derek, *Virginia Woolf and the Materiality of Theory: Sex, Animal, Life* (Edinburgh: Edinburgh University Press, 2013)

Scarry, Elaine, *Dreaming by the Book* (Princeton: Princeton University Press, 2001)

—— 'On Vivacity: The Difference between Daydreaming and Imagining-Under-Authorial-Instruction', *Representations*, 52 (Autumn 1995), 1–26

Schiller, Friedrich, *On the Aesthetic Education of Man in a Series of Letters*, trans. and ed. by Elizabeth M. Wilkinson and L. A. Willoughby (Oxford: Clarendon Press, 1967)

Schlossberg, Linda, 'Consuming Images: Women, Hunger, and the Vote', in *Scenes of the Apple: Food and the Female Body in Nineteenth- and Twentieth-Century Women's Writing*, ed. by Tamar Heller and Patricia Moran (New York: State University of New York Press, 2003), pp. 87–108

'The School Leaving Age', *Nation and Athenaeum*, 45.17 (27 July 1929), 558–9

Sedgwick, Eve Kosofsky, 'Paranoid Reading and Reparative Reading', in *Touching Feeling: Affect, Pedagogy, Performativity* (Durham, NC: Duke University Press, 2003), pp. 123–51

Shapira, Michal, *The War Inside: Psychoanalysis, Total War, and the Making of the Democratic Self in Postwar Britain* (Cambridge: Cambridge University Press, 2013)

Shelley, Percy Bysshe, *The Complete Poetical Works of Percy Bysshe Shelley*, ed. by Thomas Hutchinson, cor. by G. M. Matthews (Oxford: Oxford University Press, 1970)

Shklovsky, Viktor, 'Art as Technique', in *Russian Formalist Criticism: Four Essays*, ed. by Lee T. Lemon and Marion J. Reiss (Lincoln: University of Nebraska Press, 1965), pp. 3–24

Silver, Brenda, 'Cultural Critique', in *The Gender of Modernism: A Critical Anthology*, ed. by Bonnie Kime Scott (Indianapolis: Indiana University Press, 1990), pp. 646–58

—— ed., *Virginia Woolf's Reading Notebooks* (Princeton: Princeton University Press, 1983)

Sinclair, May, *Mary Olivier: A Life* (London: Virago, 1980)

Small, Helen, and Trudi Tate, eds, *Literature, Science, Psychoanalysis, 1830–1970: Essays in Honour of Gillian Beer* (Oxford: Oxford University Press, 2003)

Smith, Vanessa, 'Transferred Debts: Marion Milner's *A Life of One's Own* and the Limits of Analysis', *Feminist Modernist Studies*, 1–2 (2018), 96–111

Smyth, Katharine, *All the Lives We Ever Lived: Seeking Solace in Virginia Woolf* (London: Atlantic Books, 2019)

Snaith, Anna, 'Introduction', in Virginia Woolf, *The Years*, ed. by Anna Snaith (Cambridge: Cambridge University Press, 2012), pp. xxxix–xcix

—— 'Late Virginia Woolf', *Oxford Handbooks Online*, 2015, https://www.oxfordhandbooks.com/view/10.1093/oxfordhb/9780199935338.001.0001/oxfordhb-9780199935338-e-28 (accessed 27 October 2023)

—— 'Wide Circles: The *Three Guineas* Letters', *Woolf Studies Annual*, 6 (2000), 1–10

—— '*The Years* and Contradictory Time', in *A Companion to Virginia Woolf*, ed. by Jessica Berman (Oxford: Wiley Blackwell, 2016), pp. 137–50

—— ed., 'The *Three Guineas* Letters', *Woolf Studies Annual*, 6 (2000), 11–168

Sophocles, *The Plays and Fragments, Part III: Antigone*, trans. by R. C. Jebb (Cambridge: Cambridge University Press, 1888)

Spender, Stephen, 'The Road to Happiness', *The Spectator*, 23 November 1934

Steedman, Carolyn, *Strange Dislocations: Childhood and the Idea of Human Interiority, 1780–1930* (Cambridge, MA: Harvard University Press, 1995)

Stein, Gertrude, *The Gertrude Stein First Reader and Three Plays* (Dublin: Maurice Fridberg, 1946)

—— *The World Is Round*, illus. by Clement Hurd (New York: Harper, 2013)

Steiner, George, *Antigones* (Oxford: Clarendon Press, 1984)

—— *On Difficulty and Other Essays* (Oxford: Oxford University Press, 1978)

Stockton, Kathryn Bond, *The Queer Child: Or, Growing Sideways in the Twentieth Century* (Durham, NC: Duke University Press, 2009)

Stonebridge, Lyndsey, *The Destructive Element: British Psychoanalysis and Modernism* (Basingstoke: Macmillan, 1998)

—— *The Judicial Imagination: Writing After Nuremberg* (Edinburgh: Edinburgh University Press, 2011)

—— 'Once More, With Feeling', *New Humanist*, 8 June 2017, https://www.eurozine.com/once-more-with-feeling/ (accessed 8 October 2021)

—— *Placeless People: Writing, Rights, and Refugees* (Oxford: Oxford University Press, 2018)

—— 'Psychoanalysis and Literature', in *The Cambridge History of Twentieth-Century Literature*, ed. by Laura Marcus and Peter Nicholls (Cambridge: Cambridge University Press, 2004), pp. 269–85

—— *Writing and Righting: Literature in the Age of Human Rights* (Oxford: Oxford University Press, 2021)

—— and John Phillips, eds, *Reading Melanie Klein* (London and New York: Routledge, 1998)

Strachey, Alix, 'A Note on the Use of the Word "Internal"', *International Journal of Psycho-Analysis*, 22 (1941), 37–43

Strachey, James, 'Some Unconscious Factors in Reading', *International Journal of Psycho-Analysis*, 11 (1930), 322–31

Sutherland, John, 'Eimear McBride's novel doesn't fit any terms we use to categorise writing', *The Guardian*, 6 June 2014, http://www.theguardian.com/commentisfree/2014/jun/06/eimear-mcbride-novel-terms-writing-consciousness (accessed 8 October 2021)

Sutton, Emma, *Virginia Woolf and Classical Music* (Edinburgh: Edinburgh University Press, 2013)

Swanson, Diana L., 'An Antigone Complex? Psychology and Politics in *The Years* and *Three Guineas*', in *Virginia Woolf: Texts and Contexts: Selected Papers from the Fifth Annual Conference on Virginia Woolf*, ed. by Beth Rigel Daugherty and Eileen Barrett (New York: Pace University Press, 1996), pp. 35–9

Tickner, Lisa, *The Spectacle of Women: Imagery of the Suffrage Campaign 1907–14* (London: Chatto & Windus, 1988)

Trilling, Lionel, *Freud and the Crisis of Our Culture* (Boston: Beacon Press, 1955)

Trotter, David, 'A Horse Is Being Beaten: Modernism and Popular Fiction', in *Rereading the New: A Backward Glance at Modernism*, ed. by Kevin J. H. Dettmar (Michigan: University of Michigan Press, 1992), pp. 191–220

Trubowitz, Lara, et al., 'Responses', *Woolf Studies Annual*, 19 (2013), 16–25

Tyson, Helen, '"Catching Butterflies": Marion Milner and Stream of Consciousness Writing', *Literature Compass*, 17.6 (2020), https://doi.org/10.1111/lic3.12563

—— '"Forebodings about Fascism": Marion Milner and Virginia Woolf', *Feminist Modernist Studies*, 4.1 (2021), 1–21, https://www.tandfonline.com/doi/abs/10.1080/24692921.2020.1848334

—— '"Freudian Fiction" or "Wild Psycho-Analysis"? Modernism, Psychoanalysis, and Popular Fiction, 1900–1920', in *British Literature in Transition, 1900–1920: A New Age?*, ed. by James Purdon (Cambridge: Cambridge University Press, 2021), pp. 365–80

—— '"Little Mussolini" and the "Parasite Poets": Psychoanalytic Pedagogy, Modernism, and the Illegible Child', in *Wild Analysis: From the Couch to Cultural and Political Life*, ed. by Shaul Bar-Haim, Elizabeth Sarah Coles and Helen Tyson (London: Routledge, 2021), pp. 85–104

—— 'Reading Childishly? Learning to Read Modernism: Reading the Child Reader in Modernism and Psychoanalysis', *Textual Practice*, 31.7 (2017), 1435–57, https://doi.org/10.1080/0950236X.2016.1237997

Wachsmann, Nikolaus, 'The Policy of Exclusion: Repression in the Nazi State, 1933–1939', in *Nazi Germany*, ed. by Jane Kaplan (Oxford: Oxford University Press, 2008), pp. 122–49

Wagenknecht, Edward, *Cavalcade of the English Novel: From Elizabeth to George VI* (New York: H. Holt and Co., 1943)

Watson, Dana Cairns, 'Building a Better Reader: The Gertrude Stein First Reader and Three Plays', *The Lion and the Unicorn*, 35 (2011), 245–66

Watt, Adam, *Reading in Proust's À la recherche: 'le délire de la lecture'* (Oxford: Clarendon Press, 2009)

West, Rebecca, 'The Tosh Horse', in *The Strange Necessity: Essays and Reviews* (London: Jonathan Cape, 1931), pp. 319–25

White, Allon, *The Uses of Obscurity: The Fiction of Early Modernism* (London: Routledge & Kegan Paul, 1981)

Whyte, Iain Boyd, 'Berlin, 1 May 1936', in *Fascism: Fascism and Culture*, ed. by Roger Griffin and Matthew Feldman (Basingstoke: Palgrave Macmillan, 2004), pp. 292–306

Willis, J. H., Jr, *Leonard and Virginia Woolf as Publishers: The Hogarth Press, 1917–41* (Charlottesville: University Press of Virginia, 1992)

Withers, Pearkes, 'The Feminine Interest', *Stoll's Editorial News*, 16 September, 15–16

Wollstonecraft, Mary, *A Vindication of the Rights of Woman* (1792), ed. by Janet Todd (Oxford: Oxford University Press, 1993)

Wood, Alice, *Virginia Woolf's Late Cultural Criticism: The Genesis of 'The Years', 'Three Guineas' and 'Between the Acts'* (London: Bloomsbury, 2013)

Wood, Harriet Harvey, 'Dell, Ethel Mary (1881–1939)', in *Oxford Dictionary of National Biography* (Oxford: Oxford University Press, 2004)

Wood, James, 'Useless Prayers', *The New Yorker*, 29 September 2014, http://www.newyorker.com/magazine/2014/09/29/useless-prayers (accessed 8 October 2021)

Woolf, Leonard, 'Review of Freud's *Psychopathology of Everyday Life*', *New Weekly*, 1.13 (June 1914), 12; reprinted in *A Bloomsbury Group Reader*, ed. by S. P. Rosenbaum (Oxford: Blackwell, 1993), pp. 189–91

Woolf, Virginia, '"Anon" and "The Reader": Virginia Woolf's Last Essays', ed. by Brenda Silver, *Twentieth Century Literature* 25.3/4 (Autumn–Winter 1979), 356–441

—— 'Appendix B: Report on Teaching at Morley College', in Quentin Bell, *Virginia Woolf: A Biography*, 2 vols (London: Hogarth Press, 1972), I, pp. 202–4

—— *Between the Acts*, ed. by Mark Hussey (Cambridge: Cambridge University Press, 2011)

—— *The Diary of Virginia Woolf*, ed. by Anne Olivier Bell and Andrew McNeillie, 5 vols (London: Hogarth Press, 1977–1984)

—— *The Essays of Virginia Woolf*, ed. by Andrew McNeillie and Stuart N. Clarke, 6 vols (London: Hogarth Press, 1986–2011)

—— *Jacob's Room*, ed. by Kate Flint (Oxford: Oxford University Press, 1992)

—— 'Letters', *Nation and Athenaeum*, 37.24 (12 September 1925), 699

—— *The Letters of Virginia Woolf*, ed. by Nigel Nicolson and Joanne Trautmann, 6 vols (London: Hogarth Press, 1975–1980)

—— *Moments of Being*, ed. by Jeanne Schulkind, rev. by Hermione Lee (London: Pimlico, 2002)

—— *Mrs. Dalloway*, ed. by David Bradshaw (Oxford: Oxford University Press, 2000)

—— *Night and Day*, ed. by Michael Whitworth (Cambridge: Cambridge University Press, 2018)

—— *Orlando*, ed. by Rachel Bowlby (Oxford: Oxford University Press, 1992)

—— *The Pargiters: The Novel-Essay Portion of The Years*, ed. Mitchell A. Leaska (New York and London: Harcourt Brace Jovanovich, 1977)

—— *A Passionate Apprentice: The Early Journals 1897–1909*, ed. by Mitchell A. Leaska (London: Hogarth Press, 1990)

—— *Roger Fry: A Biography* (London: Vintage, 2003)

—— *A Room of One's Own and Three Guineas*, ed. by Anna Snaith (Oxford: Oxford University Press, 2015)

—— *To the Lighthouse*, ed. by David Bradshaw (Oxford: Oxford University Press, 2008)

—— *The Voyage Out*, ed. by Lorna Sage (Oxford: Oxford University Press, 2009)

—— *The Waves*, ed. by David Bradshaw (Oxford: Oxford University Press, 2015)

—— *The Waves*, ed. by Michael Herbert and Susan Sellers (Cambridge: Cambridge University Press, 2011)

—— *The Waves: The Two Holograph Drafts*, transcr. and ed. by J. W. Graham (London: Hogarth Press, 1976)

—— *The Years*, ed. by Anna Snaith (Cambridge: Cambridge University Press, 2012)

Woolmer, J. Howard, *A Checklist of the Hogarth Press, 1917–1938* (London: Hogarth Press, 1976)

Yorke, Clifford, 'Barbara Low', *International Dictionary of Psychoanalysis*, ed. by Alain de Mijolla (Detroit: Macmillan Reference USA, 2005), pp. 996–7

Zambreno, Kate, *Heroines* (Los Angeles: Semiotext(e), 2012)

INDEX

Figures are indicated by page references in *italics*.

Printed and bound by CPI Group (UK) Ltd, Croydon, CR0 4YY

20/03/2025

01835113-0002